The Secret Heresy of Hieronymus Bosch

For John, Becca and Hillie

Lynda Harris

The Secret Heresy of Hieronymus Bosch

Floris Books

First published in 1995 by Floris Books

British Library CIP Data available

ISBN 0-86315-198-1

Printed in Singapore

Contents

List of illustrations

(All paintings and drawings are by Hieronymus Bosch, unless otherwise attributed)

Colour plates

Section 1 (following p.96)

Figures in the text

Maps and diagrams

Acknowledgments

Many people have played vital roles in shaping this book. These include first and foremost my husband, John, whose patience and good humour have been boundless. Without his companionship on trips to obscure sites, and his help in numerous other ways, this work could never have been written. I have also benefited greatly from the support, advice and encouragement of my two children, Becca and Hillie (Ken), as well as various friends and family members, including (among others) Joan Ash, Annela Twitchin, Naomi Cream, Carola Beresford-Cooke, and Mike and Evelyn Harris. Other friends whom I would especially like to thank for their valuable professional help and advice include Professor Naomi Miller, Harold and Adina Bartram, Penelope Cream, and Jeannette Willis. I also greatly appreciate the time and help in translating texts given by Eve Webb, Aniche Harvey, Dr Ryan of the Warburg Institute, and Dr Puvačić of the School of Slavonic Studies.

One of my greatest debts is to Professor Walter Gibson, who very kindly read the manuscript at an early stage. The advice which he then provided has been extremely helpful during the ten years of writing. Comments on the manuscript in its later stages, which were also very useful and greatly valued, were made by Dr Georges Graner and Maridjo Graner of Paris. Professor Nicholas Davidson was also very generous in reading the section on Venice, and sharing his recent unpublished research on the subject of Venetian heresy. His help in this field is much appreciated, as is that of Dr John Martin who, with a few sentences, provided an invaluable lead.

In addition to those named above, I am grateful for the help and time given by the curators and restorers of various museums, especially Dr Carmen Diaz of the Royal Palace in Madrid, Dr Guido Jansen of the Boymans-van Beuningen Museum in Rotterdam, Dr Lore Sander of the Museum of Indian Art in Berlin, and Signor Luigi Sante Savio of the Accademia in Venice.

Last but not least I owe an enormous debt of gratitude to my editor at Floris Books, Christopher Moore. His very perceptive suggestions (all made with admirable tact) have had an important influence on the final version of the book. I will also remember his continuing patience, as I sent in yet another set of changes and additions to the manuscript. And finally, I greatly appreciate the hard work of Mary Charrington on the illustrations, and of Christian Maclean on the design and organization.

Lynda Harris
London 1995

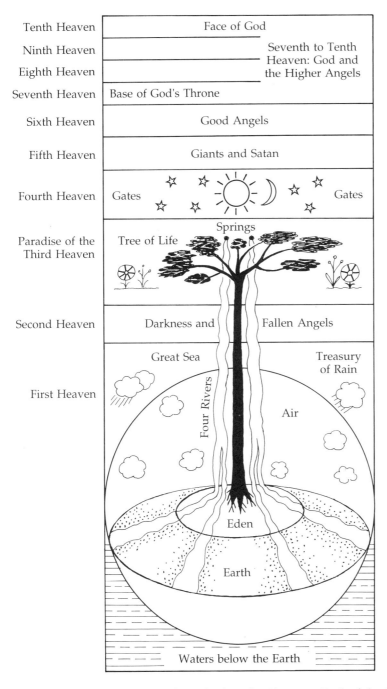

1. Model of the Universe, as described in the Slavonic *Book of the Secrets of Enoch*, written during the early first century AD and known to the Cathars.

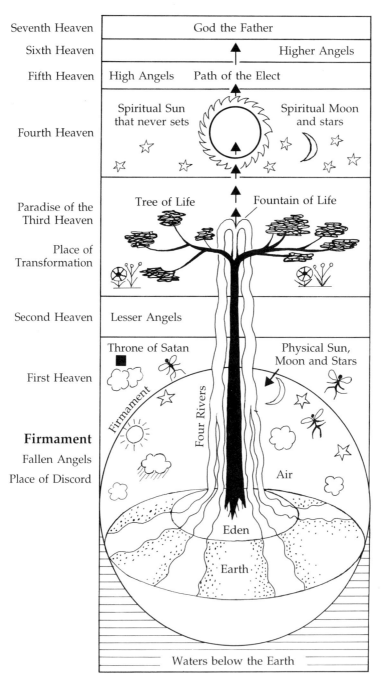

The figure is labelled as follows, from top to bottom on the left:

- Seventh Heaven — God the Father
- Sixth Heaven — Higher Angels
- Fifth Heaven — High Angels · Path of the Elect
- Fourth Heaven — Spiritual Sun that never sets · Spiritual Moon and stars
- Paradise of the Third Heaven — Tree of Life · Fountain of Life
- Place of Transformation
- Second Heaven — Lesser Angels
- First Heaven — Throne of Satan · Physical Sun, Moon and Stars
- **Firmament** — Fallen Angels · Place of Discord — Firmament · Four Rivers · Air · Eden · Earth
- Waters below the Earth

2. Cathar model of the universe: a heretical version of the early Christian model, which has much in common with Bosch's paintings.

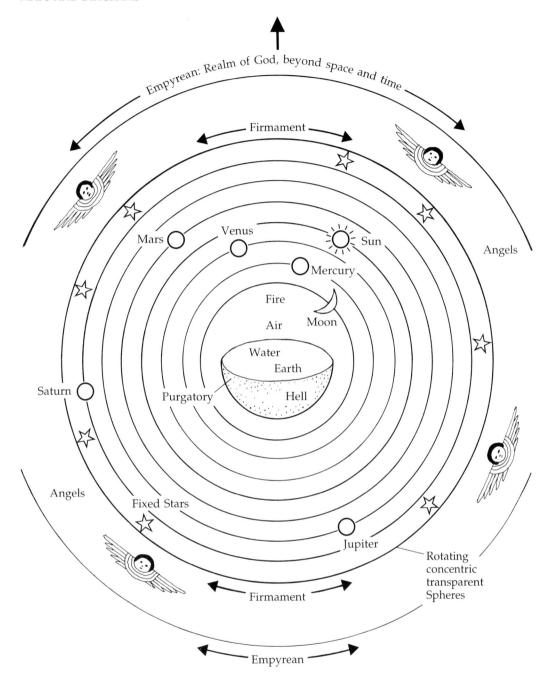

3. The established Church's model of the universe: widely accepted between the eighth and sixteenth centuries.

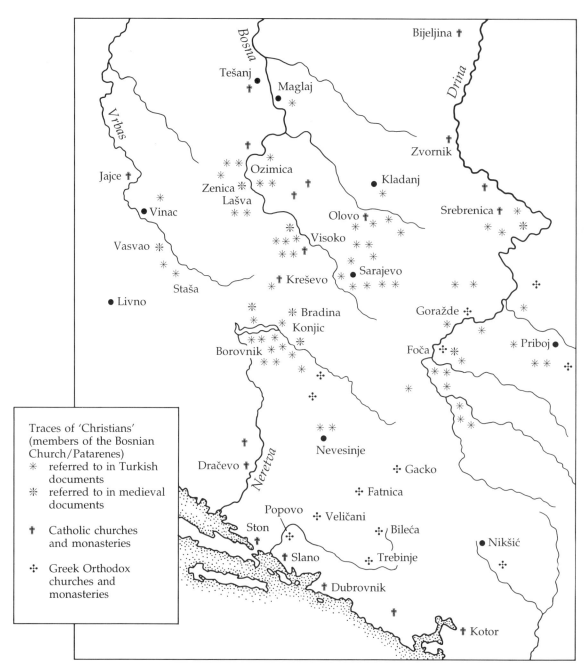

4. Map showing locations of various religious groups in Bosnia-Herzegovina from the Middle Ages through the Turkish period. (*After* Ćirković, *Istorija Srednjove-kovne bosanske države*, Belgrade 1964, p.284.)

5. Map showing main locations of stećci (Cathar tombstones) in Bosnia-Herzegovina. (*After* Bihalji-Merin and Benac, 1962, and Kutzli 1977.)

Introduction:
The Historical Background

The myths and images of the Cathars will play an important part in the chapters to come. This is because we will be looking at Bosch's eccentric and unorthodox symbols as coded records of the much persecuted Cathar heresy. Bosch's iconography has never been fully explained. Some authors have interpreted his work as heretical (see Chapter 2 for more on this), but he is most often seen as an eccentric but pious member of the Church who was influenced by alchemy, and specialized in paintings of hell and devils. This view of Bosch is understandable, but it is based on a misconception of Bosch's real motives. This artist was above all a mystic, who saw the world as dark, in comparison with the realm of the spirit. He painted luminous, otherworldly scenes, as well as hellish ones. Bosch is understood best when his entire *oeuvre* is seen as a unified expression of his spiritual message, and Baldass summarizes this idea when he says:

> Unique in the history of art, the outstanding feature of
> Bosch's achievement as a whole, which was so long
> misunderstood, is the coherence and lucidity of his
> conception of the world, manifest in every painting he
> produced. Such qualities are only to be found in the true
> spiritual leaders of humanity.[1]

In the coming chapters, we will examine the connections between Bosch's mysterious symbols and his secret, heretical and mystical faith. But first, let us set the stage with a general discussion of this faith. Just what place does Catharism have in Western religious history? What were its origins? Once established, was it just a minor medieval outburst, or was it more universal, ancient and important than this?

The ancient origins of dualism

One point which we can start with in our discussion of Catharism is the indisputable fact that it was a Gnostic religion. Like all the other members of its religious family, it was strongly dualistic, and put great stress on the contrast between the light of the spiritual realm and the darkness of the material one. The Gnostic contrast of spirit and matter was not unique in itself, for all religions, whatever they are, contain some dualism. It is the extent to which these ideas are carried which separates the truly dualistic religions from the others. The Gnostic systems, which are the most dualistic of them all, see the material world as a realm of darkness and death, governed, and even created by its own deity. The spiritual world, in contrast, is seen as a totally separate realm of light and life, ruled by a separate god. Birth into the physical body is viewed by the Gnostics as a trap from which it is very difficult to escape. The soul, fallen into the world of matter and caught in the wheel of repeated births and deaths, is seen as spiritually 'drunk,' 'asleep,' or even 'dead.' It is in a state of drugged oblivion, and has forgotten its origins in the world of spirit. But its entrapment need not be permanent, for a Saviour is sent out from the realm of light to rescue it. The soul's release begins with enlightenment, and ends with its permanent escape into the world of spiritual light and life.

But where did these dualistic ideas come from? What were the origins of the many Gnostic sects which emerged in the late BC/early AD period? The answers to this question are complex and controversial, for, as Walker says, 'Gnosticism was born at the crossroads of many ancient cultures.'[2] Myths, symbols, and ideas from all the main religions of the known world, all the way from Rome through to India, contributed to the various Gnostic sects. The most important influences include certain ideas and myths from Egypt, dualistic doctrines from the Babylonian religion of Zoroaster, philosophical theories developed in the Greek world, and, above all, concepts from Judaism and Christianity. R.M. Grant makes a particularly interesting point, when he suggests that the first Gnostics were ex-Jews, who had rejected the chief identifying characteristics of their religion. This would explain the Gnostics' typically negative attitudes towards the Old Testament, and their frequent identification of the evil creator and ruler of the physical world with the Jehovah, the God of the Jews.[3]

Whether or not Gnosticism was actually developed by renegade Jews, it is now becoming more and more obvious that a substantial proportion of early Christians, many of whom had originally been Jews, believed in a Gnostic form of their religion. It has even been suggested by several scholars that the inner teachings of Jesus himself were at least partially Gnostic. There is quite a lot of evidence to back this up, as readers who have looked at the books of authors such as Grant and Welburn will know. It may be that the Gnostic ideas which began to surface among Jews and others at this period were not actually new at all. Instead, it is possible that they were open and overt expressions of secret, inner teachings which had been hidden in many ancient religions all along.

How far did these inner dualistic teachings go back? It could well be that they were already in existence as early as the prehistoric period. There are indications of their presence in the oldest myths we know: those of the ancient Mother Goddess. The earliest versions of the Goddess myths in the Middle East and Greece all follow the same basic pattern — a pattern which might well have had a dualistic inner meaning. The stories of Tammuz and Ishtar in Mesopotamia, and those of Dionysos, or Venus and Adonis in Greece, all conform to this universal type. The Egyptian tale of Isis and Osiris is also a somewhat altered version of the same myth. Elements of the same basic story are also found in the Bible — in the story of Joseph in Genesis, for example, and even in the life story of Jesus.

The tale of Tammuz and Ishtar is a particularly old version of this ancient and widespread myth, and it therefore gives us a good idea of the original pattern. It was first written down in Mesopotamia in about 2500 BC, but its origins are likely to be much more remote. It tells the story of Tammuz, a youth whose cyclical death and rebirth are associated with the cycles of the year and the plants. Tammuz's sister, mother and lover is Ishtar, the great Goddess of heaven and earth. Tammuz enjoys a summer of unity and love with Ishtar, but it does not last. At the end of the summer he dies, and the heartbroken Ishtar goes down to Hades to rescue him. With his rescue, he is reborn in the upper world. And after this, the same cycle of love and death begins again.

The cyclical pattern of birth and death in the Tammuz story can be understood in several ways. Most often it is seen as a parable of the death and rebirth of all living things. All life is born from the womb of the earth. It enjoys a period in the sun, then it dies, and returns again to its mother. When the next season comes, the creator of all that exists will give birth to it again. This cyclical pattern clearly applies to plant life, and there is no doubt that it was also seen as a symbol of human reincarnation by many early peoples. For them, the bright land would have been the physical world, and Hades would have been seen as the dark underworld of the physically dead.

But did everyone interpret the mythological pattern in this way? Perhaps, for the inner circle of shamans, priestesses and priests, these same symbols had a second inner or esoteric significance. This hidden meaning could have been a dualistic one, in which Tammuz's death and descent into Hades symbolizes his fall into the spiritual darkness of the physical world. He is rescued from this shadowy realm by a Saviour. This Saviour is Ishtar, his sister, mother and lover. Ishtar's multiple relationships with Tammuz show that she is actually a part of him. She is his spiritual self, and she takes him back up to the spiritual world of light. The Gnostics of the late BC/early AD period repeat the same basic mythological pattern in their stories of the soul and its Saviour, but in their texts, the esoteric symbolism is made much more explicit. It is possible, of course, that the Gnostics were imposing a newly invented dualistic interpretation on the pattern of the ancient myth. But there is a good chance that they were revealing the inner meanings which had been there all along.

Support for the idea that the esoteric interpretation of the myth had ancient origins is given by the Swedish author Widengren. In his book *Mesopotamian Elements in Manichaeism*, he makes a detailed comparison between the Mesopotamian myth of Tammuz, the Indian Upanishads, and the Gnostic (in this case Manichean) drama of the soul. From our point of view, the Indian Upanishads, important as they are, are only relevant as evidence of the widespread influence of dualism. Our concern in this book is with the West and the Middle East. And, when we look at Widengren's comparisons between the ancient goddess religion of Mesopotamia and Mani's Gnostic system, we can see that there are many surprisingly close connections.

By the AD period, when Gnosticism and Manicheism evolved,

religions had become patriarchal rather than matriarchal. The Mother Goddess had now been transformed into God the Father. In the Gnostic systems, the Father became remote and entirely disconnected from the physical world. His son (the Tammuz figure of Mesopotamian mythology) split into two, and took on the identity of both the Saviour (or spirit) and the fallen soul.

In Manicheism, the fallen soul is often personified as Adam. Adam appears again in Catharism, and the two closely related religions use similar metaphors to describe his fate. These will be looked at in more detail in the text, especially in Chapters 5, 8 and 9. It is striking how much the Cathar and Manichean story of Adam the collective soul has in common with the myth of Tammuz. When Tammuz dies, for example, he falls into a pit (Hades), and Ishtar (his spirit) mourns his fall and entrapment:

> The lord is exposed to the woe in the pit ....
> My heart is sending wailing of flute to the steppe,
> to the place where the strong one is chained,
> to the place of the chains of Tammuz,
> to the lamb which is given in the power of the nether world ...[4]

In the Cathar/Manichean tradition, the same metaphors of chains and entrapment in a pit are used to symbolize the soul's fall from the world of light into the darkness of matter. In the Tammuz myth, the fallen hero also loses his beautiful robe and his crown when he falls.[5] These attributes are again found in Manichean and Cathar literature, where they represent the soul's lost shining spiritual body and aura. In Hades, the fallen and unhappy Tammuz is bitten by dogs or poisoned by serpents. He lies drugged, and is 'slumbering in an over-whelming sleep.'[6] All of these images appear again in Manichean and Cathar texts, as symbols of the forgetfulness which overtakes the soul (or Adam), once it is ensnared in the body.

The trapped Tammuz is drugged, but he is aware enough to respond to the call of his Saviour, just as Adam does in Manicheism and Catharism. In the ancient myth, Ishtar rescues Tammuz by ship:

> Fitting out a large ship at this place she sent it to the water of the
>   nether world ....
> O Lord, I shall sail away to bring thee back from the lower world.[7]

The Saviour (who is personified as Jesus in Catharism, and either Jesus or Mani in Manicheism) also descends into 'Hades,' in order to rescue the soul from its spiritual death. And, as in the Tammuz story, the soul's vehicle of escape is sometimes described as a 'ship.' This vehicle transports it to the light and joy of the upper world (see Chapter 11). The soul and spirit are now reunited, and have once again become a single entity.

Manicheism and the evolution of Catharism

Widengren compares the myth of Tammuz with the ideas and images of the Manicheans, but, as he says in his introduction, the chief doctrines of Manicheism are essentially the same as those of all the other Gnostic systems.[8] Manicheism was an amalgamation of many earlier traditions, but it emphasised and developed certain ideas and customs. It also used specific, individual metaphors to express its ideas. In addition to this, Manicheism was unique in its openness, its wide popularity and its exceptionally long lifespan. What makes it especially relevant to us is its importance in the history of Catharism.

The story of the two religions begins with the history of Manicheism. This new faith developed in Mesopotamia during the third century AD. It was an amalgamation of many earlier systems, including Gnostic Christianity, Zoroastrianism, and even Buddhism. Its creator was a mystical genius called Mani, who has since been so maligned that, even today, his name has unpleasant associations for many people. Mani came from a noble Parthian (Zoroastrian) family, and was born in what was then Babylonia, near to today's Baghdad. He was raised by his father in an ascetic baptismal Gnostic sect, but, after a split, he struck out on his own and formed a new religion. This system was even more extreme in its dualism than the other Gnostic sects. In Mani's vision, for example, the seven heavens were made of the flayed skins of demons, earth's mountains were made of the bones of dead demons, and earth's soil was made of demons' excrement. These images must have been truly horrifying to anyone who took them literally, and presumably many did. They were contrasted with descriptions of the great purity and beauty of the invisible universe of light. Such extreme views angered the established religions, but they did not put off potential converts. In spite (or perhaps even because) of them, Manicheism became a widely popular religion.

Unlike almost all the other Gnostic religions, Manicheism was open to anyone who wanted to join it. It was not necessary to be an initiate in order to belong. The Manichean doctrines were publicized overtly, and the religion's missionaries aimed to attract as many converts as possible. By 242, when Mani was 26 years old, he had already developed his basic ideas and had begun preaching to large crowds. He was martyred by the Zoroastrian establishment in Mesopotamia in 277, but by this time he had written and illustrated several books which set out his doctrines for all to see. His new Gnostic faith spread rapidly. At its height in the fourth century, the Manichean religion had gained converts all over the Roman Empire. It soon became a serious threat to the newly established Christian Church, and the Church finally suppressed it in the West, sometime during the sixth century.

After the sixth century, the Manichean religion seemed to disappear in Western Europe, but as we will see, it is more likely that it went underground. And meanwhile, other Manicheans were still able to practise their faith openly in many parts of the non-Christian world. We know, for example, that they moved eastwards along the Silk Route. Their religion flourished in the Turfan Oasis in Central Asia during the ninth century, and was active in China from the seventh to the fourteenth century. Also, according to Runciman, Obolensky, Loos, and other scholars in the field, Manicheism remained strong in the Middle East. Here, it influenced a seventh century Armenian sect called the Paulicans. According to ninth century Byzantine historians, the Paulicans kept the doctrines of the Manicheans, but forbade the reading of any books except the New Testament. They also 'reclothed' Manichean ideas in order to make them more acceptable to the Christians.[9] The Paulicans, who were to have an important influence on the development of Catharism, arrived in Turkey and the Balkans during the eighth century.

Manichean ideas must also have been incorporated into another fourth century form of Christian Gnosticism called Messalianism. This heresy originated in Mesopotamia, probably during the early fourth century. Its members soon found their way to Syria, and here, as well as in Mesopotamia, they would have had contact with the Manicheans. The two religions had access to many of the same esoteric texts, and they shared certain Gnostic Christian ideas. The Messalians were particularly ascetic, and we know that they often infiltrated Christian monasteries and converted the monks. Their numbers continued to increase, and by the fifth century, their religion had spread to Armenia, Cappadocia and the coast of Turkey. They were to be the second major influence in the development of Catharism. By the eighth century they were living alongside the Paulicans in the Balkans.

About two hundred years later — sometime in the middle of the tenth century — the doctrines and practices of both the Paulicans and the Messalians amalgamated, and contributed to the development of a new-yet-old Gnostic religion. This dynamic and revitalized heresy, which was to become extremely important in both Eastern and Western Europe, originated in the Babuna mountains in ex-Yugoslavian Macedonia, not far from present-day Bulgaria. It was called Bogomilism, after Bogomil (beloved of God), the man who was its first priest. It was to have many names during the course of its history, however. One of the best known of these, and the one which we will be using here, is Catharism.

According to Runciman among others, the newly evolved Cathar faith was a modern, Christianized version of the old and widely popular Manichean heresy. Like Manicheism, it was open to everyone. Its ordinary followers were called Hearers or Believers, and its initiated priests were known as Perfects or the Elect, just as they had been in Manicheism. Catharism was also similar to the religion of Mani in its immediate and widespread appeal. It soon spread to Bulgaria and the rest of Macedonia, and by the eleventh century it had reached Constantinople. By the twelfth century, it had become widespread in all of Thrace. It remained active in these areas until the arrival of the Turks during the fourteenth century.

Sometime during its early stages of development, Catharism split into two different sects, called the Absolute and the Mitigated Dualists. Both groups took many of their doctrines and images from the Manicheans, but the Absolute Dualists were nearer to Mani in their acceptance of the Zoroastrian idea that the dark ruler of the visible universe had always existed. They probably picked up these Manichean concepts from the Paulicans. The Mitigated Dualists, in contrast, were nearer to the Zervanites, who had been the contemporaries of the Zoroastrians in Mani's Mesopotamia.[10] The Zervanites believed in a more ancient form of dualism, which saw the two deities of darkness and light as sons of a single godhead.[11] The Mitigated Cathars probably acquired their doctrines (which include both Zervanite and Christian ideas) from the Messalians. They believed that Satan, the evil principle, had originally been the beloved elder son of God. As they saw it, he had only become the prince of the visible universe after a fall. Mitigated Catharism, which is still very near to Manicheism despite its Zervanite, Messalian and Christian influences, was the more wide-spread and longer-lasting of the two types. It is also the one which corresponds with Bosch's iconography.

Both forms of the dynamic and fast-growing Cathar heresy had their missionaries and advocates, and it was not long before they reached Western Europe. Cathars probably arrived there during the eleventh century, and by the twelfth century the heresy was spreading quickly in Germany, Flanders, France, and Italy. Catharism became most en-trenched and widespread in Lombardy and the Languedoc (Figures 1 and 2), but it was seen as a serious threat to established Christianity in many other countries. Because of this, it was persecuted with great ferocity by both the Greek Orthodox and the Roman Church. Some of the refugees from these persecutions joined the Cathars in Bosnia and the Dalmatian Coast between the twelfth and fourteenth centuries. In Bosnia, where the heretics were comparatively unmolested, Catharism actually became the leading religion. The Bosnian Cathars, who were Mitigated Dualists, were known as Patarenes or members of the Bosnian Church.[12]

The 'modern Manicheans' in Europe

In medieval Europe, the Cathars were often referred to as 'Bougres.' This was an acknowledgement of the fact that their religion had originally come from Bulgaria. Virtually all of today's experts now agree with this, and accept that West European Catharism had direct links with East European Bogomilism. In addition to this, the medi-eval populace took it for granted that Catharism had Manichean roots.

Figure 1. Ruins of the Cathar castle of Montségur (Ariège, Languedoc). Fell to the besieging anti-Albigensian forces, March 1244.

This idea was accepted for many years, but recently, a number of scholars have begun to dispute it. As they see it, Catharism and Bogomilism were unexplained revivals of primitive Christianity, which had somehow been influenced by Gnosticism. Any similarities between them and Manicheism are explained by the universal Gnostic ideas which were shared by all of them.

This new viewpoint, which is now becoming widely accepted, is based partly on the way that the Cathars and their predecessors in the Byzantine world described themselves. They always (or nearly always) referred to themselves as 'Christians,' and avoided the word 'Manichean.' There is one small but significant exception to this rule, however. Between 1043 and 1048, Anselm, the canon of the cathedral

Figure 2. Castle of Sirmione (Lake Garda, Lombardy), once a Cathar stronghold. Fell to the Scala family of Milan in 1276.

at Liège, wrote about a group of 'countryfolk' in the diocese of Châlons. According to Anselm, these people:

> ... eagerly followed the evil teachings of Manicheans and frequented their secret conventicles, in which they engaged in I know not what filthy acts .... And they lyingly asserted that their Holy Spirit is given by a sacrilegious imposition of hands; to buttress their faith in this error, they most falsely proclaim Him to have been sent by God only in their heresiarch Mani, as though Mani were none other than the Holy Spirit.[13]

This piece of evidence is important, for it shows that there were a few European heretics in the mid-eleventh century who did admit their connections with Manicheism. Later, when the heresy became more widespread, and the intolerance more severe, the heretics grew more careful. This was only to be expected, for in an age of violent persecutions, anyone in the Greek Orthodox or Roman Church dominions who admitted an association with the abhorred Mani would have been courting death. Under these circumstances, it is not surprising that the Paulicans, Messalians, Bogomils and Cathars all called themselves Christians rather than Manicheans.

When the Cathars claimed to be Christians, they would have been leaving out some of the facts, but they would not actually have been lying. Like the original Manicheans, who had also seen themselves as the true Christians, they were describing themselves accurately.[14] The difference was that their form of Christianity was esoteric and Gnostic. Its doctrines and viewpoints went back a long way, and had been influenced by a combination of many sources. These included not only the New Testament (especially the Gospel of John), but also, and very importantly, the Gnostic doctrines of Mani.

The opponents of the Cathar religion were much more outspoken about the real roots of the heresy than the heretics themselves. Over and over again, these clerics described the Cathars as 'Modern Manicheans.' The Dominican friar Bernard Gui is just one example of many. In 1323–24, Gui wrote a comprehensive, clear and accurate description of Cathar beliefs and practices. The first of its six parts begins as follows:

> (1) *Concerning the Errors of the Manichaeans of the Present Time.*- The sect and heresy of the Manichaeans and the supporters of its aberration declare and confess that there are two gods and two lords, to wit, a beneficent God and an evil one. They assert that the creation of everything visible and corporeal was wrought, not by God the Heavenly Father, whom they term the beneficent God, but by the devil, or Satan, the wicked god .... Thus, they postulate two creators ... and two creations, that is, one invisible and incorporeal, and the other visible and corporeal ...[15]

The scholars who support the non-Manichean theory discount the evidence in this and many other texts, by saying that the clergy of both the Greek Orthodox and the Western Church would have used the term 'Manichean' for any dualist heresy. But to say this is to underrate the learning and intelligence of the clerics, as well as their sources of information about both Manicheism and Catharism. The persecutors had to understand dualism in order to fight it, and there is no doubt that they made it their business to learn all they could about their adversary.

The medieval clerics should therefore be listened to carefully. They had reliable information about both Manicheism and Catharism. Their knowledge of the former came from several sources, but the best one would have been the writings of St Augustine. This late fourth century Father of the Church had been a Manichean himself for nine years. It is now generally agreed that what he says about the religion corresponds well with two collections of original Manichean writings which have only recently been discovered. These were found during the first half of the twentieth century, one in the Turfan Oasis in Chinese Turkistan, and the other in the Fayum Oasis in Egypt. These texts give more information about Manicheism than was available during the Middle Ages, but they also vindicate Augustine's descriptions of the Manichean religion.

Augustine summarizes his main points in a work called *De Haeresibus,* and elaborates on them at greater length in several other texts. All of these writings would have been easily available to clerics who were interested in the Cathars. And what they say makes it plain that Catharism did indeed have a great deal in common with Manicheism. It is not only the doctrines of the two heresies which correspond; it is also their religious customs, and the organization of their churches.

The other main Western source of information about the Manichean heresy was a text called the *Acta Archelai.* Widengren describes it as that 'hate-filled and somewhat distorted ... Christian tissue of lies about Mani which nevertheless contains so much authentic material.'[16] This work, which was written in 325, was the earliest anti-Manichean summa. What is most important about it from our point of view is its publishing (or, more accurately for the period), its reproduction history. Many new copies of it were produced in France from the ninth century onwards.[17] This shows that clerics were studying it, along with the works of St Augustine, and indicates that they were already worried about local dualist heretics. Our records of the period are incomplete and controversial, but we cannot rule out the possibility that dualist heresy did exist in Europe during the ninth and tenth centuries. If so, there seems little reason to assume that the clerics were wrong when they decided that this heresy was a resurgence of the Manichean faith. This is by far the most likely option anyway, since the only dualist heresy which had ever been widespread in Western Europe had been the religion of Mani.

There is a good chance, then, that Mani's popular religion went underground in Western Europe during the sixth century, and began to resurface again during the ninth century. And at some point, most likely during the eleventh century, this indigenous European Manicheism could have amalgamated with the Christianized form of the religion that had been brought to the West by the Balkan Bogomils.

By the twelfth century, the new 'Modern Manichean' religion had become firmly established in Western Europe. At this stage, it still kept Mani's tradition of openness. This enabled it to spread quickly, but it also gave the medieval clerics many opportunities to learn about it. By the time the Inquisition was instituted officially in about 1230, the Church had been concerned about this 'Manichean' heresy for many years, and had built up a large body of information about it. The clerics often made insulting value judgments about Cathar beliefs — Gui's treatise is called *The Conduct of the Inquisition of Heretical Depravity*, for example. But what Gui actually says about the heretical beliefs is precise and accurate. It is now widely agreed the Inquisitors' descriptions of the heresies were correct. They expressed their aversion to the beliefs, but they did not distort the facts.

Some of the Inquisitors' best information came from Church clerics who had once been Cathars themselves. The well-known thirteenth century Dominican Inquisitor, Rainerius Sacconi of Piacenza, is just one of several examples. These converts, who often became the most fanatical persecutors, told their fellow clerics a great deal about the religion's doctrines. Their inside information was written down as an aid to recognizing the heresy. It was an important part of the Inquisition material, and it is still available today.

The Inquisitors were also able to learn about Catharism from the Cathars' own religious writings. We know that there were a great many of these, and that they were easy to obtain during the Middle Ages. These original Cathar texts remained in circulation into the fourteenth century, but by the fifteenth century, when Catharism was no longer any kind of threat to the Western European Church, these books had disappeared. Many had been destroyed by the Inquisition, and others must have gone underground. Yet others had probably been hidden by the Cathars during periods of persecution. For example, the so-called Cathar treasure, which was spirited away from the castle of Montségur (Figure 1) when it fell in 1244, was most likely a cache of valuable books. These could well have been stored somewhere nearby, and with luck they will some day be rediscovered. Meanwhile, twentieth century researchers have done a very useful task in uncovering a few of the lost Cathar texts in various European libraries.

In addition to the Cathar books and the writings of the Inquisitors, there were also many descriptions of Catharism which came from the victims themselves. During about two hundred years of official and organized persecution, the Inquisitors arrested great numbers of suspected Cathars, and questioned them about their beliefs. These question sessions were written down, and the records are still available today. The information which was so meticulously recorded is useful to us, but most of it was probably not new to the Inquisitors. This is because the questions were mainly a means of identifying heresy, and were used to test the suspects' beliefs against what the Inquisition already knew about Catharism. All of this makes it plain that the medieval clergy were not careless, ignorant or uneducated. They tell us repeatedly in their records that Catharism was a Manichean religion. We should respect their knowledge of the subject, even if we do not think very highly of their cruel and ruthless persecutions.

The religion of darkness and light

The modern scholars who do not take Catharism's Manichean roots into account tend to see the heresy as less dualistic than it actually was. But its extreme contrasts of darkness and light come into focus when we compare Manichean visions of the Last Judgment and the End of the World with the images in one of the few Cathar texts available today. This Cathar work, which is often called the *Secret Book*, is also known as the *Interrogatio Johannes (Questions of John)* and the *Secret Supper.* It relates Jesus's answers to questions asked by John the Evangelist at a secret supper in heaven. The subjects covered include a Christianized version of Satan's acts of creation, descriptions of Christ's baptism and mission, and visions of the Final Days. The Cathar *Secret Book* was written or compiled by Mitigated Dualists in the Balkans. It probably dates from the eleventh century, but it may not have reached Western Europe before the end of the twelfth century. By this time it was circulating widely among the European Cathars, and it seems to have become one of their most important texts.

We will be looking at the Cathar *Secret Book* often in the chapters to come, but the part which is relevant to us at this stage concerns the End of the World and the fate of the saved and the damned. The Cathar text describes these events as follows:

> by permission of my [that is, Jesus'] father, gloomy
> darkness shall spread over the lower regions of the earth
> and a hell of fire shall burn all the land from its lowest
> depths even unto the air of the firmament .... Then Satan
> shall be bound and all his host, and he shall be cast into
> the pool of fire. The Son of God, *with his elect* [italics mine],
> shall walk above the firmament; and he shall shut up the
> devil, binding him with unbreakable bonds, with sinners
> weeping, wailing and crying out 'Swallow us up, O land,
> hide us within thyself.'[18]

A similar Manichean description of the fiery end of the world goes as follows:

> ... the Angel who has been placed in charge of the heaven
> lets go. Then the uppermost [parts of the visible universe]
> are overturned to the lowermost ones, and a Fire breaks
> out in these lowermost [parts] and continues burning until
> the portions of light that are in the World of Darkness ...
> are liberated.[19]

This is supplemented by other Manichean writings which are discussed by Jackson in his article of 1930. These describe the events which will take place after the fiery destruction. At this stage, the righteous Elect will descend to a level which is below the invisible heavens, and above the burning earth and sky. When they arrive there, they will join the company of the Gods, and look down on the evildoers suffering in the fire.[20]

The descriptions of the destruction of the earth and sky are very similar in the Manichean and Cathar texts, but they are not unique to these two heresies. Other Gnostic religions also visualized fires which would burn up the earth and the material universe. On the other hand, the picture of the Elect joining the gods (or Saviour) somewhere above the firmament, and looking down on the sufferings of the damned in the fiery 'hell' are not found anywhere else. Their unique presence in the writings of the Manicheans and the Cathars could not be a coincidence. The only way that these Manichean ideas could have reached the *Secret Book* is through a direct connection between the two religions.

These rather heartless visions may correspond with our ideas about Manichean dualism, but they don't accord very well with what we normally think of as Cathar Christianity. No one can deny that the Cathars followed the ideals of the New Testament, and viewed the ordinary people of the world with sympathy and understanding. As they saw it, the souls of these people were still spiritually alive, and could be enlightened and saved. The problem was that not everyone fitted into this category. Like the Manicheans before them, the Cathars believed that certain souls had been committed colleagues of Satan from the start. These souls were seen as spiritually dead, and beyond all hope of salvation. The Cathars carried this idea so far that they believed some people were literally demons in human form. These 'demons' were often the richest and most powerful members of society and the Church, and the Inquisitors were undoubtedly included among them.[21]

The demons in human form had been loyal followers of Satan from the beginning, and there was no possibility of their being saved. But, as the Manicheans and the Mitigated Cathars saw it, ordinary human souls could also end up sharing the fiery fate of Satan and his world. According to St Augustine, the Manicheans believed that these souls, which are 'good by nature, but which, nevertheless, have not been able to be purged from the contagion of the evil nature' would not be able to make their escape at the time of the Last Judgment. This idea is reflected in the *Secret Book*, where Jesus says 'Depart from me, you cursed, into everlasting fire, which was prepared for the devil and his angels.'[22] In this quotation from Matthew (25:41), orthodox Christians would identify the 'cursed' as sinners who had failed to believe and repent. For the Mitigated Cathars, however, the cursed were those souls which had become so enmeshed in Satan's world that they were no longer able to overcome their attraction to it. As we will see later, Bosch's paintings often depict the same fate for the ordinary, misguided people who show no interest in escaping the web of Satan.

Since the heretics believed that Satan held the reins of power on the earth, they probably thought it likely that his co-workers, the Inquisitors, would win the earthly battle against their religion of light. In any case, this is what happened. In the end, the Inquisitors' efforts to eliminate the Cathars succeeded completely. By the fifteenth century the tenets of Catharism had been forgotten in most parts of Europe, and its members were reduced to secret underground remnants. These small groups still existed during the sixteenth century, as we will see in later chapters, but by the seventeenth century, there is no longer any sign of them.

Catharism did not persist much longer in Bosnia, either. The Turks conquered Bosnia during the late fifteenth century, and, though they did not persecute the Cathars in their new territory, they did give them strong incentives to convert to Islam. By the seventeenth century, the Bosnian towns which had once been Cathar were inhabited by Muslims, and (in some cases) Roman and Greek Orthodox Christians. Some particularly committed Cathars must have continued to follow their religion without converting, but the reports of eighteenth and nineteenth century visitors to Bosnia concerning surviving 'Patarenes' or 'Manicheans' are unclear and inconclusive.[23]

Art and religion at the time of Bosch

Bosch was born in the middle of the fifteenth century, a decade or two before the Turkish invasion of Bosnia. His paintings are all undated, but most scholars think he produced his early works between the 1480's and the mid-1490's. His mature period lasted from about 1500 to his death in August, 1516.

In 1477, when Bosch was still young, the Habsburg Emperors replaced the Dukes of Burgundy as rulers of the Netherlands. In Rome, a succession of worldly Popes made great contributions to art patronage, but did little to introduce much needed Church reforms. They included Sixtus IV (1471–84), who built the Sistine Chapel; Alexander VI (1492–1503), the notorious father of Lucrezia Borgia; Julius II (1503–13), patron of Michelangelo; and the Medici Pope Leo X (1513–21), whose favourite artist was Raphael. Approximately fifteen months after Bosch died, Martin Luther inaugurated the Reformation by nailing his Ninety-five Theses on the door of All Saints Church in Wittenberg.

As can be seen from the above, Bosch lived during the last years before the Reformation, and his period of activity coincided with the development and flowering of the High Renaissance style in Italy. But in spite of this seeming modernism, Bosch's style and background belong to the late Gothic period in Northern Europe. This was because the Renaissance (which we will define here as a movement which was inspired by the styles, techniques and texts of the Classical World) did not reach the Netherlands until about 1516, the very year of Bosch's death. During the fifteenth century, the painters of the Low Countries found ways to improve their technique, but they did this without Italian influence, and they used their new realism to express traditional medieval Christian ideas.

Bosch's works grew out of the Netherlandish style, and on the surface, his iconography conforms with its traditions. His symbolism reveals a thorough knowledge of the prevailing culture of the North, and does not take the new ideas of the Renaissance into account. When Bosch visited Venice in about 1500, he did it for his own reasons (see Chapter 2). While he was there, he made contact with the great High Renaissance painters Leonardo and Giorgione, and the works of all three painters show mutual influences. Nevertheless, these influences did not make Bosch into a High Renaissance artist. His style and mentality were formed in the Netherlands during the Late Gothic period, and his trip to Italy did not change this.

Bosch's Northern Gothic background is described by Huizinga in *The Waning of the Middle Ages.* This book makes it plain that Bosch lived in highly disturbed times. The Black Death, which had hit Europe in 1345, continued to recur at intervals during the fifteenth century. The plague was particularly devastating, but it was only one of many illnesses which were difficult or impossible to treat. And there were many other dangers and insecurities. People who travelled were frequently attacked by brigands, and those who stayed at home could suffer death, rape or pillage from wandering soldiers. Wars and feuds seemed to be chronic. The nobles could do what they liked with the peasants and produce of their lands, without being called to account. The Church was notoriously corrupt, and the clergy which pontificated about sin could be at least as grasping and cruel as the nobility. The ordinary people were uneducated, ignorant, and as debauched as anyone else. These conditions were not new, but they seem to have become even more extreme during the fourteenth and fifteenth centuries than they had been in the eleventh, twelfth and thirteenth.

Not surprisingly, the people who lived during this disturbed period tried to explain the evils of the world by talk of demons, witches, and the power of the devil. These ideas had always been part of medieval folk culture, and they were absorbed by the Church. In the late Middle Ages, they became more and more of an obsession. But the more extreme they became, the more these negative views of the world contradicted the established views of the Church. On the one hand, the preachers said that the world was lost to Satan through mankind's sin, but on the other hand the Church stated firmly that God was the creator and ruler of the earth. God had planned Christ's death, resurrection and harrowing of hell from the beginning, and these all-important events had vanquished the devil. As Emile Mâle points out in his book *The Gothic Image*, the Church's doctrines stated uncompromisingly that the material world is a reflection of God's great plan. This idea was formulated by the thirteenth century writer Vincent of Beauvais, who saw every aspect of the world as a mirror of God. This view was still powerful during the fifteenth century. Even during these troubled times, the doctrines of the Church proclaimed that man and nature were creations of the deity, and the earth was very much under God's control. According to Church dogma, the material world was not demonic at all. It was a holy place, which was unified with the spiritual one.[24]

As one might expect, the contradictions between the Church's official view, and the experiences of everyday life caused a certain amount of confusion. Church dogma said that all was well, but churchmen preached about the domination of the devil. Some of the lay Christians of the Late Middle Ages began to think that Satan was the ruler of the world, but they never sorted out his position. They weren't sure whether he was acting on his own, or whether he was doing God's work in punishing mankind for its sins.[25] They continued to respect the Church and its doctrines, even if they had contempt for the clergy and the sins of humanity. This meant that they could never go as far as the heretics in their ideas about either the devil or his creation. Their dualism was only partial. It never matched the clear and uncompromising dualism of the Cathars and Manicheans. Some Christian believers in parts of France (Brittany, the Auvergne and the Pyrenees) approached a dualistic idea of creation, but even these made a compromise by saying that the devil had tried to equal God and failed. According to these stories, God had made the sun and the rain, but his evil competitor had only managed to create the moon and the hail.[26]

The prevailing confusion about the origins of evil and the place of God in a dangerous, unfair and corrupt world was not surprising. Such questions are always difficult, but they must have been especially so during the Late Middle Ages, when the troubles of the times conflicted so strongly with the established world-view of the medieval Church. The official Church view began to be modified at the Council of Trent in 1545–63.[27] It was eroded further at the first Vatican Council of 1869–70. But in Bosch's day, the idea that the world was holy still dominated the outlook of the Church, and the art which reflected it. As Lotte Brand Philip puts it:

> ... if these [fifteenth century Netherlandish] painters defy a distinction between Heaven and earth, it is a distinction which we make and not a distinction made by their predecessors. In other words, it is the intrinsic unity of the two realms which is characteristic of medieval thinking and it is only in the modern thought that Heaven and earth are clearly separated categories.[28]

Bosch's contemporaries sometimes painted saints tempted by devils, or scenes of punishment in hell, but these images did not conflict with the Church's idea that God was dominant on the earth. A second folk tradition, which was accepted by the Church, also existed alongside this traditional art. Examples of it are found in the margins of manuscripts, or among the gargoyles and misericords of the Gothic cathedrals. These works were a kind of comic relief to the more serious religious art. Their drolleries, devils and scenes of everyday life often mocked the clergy or the conventions of Church and society, but they didn't go far enough to be offensive. Bosch's paintings undoubtedly have something in common with this second tradition, but, as we will see in the following chapters, they are more rebellious and angry than folk art. Bosch was an original. He drew on earlier traditions, but he also introduced many images which were new to Western art. The inner meanings of these images reveal an intense anti-Church feeling and an uncompromising dualism.

Bosch's unconventional style had an impact on the art of his country after his death. The Spaniard Don Felipe de Guevara, who saw Bosch's works in the collection of Philip II, wrote a commentary on painting in about 1560. In it, he said that Bosch's strange paintings were often imitated, and that some artists signed Bosch's name to their forgeries.[29] Twentieth century art historians have sorted out many of the forgeries by now, though X-rays are still adding to our understanding. The questions of which works were or were not originals will be discussed in the text, as we go along.

Bosch may have had many imitators, but it would be wrong to think they were all forgers. He also had an important influence on sixteenth century painting, especially in the Netherlands. The fires, monsters and small, lively figures which are found so often in Bosch's works were taken up with great enthusiasm. In many cases, these images were integrated into the Mannerist style which had been imported from Italy. Pieter Brueghel the Elder is Bosch's most famous follower, but there are numerous others. They used Bosch's symbols, but none of them understood their hidden messages. This is because Bosch's paintings are coded records of a secret heresy. By the sixteenth century, this heresy had been forgotten, and neither the Church nor the general public looked for it or even thought about it. The mood in Europe had changed, and even without the Inquisition, the heresy of the Cathars would probably have lost its hold on the popular imagination. Public interest in the Gnostic tradition to which it belonged did not revive until the end of the nineteenth century.

44

1. Bosch and the Christian Faith

Bosch's background

Hieronymus Bosch was born sometime between 1450 and 1460, in the small market town of 's-Hertogenbosch. He lived all (or, as we will see later, nearly all) of his life in the town, and he died there in 1516. 's-Hertogenbosch, which is also known by the more pronounceable name of Den Bosch, is in the Brabant region of present day Holland, not far from the Belgian border. Today it has lost many of its medieval buildings, but it is still a pleasant and quiet place. Motorized traffic is not particularly heavy, and people cycle freely on the streets and pavements, and shop in a large pedestrianized precinct. When the weather permits, they sit in outdoor cafes in the area around the Cathedral of St-Jan.

St-Jan was built mainly between the fourteenth and sixteenth centuries. It became a Dutch Reform church when the town was conquered by the Protestants in 1629, but is now Catholic again. It is an elaborate example of Late Gothic architecture, supported by double flying buttresses which are decorated with tracery, pinnacles, gargoyles and numerous small carvings and statues. Seen from below, these give the viewer the feeling of a world populated by numerous fantastic and supernatural beings (Figures 3 and 4). The impression must have been the same in Bosch's day, but with certain differences, which are the result of nineteenth century restorations. Originally, there were not quite so many statues, and, perhaps surprisingly, they were more lewd. It is possible that they were more unconventional than traditional church gargoyles, for they looked very much like the figures in Bosch's paintings. We can still see something of their original appearance in the weathered originals preserved in the local Museum of North Brabant (see for example Figure 4). These statues were designed by Bosch's colleague Allart du Hameel in the late fifteenth century, and

Figure 3. Restored buttress figures on the Cathedral of St-Jan, 's-Hertogenbosch.

Figure 4. Bagpipe player, buttress figure from the Cathedral of St-Jan, late fifteenth/early sixteenth century.

it is possible that Allart might have consulted Bosch when making his plans. Perhaps Bosch even made some of the drawings.

Bosch, like du Hameel, was accepted universally as a sincere and traditional Christian. He was prosperous, and lived an outwardly conventional and respectable life. He was not referred to as 'Bosch' until after 1500.[1] Before this, he used his family name, Van Aken. Many members of his family, including his grandfather, father, uncles and brother were active as artists. None of them except Bosch ever became well-known outside their home town, but by 1462, Bosch's father Anthonius Van Aken had made enough money to buy a stone house with grounds in the main square of 's-Hertogenbosch.[2]

By June 1481 Bosch had married. His wife was a rich woman called Aleit Goyarts van den Meervenne. There is no record that the couple ever had any children, but there are many documents which are concerned in one way or another with their negotiations over property. Other documents refer to Bosch's membership of the important and respected Brotherhood of Our Lady. Bosch became a member of this pious confraternity between June 1486 and June 1487. According to the records, he produced various works of art for the Brotherhood (all now lost or destroyed), as well as for various churches. The Brotherhood still exists today, in a new building on its original site behind the Cathedral. Its members say very little about their famous predecessor in their leaflet, and they do not appear to take much pride in his association with them. This indicates that they no longer feel he was quite as sincere and genuine as he once seemed to be.

Whatever the members of the present Brotherhood of Our Lady may feel, most art historians today take the view that Bosch was a conventional Christian. The outward facts of Bosch's life seem to confirm this, and because his iconography always corresponds on some level with Church dogma, those who see him as orthodox can always find something to support their point of view. And yet, somehow, Bosch's Christian images are never quite as straightforward as they ought to be. Bosch's life may have been conventional (at least outwardly), but his works never really are. There are invariably elements in the paintings that are eccentric or unique. Some scholars ignore this side of Bosch's art. Others give various explanations for it. The oddities can be seen as the result of a disturbed or even psychotic obsession with sin and witchcraft, typical of the eve of the Reformation. Alternatively, they can be viewed as the products of an amazingly erudite knowledge of abstruse Christian texts or sermons.

Bosch may have appeared to be a conventional Christian, but his apparent piety was only superficial. It is true that he was mystical but he was not among the followers of the accepted fourteenth century mystic Jan van Ruysbroeck, or the fifteenth century Brothers of the Common Life, as some scholars suggest. These sects were dualistic but less fundamentally so than Bosch. They criticized the clergy, as Bosch did, but they supported the Church and the Papacy. As we will see later, Bosch's depictions of the Church and Papacy are far from friendly. The various efforts to fit his symbolism into patterns of orthodoxy can account for some of Bosch's oddities but never cover them all. They always leave gaps. This is because they are based on misconceptions of the artist's real religious views.

Dualism in Bosch's works

What, then, were these real religious views? The art historian Baldass, writing in the first half of this century, shows what is surely a particularly acute understanding of Bosch. Baldass points the way towards a real comprehension of the artist's underlying message, when he describes Bosch's view of the world as not only spiritual, but also dualistic. According to Baldass, 'Bosch painted, in the last analysis, a paraphrase of the ancient Parsee (Zoroastrian) philosophy, though he clothed it in the garb of late medieval Catholicism.'[3] Baldass also suggests that Bosch might have believed 'the earth had been initially created evil ... as a world of unbelief and heresy.'[4]

These interpretations of Bosch's iconography are certainly perceptive, but they are flawed by one crucial misinterpretation. This major misconception is Baldass's belief that Bosch was not just a dualist, but also a traditional Christian. This could not have been the case, for although medieval Christianity did contain elements of dualism, the two belief systems were basically in conflict. One of their most fundamental differences lay in their views of the natural world. The Church did not ignore sin and the devil, but, as we saw in the Introduction, it always insisted that the earth was a holy place, in which God's creation was manifest.

Erwin Panofsky, who is a particularly respected expert on Early Netherlandish art and iconography, has analysed the way in which these traditional Christian views of God and nature are expressed in fifteenth century Netherlandish art. He does not think that Bosch was a heretic, but on the other hand, he cannot deny that his works differ from the norm. As Panofsky sees it, Bosch's iconography is a 'lonely and inaccessible ... island in the stream of [the Early Netherlandish] tradition.' He adds that 'the real secret of his magnificent nightmares and daydreams has still to be disclosed. We have bored a few holes through the door of the locked room; but somehow we do not seem to have discovered the key.'[5] Bosch, clearly, was a misfit. He could not have been an orthodox Christian because his attitudes towards the world and the established religion of his country were entirely different from those of his contemporaries.

As the coming chapters will show, Bosch's work can only be

explained if we see him as a true dualist, who believed that God and nature were completely separate. For Bosch, the physical world was *entirely* evil, created by Satan, and totally within his sphere of influence. Where Jesus, a personification of the light, appears in this world of spiritual darkness, he is ignored or attacked. As the genuine dualists saw it, Jesus and the human spirit were strangers in the physical world. They belonged to an entirely different one: the realm of the Father. This was an immaterial world of light, which was located far beyond the malign influences of the visible universe. Bosch could not express these views with entire openness, for if he had he would have been condemned as a heretic. Catharism had been more or less forgotten by his day, but extreme dualistic beliefs could still be condemned.[6] Bosch pretends to be a conventional Christian, but at the same time he makes his dualism plain by his double symbols, and his continual contrasting of good and evil; spirit and matter.

The physical world, as depicted by Bosch, can be shown as literally dark. More often, however, it is temptingly bright and beautiful, but basically unsound. Bosch frequently represents it as a circle, surrounded by clouds which often swarm with devils. Its surface is always populated by demons and oddly formed, evil looking plants. It is not only the province, but, as we will see later, it is actually the construction of an evil deity. Only those who can manage to separate themselves completely from this material realm and its influences will be able to achieve salvation. This separation must be mental as well as physical. Such a disconnection is extremely difficult, but a few of Bosch's more enlightened characters, who will be described later on, do manage to achieve it.

Bosch as seen by his contemporaries

Nowadays, when people spend so much time on the interpretation of Bosch's symbols, they assume that the artist's contemporaries did the same. They therefore believe that if Bosch had been a heretic, the Church of his day would have known it. In fact, this does not seem to have been the case. All of the written evidence that we have shows that during the late fifteenth and sixteenth centuries, Bosch's paintings were interpreted more simply and uncritically than they are today.

Scholarly explanations of Bosch's eccentricities were not made then, as far as we know. Instead, the authors whose works survive from this period tell us that Bosch was universally viewed as an inventor of devils, strange and fantastic things, 'disparates,' horrible dreams, and so forth.[7] It would seem that people — both ordinary and educated — expected this artist to frighten or amuse them with his drolleries. The dubious implications of his monsters and landscapes, and the generally symbolic nature of his work apparently went unobserved by his conventionally Christian viewers. Bosch's oddities were never thought of as suspicious during his lifetime because people saw them as nothing more than entertainment. The religious side of the iconography was just conventional enough to be taken for granted, and appears to have been accepted without question. As a result, symbolism which was surprisingly heretical and anti-Church went unnoticed. Bosch had the reputation of being an acceptably pious painter who specialized in monsters and drolleries, and people saw what they expected.

Even Bosch's most literate viewers seem to have had preconceived ideas about what to look for in his works. If such people did not see Bosch as amusing, they were probably attracted, even if unconsciously, by the various images of eroticism, sin and punishment in his works. Like the general public, they did not expect Bosch's works to have underlying subversive meanings, and therefore they did not see them. This could account for Bosch's appeal during the sixteenth century to the intensely Catholic monarch, Philip II of Spain. The many paintings of voluptuous mythological nudes which Philip commissioned from Titian show that he must have had an interest in sensuality. But at the same time, he was deeply concerned with questions of sin and punishment.[8] Philip must have looked at Bosch's work for their eroticism as well as their hell scenes, while assuming that Bosch was a traditional Christian. Unlike twentieth century observers, he would not have worried about the deeper levels of symbolism or noticed the details that now appear subversive, and would therefore have had no need to find explanations for them.

Surely, if Bosch really was a secret heretic, his life and the survival of his works would have depended on his finding ways to hide this fact from the public. He would have had to appear an orthodox Christian at least on the surface. And, as we have seen, he succeeded in doing this. Nevertheless, many people today will agree that some of his oddest and most puzzling symbols are actually those that are most traditional. As Lotte Brand Philip points out, Bosch takes a traditional feature, 'transforms it for his own purpose, and thus turns its meaning into the very opposite.'[9] This is certainly a surprising way of expressing a genuinely pious faith. It makes much more sense to see Bosch as an artist who had to put on a pretence of orthodoxy in order to hide his secret beliefs. When his symbols are looked at from this point of view, many of his previously puzzling 'traditional' images fall into place, and are revealed as disguised (and sometimes even overt) anti-Church symbols.

Seventeenth century doubts about Bosch

Bosch's negative attitudes towards established Christianity must at last have been noticed for what they were about eighty years after his death. The suspicions seem to have arisen among some of the early seventeenth century Spanish Catholics. Those people who were permitted to see the royal collection would have been in a good position to note the numerous examples of Bosch's work which had been amassed during the sixteenth century by Philip II. Their doubts about Bosch's orthodoxy are hinted at in the writings of Fray José de Sigüenza, who might well have saved Bosch's works when he set out in 1605 to prove that Philip II, the founder of Sigüenza's monastery the Escorial, could not have been mistaken in his liking for Bosch. Sigüenza does not name the doubters. He also refrains from giving any details of their criticisms of Bosch, but perhaps a hint of what these were can be found in the writings of the seventeenth century courtier, Don Francisco de Melo. Reminiscing in 1657 about his stay in Madrid in 1628–40, Melo refers to a lampoon of that period which denounced Bosch as a mocking unbeliever. Sigüenza says nothing of this but he does tell us that he is arguing against certain people who call Bosch a heretic. According to Sigüenza, these people misunderstand Bosch because they have not observed his works properly.

Sigüenza was perceptive in many ways, and saw Bosch as a spiritual artist, and not just a painter of drolleries. For this reason, his views have had a great influence. Nevertheless, it is possible to argue that he was not totally observant and objective. For example, Sigüenza calls

Bosch's Prado triptych, the *Adoration of the Magi,* 'the pious and honest action of the wise and just, in which one sees no strangeness and no extravagance.'[10] In fact, if we look carefully at this work we will see that it is one of Bosch's oddest paintings, and one of his most anti-Catholic ones. Its chief message seems to be a criticism of the Mass, but there are many other subversive details, all of which Sigüenza appears to have missed.

Bosch's Prado Adoration of the Magi

Once one looks closely, it becomes apparent that all parts of Bosch's Prado *Adoration of the Magi* reveal an unconventional point of view. As Baldass has pointed out, even the outer panels, which illustrate the well-known religious subject of the Mass of St Gregory the Great (Plate 1), do not depict the scene in the normal way.[11] A painting attributed by Panofsky to the Master of Flemalle (*Early Netherlandish Painting,* Vol.II, pl.105, #227) is an example of a more conventional version of the scene. In it, Christ moves and walks towards Pope Gregory I, who has brought him to life by celebrating the Mass. Symbols of the Passion are visible against the wall above the altar.

Bosch's depiction of the same Mass is different. His Jesus does not move or even gesture, but stands tied and bound as a Man of Sorrows above the altar. The traditional symbols of the Passion have been replaced by a hill of Golgotha, on which the scenes of Christ's sacrifice are enacted amid demons and devilish tormentors. Jesus stands within the hill, as though imprisoned. This depiction of Jesus as a suffering Saviour, surrounded, and even, at times, engulfed by the forces of darkness, is typical of Bosch. It will be looked at in more detail in Chapter 5. In the meantime, it is enough to see this as a scene in which the demons, rather than Jesus, have been enlivened by the Church sacrament. Viewed in this way, the picture is a negative comment on the Mass, rather than a confirmation of it. It is certainly not the usual way of depicting the Mass of St Gregory. Nevertheless, it does not outwardly contradict accepted Church dogma. It could therefore be overlooked if it were not for the scenes which are revealed once the triptych is opened.

The Nativity scene in the central panel (Plate 2, see also Plates 5–8) is so odd, eccentric and disturbing that one wonders how Sigüenza could have accepted it as normal. In fact, what its symbolism reveals is surely not traditional piety, but negativity towards the Church. In the foreground, Bosch has represented the Magi in front of the stable. The three kings pay homage to a Madonna and Child who look stiff and unreal (Plate 5). They have been compared by Gibson to cult statues rather than living figures.[12] This concept is very unusual, but it is not heretical in itself. What is odd and completely unprecedented is Bosch's implied opinion of the Magi who worship the 'cult statues.' These kings are not the positive figures which are depicted so often in traditional Christian art. Instead, they are shown to be sinful and unsound in some way by the demons and other images of evil that decorate their clothes and gifts.

A number of writers explain the collective images of evil that surround the Magi as references to the sin and paganism of the world before the advent of Christ. This explanation might account for the eccentric demons decorating the clothes of the kings, but it does not cover the meaning of their most significant gift. This present is a piece of sculpture, made of brass or gold, which depicts the sacrifice of Isaac (Plate 6). Isaac's sacrifice was seen in the Middle Ages as an Old Testament prefiguration of the sacrifice of Christ. According to Charles de Tolnay and other scholars, Bosch uses this sacrificial image to associate the homage of the Magi with the celebration of the Mass. This identification of Mass and Nativity is also found in the *Portinari Altarpiece* of *c.*1475 by Hugo van der Goes, and the Birmingham *Nativity* of *c.*1515 by Jan de Beer. In both of these highly reverent works, the artist includes a large sheaf of wheat (Eucharistic bread), and the angels wear vestments associated with the Mass.[13]

In Bosch's version of the scene, the angels are absent and it is the Magi who wear the vestments. The Mass is alluded to by the sacrifice of Isaac, as well as the straw of the false star hanging down from the eves of the stable (more on this 'star' a little later). Bosch's symbols refer to the same religious ideas, but subtle (or not so subtle) nuances reveal that his attitudes towards them are far from reverent. It is extremely odd, for example, that Bosch, supposedly a pious Christian believer, depicts toads peeping out from beneath the image of the Sacrifice of Isaac. This statue literally stands on and is supported by reptiles. The toads identify the Old Testament story, its New Testament counterpart, and, by implication, the Mass itself, with darkness and demons. What Bosch is really telling us here is not that the Magi will be saved by the Mass, but that the Mass and the kings' participation in it are evil. He is also saying that the kings are sinful, because they worship the false idols of a false religion. This is the real explanation of the eccentric symbols that Bosch has associated with the three Magi.

In addition to this, there are many other odd features in the central panel of the Prado *Adoration of the Magi*. Who, for example, are the strange and totally unconventional figures that stare out from the door of the stable? Who, in particular, is the half naked man at the front of this wild and evil looking crowd? He wears a fantastic hat, whose base is a crown of thorns, and he has a bleeding, festering sore just above his right ankle (Plate 7). This sore, covered by a glass tube, has reminded Brand Philip of a reliquary.[14] In other words, it is in some way a religious object of worship.

But just what, here, is Bosch depicting as an object which the Christian faithful revere? The answer to this question is again an indication of Bosch's negative attitude towards the Church. The wounded leg or foot was for heretics (and also, though much less frequently, for traditional Christians) a symbol of sinfulness. A collection of fourth century Manichean psalms discovered in Egypt's Fayum use metaphors such as 'the wound of my sins,' or 'the grievous wound of lawlessness,' for example.[15] Perhaps this image was passed on to the Cathars. In any case, in the mid-thirteenth century, the Dominican friar Moneta of Cremona commented on the fact that the 'Modern Manicheans' thought of the wound as a symbol of sinfulness.[16] In the more conventional Christian tradition, Dante, who is usually taken to have been a sincere believer, uses the injured left leg or foot to represent the sin of lust, and the right one to symbolize the sin of ignorance.[17] Bosch's figure has a bleeding sore on his right leg, and (assuming Bosch has also assimilated Dante's symbolism) this would therefore be an indication that he is ignorant. It reveals that he is unaware of the true nature of Christianity and Christ. This sinfully misguided ignorance is enshrined within the Roman faith, as the sore is enshrined within the glass reliquary.

The figure's fake Christianity is further indicated by the imitation star in the eaves of the stable above his head (Plate 8). This 'star,' which has been brought to our notice by Brand Philip, is made up of a bundle of straw, with ray-like strands radiating down from it. It hangs in a false heaven, among 'clouds' made of broken roofing felt.[18] The fake star in its false heaven is an integral part of the unholy figure's illusory and corrupt world. He shows no sign of being aware of the real holy star, which is depicted as a small point of light in the sky, far above the stable.

The imitation crown of thorns on the head of Bosch's demonic figure is another symbol of his outlandish and perverted form of Christianity, and, as we will see later, the shape of his hat is also significant.[19] The strip of cloth hanging between his legs gives us further clues to his identity; it resembles a Roman ecclesiastical garment, the maniple, which is normally worn over the left arm of the celebrant of the Mass. Bosch's repositioning of the maniple has corrupt and lewd implications, which are reinforced by the devilish monsters with which it is decorated. In addition, according to Brand Philip, the bell at its end is a reminder of the Jewish high priest Caiaphas, who condemned Christ.[20]

Other features of Bosch's strange character, including the wound, have led Brand Philip to associate him with the leprous Antichrist.[21] Gombrich, in another convincing and scholarly study, has identified him with Herod. Herod, as described by Josephus and depicted in certain medieval mystery plays, had a skin disease that caused a sore on his leg.[22] These various identities given to the same man may seem contradictory, but in fact they all point to one conclusion. The figure is a corrupt, false and misguided leader, with a negative attitude to Christ. If we look at his symbolism from the point of view of a medieval heretic, his identity becomes clear. This evil character is an image of the Pope. According to the Inquisitor Bernardo Gui, writing in 1323–24, a group of 'Beguins,' who had been condemned as heretics in 1317, associated the Pope with Caiaphas and Herod, as well as the Antichrist — in other words, with all of the various characters whose symbols are found on this figure.[23] Gui's 'Beguins,' who were actually Spiritual Franciscans, could have been influenced by the metaphors of the Cathars.[24] The latter believed that Pope Sylvester, who had been appointed by Constantine in 314, had been an incarnation of the Antichrist. They saw him and all his successors as accomplices of Satan, who had invented the Mass and the Eucharist to further Satan's aims.[25] The Cathars also used Herod as a metaphor for the established church, which wanted to kill Christ (that is, the word of God).[26]

Most of the members of the 'Pope's' entourage within the stable are fantastically dressed, but one of them is clearly a straightforward monk or friar, seen in profile. This man is not simply an anachronism, or a sign of Bosch's typical medieval anti-clericalism, as some writers suggest. Instead, his presence is a subtle indication that the followers of the 'Antichrist' or 'Pope' figure in the stable are his entourage among the Roman clergy. The stable itself is a traditional Christian symbol of the Jewish Synagogue. In Bosch's symbolic language, however, this building is not just the Synagogue of the Old Testament. It is also a depiction of the 'Synagogue of Satan,' a term which, as is well-known, was commonly used by the Cathar heretics for the Roman Church. The ass, a traditional Netherlandish image of Judaism and the Old Testament, is clearly visible in its doorway. The ox, representing true Christianity and the New Testament, is hidden away inside. It is imprisoned in Satan's Synagogue, as the shackled Christ is imprisoned on the altar by the Mass of St Gregory. The stable is clearly the province of Satan, and the Magi who worship at its doorway, are taken in and deceived by the devil.

Some of the disguised images in the central panel of the Prado triptych appear again in different forms on the right wing of the painting (Plate 4). The Pope, for example, was sometimes described by the heretical 'Beguins' as 'the boar who comes out of the woods.'[27] It is interesting, in view of this, that Bosch paints a small boar emerging from the woods in the upper half of the right panel (Plate 9). It is followed by a small group of its young, as the 'Pope' in the stable is followed by his demonic entourage. In the centre of this wing is a sheep, left alone by the 'bad shepherds' who climb and peer irreverently and almost insolently at the baby in the central panel (see Plates 2 and 4). This animal sits beside a rock that has a dead tree growing out of it. The sheep appears to represent a member of the ordinary Christian flock, sitting deserted and unprotected beneath the barren and dead rock of the Church. Behind it, a man and a woman are set upon by wolves. These figures could be either ordinary members of the Church attacked by demons because they are not protected by their clergy, or heretics persecuted by the Church. The Manicheans and Cathars often referred to their initiates as the 'sheep of Light,' and their enemies as wolves, dogs or wild beasts.[28]

The anti-Church symbols discussed above are just some examples of what can be seen in this particular painting. As the following chapters will show, numerous other disguised subversive symbols can be found in this and other works by Bosch. Once one looks at Bosch's works in this much detail, he begins to appear less and less like a pious member of the Church faithful. Instead, it becomes increasingly apparent that he was a heretic. His heresy was a medieval version of the ancient dualist tradition, which (as we saw in the Introduction) can be traced back to the earliest myths. We will examine Bosch's connections with this heresy in the next chapter.

2. Bosch and the Cathar/Manichean Tradition

As we have just seen, Bosch's great hostility towards the Church, and his uncompromising dualism reveal that he was a heretic. If he had been a conventional Christian, he would certainly have been a very odd one. But although Bosch was anti-Church, he was not anti-Christian. Jesus clearly plays an important part in Bosch's world, and there is no doubt that he is seen as a holy figure. This positive view of Jesus, combined with a negativity towards the established Church, shows that Bosch's secret religion was some sort of non-Roman Christianity. He was clearly a Christian heretic, and, ever since the seventeenth century, some viewers have seen him in this way.

Fraenger's interpretation of Bosch's art

The medieval Church was plagued with a number of heretical Christian sects, including the Spiritual Franciscans, and the Poor Men of Lyons, or Waldensians. Both of these heresies were still in existence during the late Middle Ages, but neither of them was dualistic. Another important group of dissident Christians was known as the Adamites, or Brethren of the Free Spirit. These heretics were particularly numerous in Germany during Bosch's lifetime, and during the 1940's, the German Art Historian Wilhelm Fraenger suggested that Bosch might have been a member of this group.

Fraenger's interpretations of Bosch's major paintings, based on the real and imagined tenets of the Brothers of the Free Spirit, have had a great impact. But most of today's art historians disagree with Fraenger, because they believe that his views are based on some major misinterpretations of both the Brethren of the Free Spirit and the iconography of Bosch. Not much is known of the real beliefs of the Brethren, who emerged in the thirteenth century and continued into the sixteenth.

Nevertheless, as Fraenger often emphasises, there is no doubt that these dissidents were pantheists rather than dualists. They believed that God was present in every part of the natural world, and that the material realm and everything in it was therefore holy. According to them, everyone was destined to be saved, because all of humanity came from God and was thus essentially divine. There was no Trinity, no hell, no purgatory, no resurrection, and no need for the sacraments of the Church. The Brethren were divided into sub-sects, and at least some of these believed that for true followers of the free spirit, there was no virtue and no vice. The sub-sect known as the Adamites seems also to have included 'promiscuous nakedness' and sensuality among its practices.[1]

Fraenger's belief that Bosch was a member of the Brethren of the Free Spirit, and most likely an Adamite, is largely inspired by the iconography of the central panel of the *Garden of Earthly Delights* (Plate 21). Because of the hedonistic and sensuous naked figures in this one panel, Fraenger assumes that Bosch was in favour of promiscuous nakedness, sensuality, and even pagan fertility rites. He interprets the entire triptych, as well as other works by Bosch such as the *Marriage of Cana*, in this vein. Fraenger observes Bosch's works carefully, and notices the details, but in most of his interpretations he ignores the artist's clear condemnations of sensuality and the material world. Because he is determined to view Bosch as an optimistic pantheist, he often has to go through complicated convolutions in order to reconcile his theories with what one actually sees in the artist's works. He also attributes all sorts of arcane and complex beliefs to the Brethren of the Free Spirit, as an explanation for the elaborate interpretations he makes of Bosch's symbolism. There is no evidence that the real members of this very secretive religion held these particular beliefs.

In Fraenger's favour, however, it must be said that one of the reasons for his great impact is his recognition of Bosch's unconforming and esoteric nature. Fraenger might have misinterpreted and distorted Bosch's esoteric symbols in his efforts to make them conform to a pantheistic belief system to which they did not belong, but he did realize that they had meanings which were outside the mainstream Christian tradition. It is probably for this reason that Fraenger's works are still read with interest today, despite their complexities and convolutions.

Other interpretations

Fraenger's influence still continues among certain authors, who use his complex and fanciful approach to symbolism in their own interpretations of Bosch's works. We see this trend (combined with some perceptive insights) in the writings of Wertheim Aymès, who believes that Bosch was a Rosicrucian, and Reutersward, who also interprets the master's works from an esoteric point of view. Stein Schneider is another writer who has been influenced by Fraenger's esoteric but free approach to artistic symbols. He is different from all the others, however, in that he thinks that Bosch (along with Brueghel, Michelangelo and a number of other Renaissance artists) believed in a mixture of Catharism and Neo-Platonism. Stein Schneider's ideas are expressed in a series of articles published in the *Cahiers d'Etudes Cathares* between 1983 and 1985. His discussions of the Italian works are far-fetched and unconvincing, and he does not say much about Bosch's dualism, but he does make some interesting and relevant points about Bosch's *Tabletop of the Seven Deadly Sins* and *Stone Operation* (see Chapters 5 and 7).

Other art historians, who think that Bosch's symbolism is odd, but not quite heretical, explain his meanings in terms of alchemy and astrology. These two ancient traditions co-existed with Christianity and were tolerated by the Roman Church. It is certainly possible that Bosch did include some of their images in his paintings, but this does not mean that he was a committed alchemist or astrologer. He could have used their symbols for his own purposes, just as he used the sayings and drolleries of the folk tradition. Above all, Bosch was a dualist, and, as far as we know, there was only one dualistic heresy in medieval Europe. This was the 'Modern Manichean' religion of the Cathars.

It would be reasonable to wonder at this stage whether Bosch could possibly have been a Cathar at a time when this heresy had supposedly been wiped out, and in a town where it never seems to have existed. However well Bosch's symbols may correspond with the doctrines, myths and metaphors of the Cathars, the artist could not have unearthed and depicted this religion all on his own. Bosch would only have expressed Catharism in his works if he shared his faith with other believers. And in fact, as we will see later, such believers did still exist. It is not easy to wipe out a strongly felt religion, and as one should really expect, Catharism remained active in underground pockets well into the sixteenth century. There is clear evidence that it still existed in Venice, Northern Italy and Germany during Bosch's lifetime, and it could well have persisted undiscovered in other areas, too. Venice and Germany may seem remote from the Netherlands and 's-Hertogenbosch, but as it turns out, Bosch had connections with both of them. Bosch and his family could indeed have been Cathars, and in order to see why, we must look first at effects that the persecutions had on the people who remained loyal to this persistent and much maligned heresy.

Cathars and the Inquisition

As we saw in the Introduction, the Cathar/Manichean heresy had a great appeal to people in all social strata. It became especially widespread in Lombardy and the Languedoc, but it was also important in Northern Europe. We know that Cathars lived in Flanders, for example, because there are records of persecutions there in c.1114, 1162, 1182 and 1235. They also found their way to some parts of Germany. Cathar heretics were discovered Cologne in 1143, and were burned at the stake at Cologne and Bonn in 1163.[2]

With its highly motivated missionaries, and its intensely committed believers, Catharism became more and more of a rival to the Church in both Northern and Southern Europe. Attempts at persuasion, and sporadic persecutions had little effect on its growth. In the end, the Church was only able to eliminate its threat by establishing the thorough and painstaking investigations of the Inquisition. These were introduced during the first half of the thirteenth century.

Once the Inquisition was established, it set up a regime which, for many, was a reign of terror. Those who suffered under it included not only the Cathars, but also other heretics, and people who were accused of witchcraft. In 1231, for example, a fanatical agent of Pope Gregory IX called Conrad of Marburg organized a series of particularly violent persecutions all over Germany. Cathars were among the dissidents whom he attacked at Trier.[3] Conrad's aim was to convert or exterminate every Christian who did not subscribe to the Roman norms, but sweeping as his attacks were, he could not have rooted out and executed every last heretic in Germany. Some must have fled the country or gone underground, as always happens during periods of persecution.

Flight was a common means of attempting to escape the Inquisition. During the thirteenth and fourteenth centuries, when the attacks on the Cathars were at their height, the unfortunate members of this religion moved from country to country in a desperate effort to find safety. Safety was extremely difficult to find, however, for wherever the heretics were known to have congregated, the Inquisition followed.[4] And once the Inquisitors were installed, even total secrecy and an appearance of great orthodoxy could not be guaranteed to give full protection. The cases of Armanno Pongilupo in late thirteenth century Ferrara and Guido Lacha in early fourteenth century Brescia are particularly striking examples of the Inquisition's methods of rooting out those who tried to hide their identities. On the surface, these two Lombard citizens appeared to be such pious members of the faithful that the local people actually revered them as saints after their deaths. The Inquisition was in full force in Lombardy at this time, however, and in the end the Inquisitors discovered that, beneath their conventionally pious exteriors, both of these men had spent years as active and committed Cathars. After these discoveries, canonization was ruled out, and instead, the bodies of both men were exhumed and burned.[5]

The Cathars who fell into the hands of the Inquisition while they were still alive were frequently tortured. Lashings and other means of punishment were used to force them to reveal the identities of their co-religionists, and to make a full conversion to orthodox Christianity. Those who would not convert were turned over to the so-called 'secular arm,' and were burned at the stake. Even the Cathars who had converted were not guaranteed a return to the normal world. Instead, many of them were imprisoned for life, because the Inquisitors felt, with good reason, that they were likely to revert to Catharism.

Catharism after the fourteenth century

By the fifteenth century, the Inquisition had done its job so well that it had wiped out all but the most fragmentary remnants of open Catharism in Western Europe. Nevertheless, there was still one location, just across the Adriatic from Italy, where the religion still flourished undisguised. This place was Bosnia. Bosnian Cathars were numerous inland, and were also found in the Venetian controlled towns of Split and Trogir on the Dalmatian Coast (see Map 4). These Cathar dualists were known locally as members of the Bosnian Church. They were also called Patarenes, the same name that had been given to the Cathars of Lombardy and Piedmont.

The dualism and Catharism of the Bosnian Church has been disputed by Fine, who makes an effort to reinterpret the records. But most other scholars accept the overwhelming evidence that the Patarenes of Bosnia were Cathars. The book which discusses this evidence most fully is *Dualist Heresy in the Middle Ages* by M. Loos. The documents covered by Loos are too numerous to discuss in full here, but certain records in the archives of the late fourteenth century Inquisition in Turin are good examples. These describe visits between people from Bosnia and citizens of the small town of Chieri, near Turin. The records show that all of these trips, which took place during the years 1348 to 1382, were made for the purpose of teaching or learning about the Cathar religion.[6]

The Cathar nature of the Bosnian Church is also shown by a number of letters that were exchanged between various Popes and their mainly Franciscan envoys in Bosnia. The letters demonstrate the unsuccessful attempts that were made by the western Church to combat the 'heretics' and 'Patarenes' who were widespread in Bosnian territory during the thirteenth, fourteenth and fifteenth centuries.[7] As Loos shows, many of the Patarenes continued to live in Bosnia after the Turks had invaded the country in 1460 (see Map 4).[8] It is generally believed that these members of the Bosnian Church converted to Islam sometime during the sixteenth century.

Not all of the Patarenes remained in Bosnia after the Turks invaded, however. A considerable number of them were given the protection of the Venetian Republic and allowed to settle in Venetian territory. In

March 1466, for example, the Venetians gave land along the Dalmatian Coast to a Bosnian Patarene nobleman called Stephen Vukčić. They also gave refuge, presumably along the coast, to a gost (priest of the Bosnian Church) whose name was Radin. We know that Gost Radin died in Dubrovnik in 1467, but we do not know what happened to the fifty or sixty other members of the gost's entourage (people of his 'law and sect') who had also been given asylum by Venice.[9]

Venice's liberal attitude towards heretics was not new or sudden. This city had always had an independent and tolerant attitude. In 1249, for example, the tribunal of the Venetian Inquisition classified Cathars and usurers together, and punished only those who were not citizens by banishment. By medieval standards, this was exceptionally liberal. On certain occasions the Pope insisted on laws against heresy, but Venice still did not enforce them. Even in 1542, when the Congregation of Rome was set up in order to direct the entire Italian Inquisition from a central source, the Venetian tribunal continued to remain comparatively independent, and to sentence mildly.[10] As before, people of various religious faiths were not looked at too closely in Venice, or given much trouble, as long as they behaved discreetly and did not attract the attention of the authorities in Rome.

As we have seen, some of the Bosnian Cathar refugees settled in the Venetian territories on the Adriatic during the 1460's. But did any of these Bosnian heretics move on to the city itself, or into its mainland territories? No records of this have been discovered so far, but perhaps new research will reveal further information on this subject. More and more evidence of heresy in Renaissance Venice and Northern Italy is continually being unearthed by scholars such as Carlo Ginzburg, Andrea del Col, John Martin and Nicholas Davidson. It is becoming increasingly clear that the apparently smooth and uniform surface of western Christianity (at this period, as well as earlier ones) actually covered a variety of religious beliefs. Venice's territories in Northern Italy were less safe for dissidents than the city itself, for the Roman Holy Office had a freer hand there. Nevertheless, the records show that various heresies, including Catharism, persisted on the mainland as well as in the city, despite all the efforts of the Holy Office.

Much of the evidence for this is brought to light by the trials of a heretical miller called Domenico Scandella. Scandella came from the small hilltown of Montereale near Pordenone in the Friuli, an area to the north of Venice which had been ruled by the city since 1420. The documents of Scandella's trials, which took place in various towns in the Friuli, were first examined by Carlo Ginzburg during the 1970's and are discussed in his book *The Cheese and the Worms*. The records show that after about thirty years of imprudently broadcasting his heretical beliefs to all who would listen, Scandella was finally denounced to the Holy Office by his enemy the parish priest. He was tried in 1583 and found guilty of several heresies, including a revival of Manichean dualism. After his first trial, Scandella was sentenced to life imprisonment. He was released from prison after only two years, on grounds of mercy and repentance, but he continued to discuss his unaltered beliefs in public. As a result, he was re-tried in 1599 and finally burnt at the stake.

Ginzburg concludes that Scandella's beliefs reflect a complex set of doctrines, some very ancient, which were communicated orally between peasants and members of the upper classes. He does not think that the miller's complicated views associate him with any single known heresy, but in fact, as Andrea del Col points out in the introduction to his book *Domenico Scandella detto Menocchio*, the majority of Scandella's beliefs show a clear connection with Catharism. For example (and there are numerous examples to choose from) the Friulian miller thought that each human soul was a fallen angel trapped in a body of mud, and that each person had a spirit as well as a soul. These are classical Cathar doctrines, as we will see later. But Scandella's Catharism can be oddly distorted. He held the usual view that God the Father had not formed the visible universe, for example, but instead of following the true Cathar tradition and believing that it was the devil who was responsible for the material realm, he thought that the creators had been the Holy Spirit and the angels.

Scandella's contradictions can be very baffling. Could this miller really have been a Cathar heretic when some of his ideas were so very untypical of the religion? Andrea del Col offers a good solution to the problem by concluding that Scandella's doctrines were Cathar, but with some profound modifications. These variations in the Cathar heresy, which had been developing during the fifteenth and sixteenth centuries, tended to incorporate doctrines from established Christianity, as well as from heresies such as Anabaptism.

In summary, it appears that Scandella was indeed a Cathar but that his version of the heresy was more fluid than it had been in the past and was in the process of changing its traditional forms. These facts are very relevant to the subject of Bosch, for if Catharism was still alive in Northern Italy during the sixteenth century, it must also have been around in the fifteenth, even if it was beginning to change.

Another fascinating and important aspect of the story of Scandella is the question of how he acquired his neo-Cathar beliefs. This Friulian miller (who read Italian but not Latin) told the Holy Office that he had looked at certain books. These texts contained some passages which showed connections with a few of Scandella's ideas, but the books themselves were not heretical. It therefore seems likely, as both Ginzburg and del Col have said, that the heretic's main sources had been oral. Who, then, were Scandella's contacts? How many of them were there, and where did they live? One likely candidate is a painter called Nicola, who was known to be a heretic but had not been tried, because two ecclesiastics from his town spoke highly of his character. Nicola came from the town of Porcia, not far from Montereale where Scandella lived. According to certain witnesses, Scandella had learned his heresies from this man. Nicola, in his turn, might have been in contact with a group of heretical artisans who also lived in Porcia. These people, who were imprisoned by the Holy Office in 1557, had met regularly to discuss 'the renewal of life, ... the purity of the Gospel and abstention from sins.'[11] Ginzburg thinks these heretics could have been Anabaptists, but their discussion subjects also correspond with Cathar concepts and aims.

Nicola of Porcia is likely to have been Scandella's main contact, though there could have been others, such as his old friend the priest of Polcenigo, who discussed the typically Cathar contrast between physical and spiritual death during his own heresy trial. A converted Jew called Simon, who wandered about living on charity and spent an entire night discussing heretical ideas with Scandella, might possibly have been another. Simon and his connections with Scandella will be referred to again later.

In addition to Scandella's possible Cathar contacts, there were other known heretics, with similar opinions, who were unknown to the Friulian miller. These heretics, who lived in other parts of Northern Italy, are discussed towards the end of Ginzburg's book. For example, there was a miller called Pelegrino Baroni, nicknamed Pighino ('the fat and lazy') who came from the Modenese Appenines. Pighino, who appears to have been less well-liked than Scandella, was denounced by his fellow-villagers. His heretical views, revealed in his trial at Ferrara in 1570, were almost exactly the same as those of the miller from the Friuli. Ginzburg suggests that Pighino picked up his ideas in Bologna as early as 1530 or 1540, when he was a servant in the house of a nobleman who had heretical connections.

The stories of these various North Italian heretics with their neo-Cathar ideas are probably only the tip of a well-hidden iceberg. They show that the concentrated persecutions of the fourteenth century did not kill Catharism off, after all. Instead, it persisted in various forms on the mainland until at least the end of the sixteenth century.

What about Venice itself, then? Here, the records of the Inquisition also point to a number of heretics whose doctrines might have been Cathar. In each of these cases, however, the descriptions of the dissidents' beliefs are much less detailed than those of Scandella. As a result, they remain inconclusive. The comparatively early case of Amadeo de Lando, who was investigated by members of the Tribunal in 1461, is an example of this. The records of his case have been discovered recently in the Venetian Archives by Nicholas Davidson of Leicester University, and are not yet published. According to them, Amadeo did not believe that the Roman Church was subject to Christ, and did not support the spending of money on church buildings. He also opposed the practice of praying to the saints, and he did not think that it was necessary to confess one's sins to a priest. All of these heretical ideas were held by the Cathars, but were not unique to them.

The Venetian trial records can do no more than hint that Catharism existed in this city during the periods which are relevant to Bosch, but there is one interesting piece of evidence which is much more significant. It seems extremely likely that these dualist heretics were responsible for the publication in Venice, in 1522, of a key Cathar text. Venice was a cosmopolitan and liberal sea-port, and publishers in this city were particularly free, especially before 1542 when the Congregation of Rome was set up. They would have been able to print a book for a group of heretics without drawing attention to it and attracting the unwelcome interest of the authorities.

This particular Cathar text (which, as we shall see later, is especially relevant to the subject of Bosch) was a Latin translation of the heretical

— rather than the accepted canonical — version of the *Vision of Isaiah*. According to Ivanov, this apocryphal book, which had been one of the most important Cathar texts of the Middle Ages, was used by the Cathar adepts to induce mystical visions of ascension to the Seventh Heaven. The chances are that similar adepts were still living in Venice during the early sixteenth century, and it was they who commissioned the book. It is even possible that an Italian version of this work existed, and was known to Domenico Scandella, the heretical miller of the Friuli. Towards the end of his life, Scandella became more mystical. He was heard talking about the moon and stars, and though no one seems to have understood what he was saying about them, his ideas appear to have been connected with 'a most beautiful book' which he had acquired and lost. He discussed this book with Simon, the converted Jew mentioned above. Simon, who was a witness during Scandella's second trial, said he thought that the book might have been the Koran. As Ginzburg points out, however, the Koran would probably have been incomprehensible to Scandella. It was too foreign to his culture and experience. The Cathar *Vision of Isaiah* would have been much nearer and can certainly be described as a beautiful book which gives mystical descriptions of the moon and stars.[12]

Taken together, the accumulated evidence already unearthed points clearly to the persistence of Catharism in Venice and Northern Italy. But did this heresy also survive underground in the countries north of the Alps? In fact, there is some very good evidence that another small group of Cathars, which believed in a classical form of the heresy, did exist in Germany during the sixteenth century. The documents which show this are discussed by C.-P. Clasen. They report the case of a man called Hans Thon. Thon was a wandering shepherd who was picked up by the authorities in 1564 in the area near Mühlhausen, in Thuringia. He was arrested and imprisoned for his religious beliefs. He escaped, but was arrested again in August 1583. He still refused to recant, and was finally put to death in January 1584.

The theologians who questioned Thon wrote down his doctrines as he described them. They recognized these beliefs as heretical and very dangerous, but they did not realize what would have been plain to the Northern Inquisitors of earlier centuries. Thon's doctrines, as Clasen says, were unquestionably Cathar. Thon told the theologians that there were two 'masters.' The good one was the God of light, who had created everything that was invisible and eternal, pure and holy. The evil master was the devil, the principle of darkness, who had made all that was visible and passing. This included the earth and everything on it, as well as the visible heavens, including the physical sun, moon and stars. Thon also denied the human nature of Jesus, and the conventional Christian belief that he had suffered, died and risen for mankind. He spoke of the Father, Son and Holy Ghost as one person. In addition to this, he viewed marriage as the unchaste creation of the evil master. He also rejected the resurrection of the dead, and said that both the Old and the New Testament were worthless. All of these beliefs except the total (if it was total) rejection of the New Testament are precisely those of the Cathars.[13] It seems that Thon, unlike Scandella and his contacts, had retained the classic Cathar beliefs.

Several of Thon's personal characteristics, which are also brought out in the records of the theologians, point to the likelihood that he was not just an ordinary believer in the Cathar faith, but a Cathar priest or Perfect. The priests and priestesses of this religion wandered around, as Thon did, caring for their human flocks. Even if they were not working-class by birth, they usually did labouring jobs as a cover, and to create a feeling of unity with the ordinary Cathar believers. The fact that Thon was a shepherd would therefore not be out of character. In addition to this, Thon did not lie when questioned about his religious beliefs, and he put his view that marriage was unchaste into practice by staying single. These traits again point to Thon's religious vocation, for every member of the Cathar priesthood had to follow strict rules of honesty and chastity.[14]

If Thon was a priest, he would also have had a flock. But where were they? There is no record whatsoever that any of them existed, and yet they must have. They were no doubt present somewhere in Thuringia, practising their religion under cover. Most likely, they were an indigenous group which had existed secretly in Germany for many centuries. They could well have been descendants of the few Cathars who had survived the horrors of Conrad of Marburg's persecutions in the early 1230's. These few survivors must have decided that total secrecy was the only means by which they could continue to exist. Nothing was heard of them again until the time of Hans Thon. Nevertheless, they appear to have clung defiantly to their faith, and passed it on to their children. As Clasen says, strongly held beliefs can be handed down in families for generations.[15] The underground continuation of the forbidden beliefs and practices of the Marranos (secret Jews) in Catholic Spain is one well-known example of this.

Bosch's family and workshop

Bosch's family name was Van Aken — evidence that his relatives had originally come from the town of Aachen. Aachen is near to Cologne, Bonn and Trier, the areas along the Rhine where Cathar heretics are known to have lived during the twelfth and thirteenth centuries. Bosch's family records have been studied by Mosmans. He believes that the Van Akens arrived in 's-Hertogenbosch sometime around the middle of the thirteenth century, because it is not long after this that their names first appear in the town records. The earliest relevant document mentions a wool merchant of 's-Hertogenbosch who did business with England in 1271. The merchant was called van Aken with a small 'v.' This apparently minor detail reveals that the man had taken a new name which showed that he had come from the town of Aachen. Once his descendants were established in North Brabant, they began to be called Van Aken with a large 'V.' This was now simply a name, rather than a sign that they had recently arrived. Mosmans believes that the wool merchant established himself in 's-Hertogenbosch in about 1250.[16]

Is it a coincidence, then, that Bosch's family surfaced in 's-Hertogenbosch so soon after Conrad of Marburg's efforts to eliminate every last heretic in Germany? The chances are that it is not a coincidence. Instead, it is an important additional piece in our jigsaw puzzle. It suggests that Bosch's forebears were Cathar refugees, people who fled to a place they hoped would be safe, just as so many of their co-religionists had done, and would do in the future. The fact that the earliest recorded van Aken was a wool merchant could also be significant, for it is a well-known fact that many Cathars were involved in the cloth trade. Like Hans Thon and his invisible flock, this merchant and his descendants held onto their faith in secret, and passed it on to the generations which followed them.

North Brabant, where 's-Hertogenbosch is located, was somewhat safer than Germany had been, for it never had an Inquisition.

Suspected cases of heresy in the area were normally investigated by the Bishop of Utrecht, and as far as we know, no one ever suggested that any of the local heretics were Cathars. It was therefore not quite as dangerous to be a secret member of this faith in 's-Hertogenbosch as in some parts of Europe. Catharism could have been passed down unnoticed or unreported from generation to generation within a small group of Netherlandish families, as long as it was kept well hidden beneath an outward show of conventional religious observance.

It would have been essential, however, even in 's-Hertogenbosch, for those who believed in the notorious Cathar heresy to have done their best to hide their true beliefs from lay Christians as well as clergy. Even if most of their neighbours were discreet, there was always the risk that someone might report them. Memories of earlier disasters would not have been forgotten. The fate of a group of twelfth century Cathar refugees, who had fled to Cologne from recent persecutions in Flanders, is one example of the dangers posed by unreliable neighbours. The unfortunate fugitives, who had been found hiding in a barn in 1163, were handed over to the local bishop by neighbours who suspected them because they kept to themselves, and did not go to church. All of them were subsequently burned at the stake.[17] With examples such as this on their minds, Bosch's family, which included a number of apparently pious painters, would have had to be discreet with all outsiders, making certain that they did not suspect that the Van Akens were not conventional Christians. If their secret had been revealed to the wrong person, the ensuing investigations and exposures would have led to the execution or life imprisonment of many whose faith had never previously been questioned.

By the fifteenth century, when Bosch was alive, the Inquisition was no longer looking for Cathars. This heresy now appeared to have been totally eliminated in Western Europe, and as a result, it was thought about much less than it had been during the thirteenth and fourteenth centuries. The Church hierarchy of the fifteenth and sixteenth centuries was especially concerned with budding and then overt Protestantism in Northern Europe, and with Judaism and Islam in Spain. Catharism was only considered to be a problem in Bosnia, and after the Turkish invasion it was forgotten, particularly in Northern Europe. It was because of this decreased awareness of Catharism that Hans Thon was not recognized for what he was, and the other members of his group were not exposed. It is for this same reason that the real meanings behind Bosch's drolleries and odd symbols managed to pass without being understood or investigated.

Bosch could not be completely complacent, of course. It was still necessary for him to keep up an apparently pious Christian front. This would explain his well-known activities as an apparently devoted member of the lay Brotherhood of Our Lady, and his outwardly impeccable social behaviour. Unlike Hans Thon and perhaps Scandella's teacher, Nicola of Porcia, he does not appear to have been an initiated Cathar Perfect or priest. If he had given his life over to his religion to this extent, he would have had to follow the rules of honesty, and would not have been able to put on such an actively conventional front or continue living with his wife. Bosch would have had to be particularly careful if he wanted the heresy in his paintings to pass without suspicion. Once he had established his reputation as a respectable and pious citizen, he would have been able to express his true feelings and beliefs through his supposedly amusing double meanings and eccentric symbols.

People sometimes argue that Bosch could not have included heretical ideas in his paintings without the members of his workshop finding out about it, and reporting him to the authorities. But, as so often, we do not know all the facts here. As far as we can tell, Bosch seems to have made less use of the workshop than many other painters of his day. A number of artists imitated his style and symbols, but there is no evidence that he ever taught them, or even knew them. Did he have collaborators? As we will see later, he did have copies made of his works. On the other hand, there is little sign that anyone actually helped him to execute his originals. X-rays show that he put the colours directly onto the panel, making numerous alterations to underdrawings which were often just sketchy outlines.[18] Many of his pictures have also been restored and repainted, but this work was done later, and is not by his shop.

Bosch must have had some workshop helpers of course. If nothing else, he would have needed them to copy his works and do technical jobs such as mixing paints. But why should we assume that these members of his shop were outsiders? Bosch did not need to look further than his own family for assistance, since his father, three of his uncles, and his brother were all painters. Even his nephew was a woodcarver.[19] The works of all these artists seem to have disappeared without trace, but perhaps we have been looking at them all along without even realizing it. The many copies of the artist's paintings might well have been executed by Bosch's brother, uncles, or father. These members of Bosch's family could also have been responsible for some of the paintings with disputed attributions.

Bosch and Venice

If Bosch was born into a long-standing underground Cathar family, as the evidence discussed above indicates, he would have been a member of a small and secretive group which lived unreported among the ordinary people of a provincial market town. Under these circumstances, he would have had to spend much of his time acting out a lie, and would surely have felt very isolated among most of the citizens of his home town. As a result, it is likely that he would have wanted to travel to places such as Venice, where other members of his religion could still be found. And in fact it appears that this is just what he did do. This is revealed by some very good evidence, discussed in an article by Slatkes. As Slatkes shows, there are many indications that Bosch spent a year or two in Venice and the Veneto at the turn of the fifteenth century.

One of the signs that Bosch was in Venice is the fact that several of his paintings were located in that city by or before 1521. Slatkes suggests, very reasonably, that these works, which show certain Italian influences, were executed in Venice, or, in one case, Brescia. The latter town was within the Venetian dominions on the mainland, and the painting which might have been commissioned for one of its churches is the *Altarpiece of St Julia*. Slatkes makes the connection between the painting and the town because Brescia owned the relics of St Julia, and was one of the few centres of her cult.[20] The *St Julia Altarpiece*, which is now in the Doge's Palace in Venice, depicts a crucified female saint surrounded by demonic persecutors. As an image of a figure of light, suffering in the world of darkness, it has much in common with Bosch's various depictions of the Passion of Jesus (see Chapter 5). But what could also be important from the Cathar point of view is its con-

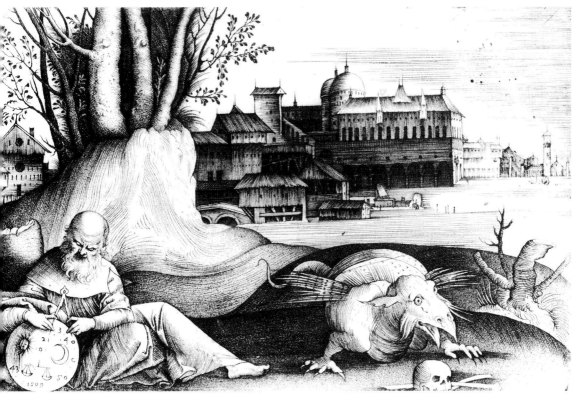

Figure 5. Giulio Campagnola *(c.1482–c.1515)*, *Sage, Death and the Devil* (also called *The Astrologer)*. Engraving, probably after Giorgione, *c.*1509.

nections with the town of Brescia. We know that Brescia had been one of the most important late thirteenth/early fourteenth century centres of Catharism in Northern Italy, and, though there is no known evidence that the heresy still existed there in Bosch's day, the artist's possible visit to the town could indicate that some Cathars still survived there underground.

The question of whether or not Cathars survived in fifteenth century Brescia and were visited there by Bosch is interesting, but it is not as important as Bosch's connections with Venice itself. There is virtually no doubt that Cathars were still present in Venice and its territories during Bosch's lifetime, for, as we have already seen, the evidence for this is particularly good. And, significantly, it is the art of this city which shows the greatest connections with the works of Bosch. As Slatkes points out, Bosch's effect on the art of Venice is a further sign that he visited the city in person. His influence is found in a number of early sixteenth century Venetian paintings and engravings. For example, Giulio Campagnola's engraving *Sage, Death and the Devil* (also called *The Astrologer;* see Figure 5) which was executed in Venice in 1509, contains a Bosch-like devil. Further influences of Bosch, in the shape of more devils and a burning building, can be seen in another engraving called *The Dream of Raphael,* executed in *c*.1505–8, by Marcantonio Raimondi (Figure 6). Both of these engravings are believed to be copies of lost works by Giorgione, the Venetian artist whose works show the most connections with those of Bosch. The Venetian art collector Cardinal Grimani, who was a friend of Giorgione's, owned

Figure 6. Marcantonio Raimondi (*c*.1480–*c*.1534), *The Dream of Raphael*. Engraving, probably after Giorgione, *c*.1505–8.

some of his works, as well as some of the ones by Bosch that are still in Venice. Slatkes suggests that Grimani might have been the link between the two artists.[21]

An example of another work attributed to Giorgione which is not mentioned by Slatkes, but which is also particularly near to Bosch, is the *Tramonto,* or *Sunset Landscape* at the London National Gallery (Plate 10). The sinister appearance of the rocks in this work, and the small Bosch-like devils moving in and out of the water, imply that the earth itself is unsound and demonic. But this painting is not entirely pessimistic, for the image of a knight fighting a dragon in the middleground symbolizes the struggle with evil. The same idea is repeated again more subtly in the scene in the foreground, where a man, who might be a doctor, is tending another's injured leg. As we saw in Chapter 1, Bosch uses the wounded leg as a symbol of sinfulness. The attempt to cure it in Giorgione's painting therefore hints at the overcoming of sin. We don't know whether Bosch had any direct connection with the actual message of this painting, but there is no doubt that many of its images show his influence.

In addition to the similarities of subject matter, Bosch's painting style also has something in common with that of Giorgione. Both artists use light brush-strokes and paint delicate, wispy highlights on details such as waterfalls, embroideries or metals. Problems of dating and establishing their earlier works makes it difficult to know which of them was the first to use these techniques, but perhaps it was Bosch, the older artist, who influenced Giorgione's style.

Painters who were working in other parts of Italy when Bosch made his trip to Venice and the Veneto were not influenced by either his style or his symbols. On the other hand, there is one important Florentine artist who did visit Venice at this time, and whose paintings do show a clear and particularly interesting connection with those of both Bosch and Giorgione. This artist is Leonardo da Vinci. Leonardo had been living in Milan between *c.*1482 and the second half of 1499. He spent some time in Venice soon after leaving Milan, and was there again in March 1500. The clear mutual influence between his work and that of Giorgione and Bosch show that the three artists must have met together during one or both of Leonardo's visits. This does not prove that either Giorgione or Leonardo shared Bosch's strong commitment to Catharism, but it *is* possible that they knew about Bosch's religion,

Figure 7. Leonardo, *Allegory with Wolf and Eagle*. Drawing in red chalk, *c*.1515.

and were flirting with some of its ideas. There is no doubt, in any case, that there was a relationship of style and subject matter between the three of them. Giorgione, who was only about twenty-three at the time, seems to have been affected by Leonardo's spirituality and *sfumato* (smoky softness of style). He was also influenced by Bosch's subject matter and style, as seen above.

Bosch and Leonardo were near in age (Leonardo was about fifty in 1500, and Bosch was between forty and fifty), and they seem to have influenced each other. Slatkes suggests that Bosch may have picked up some of Leonardo's *sfumato*, and, in addition to this, both artists depicted similar grotesque and jeering faces in a number of their paintings and drawings.[22] It is difficult to say who influenced whose caricatural faces, but there is a good chance that Leonardo's were earlier. This is certainly the case where the connections between Leonardo's *Adoration of the Magi* (Plate 11), painted in Florence in *c*.1481–82, and Bosch's later Prado *Adoration of the Magi* of *c*.1510 are concerned. Bosch must have seen a drawing of Leonardo's version of the scene, for his peering shepherds and fighting horsemen show a distinct similarity to Leonardo's images.

But Bosch did not just take influences from Leonardo. He also gave some back. There is a good likelihood that the Italian artist based his undated drawing at Windsor called *Allegory with a Wolf and Eagle* (Figure 7) on an early version of Bosch's frequently depicted *Ship of Fools*. In the painting at the Louvre (Plate 15), which is the best known example of Bosch's depictions of the *Ship of Fools*, the gluttonous and lustful figures ride in a boat which has a tree for a mast. Leonardo's wolflike creature, which represents humanity's animal side, rides in a similar boat. Leonardo's version of the scene is more optimistic than Bosch's, however. Bosch's fools are determinedly unaware, but Leonardo's animal steers its way by an eagle, a symbol of the higher self.

Much more could be said about the relationship between these three major artists. Could there be any connection, for example, between their meeting in Venice, and the group of three thoughtful men depicted in Giorgione's *The Three Philosophers*? Perhaps this painting (Plate 12), which is thought to date from about 1507, is a private commemoration of the visit. It has already been suggested by several scholars that the young man who sits on the left of the group is a self-portrait of Giorgione. As we will see soon, the man in the centre could be a portrait of Bosch, while the one at the far right could be Leonardo.

Certain details revealed by X-rays indicate that *The Three Philosophers* might originally have been a depiction of the Three Magi. The final version, however, is less straightforward and more controversial. Edgar Wind's interpretation of the finished painting is particularly interesting. According to him, the three figures represent philosophers at different stages of spiritual development, who are identified with three different cultures.[23] Of the three, it is the young 'Greek' Giorgione figure who is the most earthly, and the novice of the group. He sits on a slab of rock, holding a set square and compass.

The older philosophers in Giorgione's painting are standing. The middle-aged one in the centre wears an oriental turban and robe (Figure 8). Wind suggests that he is a Persian and a spiritual Zoroastrian sage. This identity would be particularly significant if this figure was a portrait of Bosch, for it would associate him with dualism. It is well-

Figure 8 (left). Head of 'Persian' Philosopher, probable portrait of Bosch. Detail of Giorgione's *The Three Philosophers* (Plate 12).

Figure 9 (opposite left). Engraving after a lost portrait of Bosch. Lampsonius Collection, Antwerp.

Figure 10 (opposite right). Drawing after a lost portrait of Bosch. Recueil d'Arras.

known that the Zoroastrian religion put a great stress on the conflict between darkness and light.

The third philosopher, who is seen by Wind as a 'celestial' Egyptian priest, has a long white beard. He is similar in appearance to the portrait of Leonardo in Raphael's *School of Athens* from the Vatican (1509–10). Giorgione's Leonardo figure holds a sheet or tablet covered with celestial calculations, and Raphael's Leonardo shows similar interest, for he points upwards towards the sky.

The general appearance of all three philosophers has been affected by Giorgione's poetic, soft-edged style. Nevertheless, if we look closely at their features, they correspond well with the known portraits of the three artists. The two Italians may be easier to accept than the 'Bosch' figure, who does not look as Northern or as tormented as we would expect. If we mentally remove his 'Persian' beard and turban, however, he does have quite a lot in common with a later portrait of Bosch. This work was executed near to the end of the artist's life, when Bosch was around the age of sixty. The original portrait is lost, but an engraving

and a drawing after it (Figures 9 and 10) give us an idea of the original. They depict a man who resembles Giorgione's 'Persian' in the shape of his face and neck, as well as his eyebrows and eyes, and the lines around them. The noses are also similar, though Giorgione's version is shorter and more idealized. The mouth in the drawing is longer than in Giorgione's painting, but the one in the engraving is similarly small and curved.

It would be interesting to speculate further about these three philosophical painters and the connections between their works, but to go into any more detail about them here would be to digress. What is relevant to us now is the subject of Bosch's presence in Venice at the turn of the fifteenth century. No written records survive to prove that Bosch was in Venice at this date, but in the late fifteenth century, this lack of documentation would not have been unusual. And records of the visit would have been especially sparse if Bosch had not wanted his presence in the city to be noticed by the authorities. He might well have gone to Venice in order to meet secretly with an established group of Cathars, and, for reasons of safety, it would have been best to keep his visit as unpublicized as possible.

The particularly interesting point, in connection with these possible meetings with his underground co-religionists, is the fact that the images in at least two of Bosch's Venetian paintings have a great deal in common with the mystical visions that must have been inspired by the Cathar *Vision of Isaiah*. This text was not printed in Venice until about twenty-two years after Bosch's visit, but the printed version would have reproduced an earlier, handwritten manuscript which was already in the city. Was Bosch inspired by the manuscript, its local owners, or both, when he painted the works which are now in Venice? This question will be discussed further in Chapter 10.

Bosch's patrons

There is a good chance, then, that a few (though certainly not all) of the paintings which Bosch executed in Venice were done for Cathar patrons. But this could not have been the case with the majority of Bosch's works. Bosch painted a great many pictures, and, since there were not many Cathars left to buy what he produced, he must have had numerous other customers. We know from Netherlandish documents that he executed some works for churches, for example, and that a number of his paintings were owned by the nobility. His most obviously eccentric work, the *Garden of Earthly Delights*, was on display in the palace of Henry III of Nassau in Brussels in 1517, only a year after Bosch's death. It is recorded in the diary of Antonio de Beatis, who was travelling with the Cardinal of Aragon and his entourage. Beatis describes it as a painting full of black and white figures, in various positions, as well as birds, animals, and strange oddities. It provoked interest, but, typically, it was enjoyed for its entertaining details, and no one looked for its overall meaning.[24]

Whoever Bosch's patrons were, however, they were probably not the audience which Bosch really had in mind. Most likely, his main aim in planning his works was not the edification of any of his contemporaries, whatever their faith. Instead, it was the preservation of the classical form of his dying and changing religion for future generations — people of a more open-minded age, who might understand and appreciate them for what they really were. For this reason it did not matter who bought his paintings, as long as the works and their coded message had a chance of lasting well into the future.

With this in mind, Bosch would have felt that the more copies that were made of a work, and the more people who bought them, the better. These factors would increase their chances of survival, and the likelihood that they would eventually reach the people who would be receptive to them. He would certainly *not* have executed his baffling and esoteric paintings for small and arcane groups, as some scholars have suggested. If he had done this, there would be far fewer versions and copies of them, and not so many examples would have survived into the twentieth century.

Bosch's *Marriage at Cana* at Rotterdam (Plate 60) is a good example of a work which has survived through what might be called the proliferation method. In this painting, which contains some of Bosch's most puzzling eccentricities, a self-contained group of holy figures is contrasted with a corrupt and depraved crowd of revellers at a feast. One might assume that this subject was commissioned privately by the small and holy group, but in fact, this was not the case. The example which is preserved at Rotterdam is not, as it turns out, a privately executed original at all, but a contemporary copy. Bosch's tendency to paint directly onto the canvas using only sketchy underdrawings always led to numerous corrections and amendments, and the X-rays of this work do not show his typical alterations. In view of this, Guido Jansen of the Boymans Museum at Rotterdam suggests that the version in his museum was one of several copies made from a prototype. The original would have been on display in Bosch's studio, so that any visitors who saw it and found it appealing could order a similar painting for themselves. According to Jansen, the anonymous *Marriage at Cana* drawing at Philadelphia reproduces another copy of the prototype, to which a donor, introduced by a bishop, has been added.[25]

This evidence, as well as what we know of other examples of Bosch's works, makes it plain that the majority of his patrons were traditional Christians. But we should not assume, as so many scholars do, that Bosch's contemporaries understood all the meanings of his symbols. The fact is that, whether they were noblemen, members of the middle class, or even clerics, Bosch's fifteenth and sixteenth century patrons do not seem to have picked up his real, underlying message.

What they saw was what they expected to see: religious subjects which amused, intrigued and in some cases frightened, much as horror films do today. What these patrons missed were Bosch's hidden Cathar doctrines, and his only partially disguised hatred of both the established Church and the pious confraternity that he was forced to join as a cover for his secret beliefs.

Bosch and the Brotherhood of Our Lady

As we saw in the last chapter, Bosch's *Adoration of the Magi* at the Prado contains many half-hidden criticisms of the Roman religion and its priesthood. One of these is the portrayal of the Madonna and Child as statues or cult images, surrounded by evil or sinfully deluded members of the Church hierarchy. This manner of representing the Nativity, which reveals Bosch's real feelings, would be surprising in any conventional Christian believer, but it is especially odd in a member of a confraternity dedicated to the worship of Our Lady. If we see Bosch as a Cathar, however, those feelings can be explained not only by his reactions to persecutions by the Church, but also by the theology of his heretical religion.

All Gnostics, including the Manicheans and Cathars, saw the physical body as corrupt. In their view, flesh belonged only to Satan's world. As one of the Coptic Manichean psalms from Egypt puts it, the Saviour was not (could not have been) 'born in a womb corrupted.'[26] The Cathars shared this view. Their explanations of how and at what age Jesus had arrived on earth varied, but many of them believed the Saviour (the emissary or Word of God) had entered Mary through her ear, taken form, and emerged again unnoticed.[27] All of them thought that Jesus, and usually Mary as well, were angels who were not made of human flesh. In their view, the body and nature of Jesus was not and never had been in any way physical. In contrast to the orthodox Christians, they believed that the human appearance of Jesus had merely been an illusion.

This docetic Gnostic view of Jesus and Mary can also explain the strange fact that Bosch, a member of a brotherhood dedicated to Our Lady, has left us no extant paintings of the Annunciation or the Virgin and Child on their own. As many authors have observed, these common fifteenth century themes are remarkable for their absence in Bosch's works. The Madonna and Child are represented only in Bosch's Nativity scenes and no more than two of these are generally considered to be authentic. One of them is the Prado *Adoration of the Magi*. The other is a panel which depicts the same theme, located in Philadelphia (Figure 11).

Bosch's *Adoration of the Magi* at Philadelphia appears to be executed before Bosch's trip to Venice. All of its figures are stiff and awkward, with the result that in this painting, the Madonna and Child do not look any more like statues than the rest of the characters. This early painting is also comparatively conventional. There are no strange figures bursting from the stable, no false straw stars, and no small and unexplained toads. But beneath the comparatively simple appearance, Bosch has already started to express heretical ideas. He has begun to use small signs and symbols which hint at his disagreement with the Church's belief in Christ's physical incarnation. From the point of view of Bosch and the Cathars, this belief is a delusion.

The Philadelphia *Adoration* expresses Bosch's views on the subject of the incarnation in two main ways. One of these is subtle comment on a surprising but not uncommon motif in Renaissance art. Leo Steinberg discusses this motif and its meanings in his book *The Sexuality of Christ*. As Steinberg convincingly points out, the kneeling king in Nativity scenes by fifteenth and sixteenth century artists such as Ghirlandaio, Botticelli and Brueghel, is often shown taking a good look at the Child's private parts. There are theological reasons for this. Christ's circumcision took place when he was eight days old, and the feast of the Epiphany, when the baby manifested himself to the Magi, was celebrated on the sixth of January, four days later. The Magi in Renaissance paintings are particularly interested in looking for signs of the circumcision, for, as the theologians of the period saw it, this was the first occasion when Jesus undertook to 'spill his blood.' They believed that the circumcision provided evidence that the Gnostics and Manicheans were wrong about the nature of Jesus. It showed that he was made of solid flesh and blood, and it was also a sign that he would later consent to suffer another, greater physical sacrifice.[28]

Bosch, who held the docetic view of Jesus, would have disagreed strongly with these ideas. He expresses his dissident views with one small but significant aberration in the traditional scene. In his depiction, Jesus absents himself from the fixed stare of the kneeling Magus and gazes into the sky, far above the heads of all three kings. In the conventional version of the scene, the Child always focuses his eyes on the Magus who examines him, appearing to give approval and consent. Bosch's apparently minor change in the tradition can easily be overlooked, but it is an early and experimental way of expressing his real views of the subject.

Bosch's second means of expressing his heretical ideas about the Nativity is through the gifts of the Magi. These, as Tolnay has pointed out, are not the usual presents offered to the Child. As in the Prado *Adoration of the Magi,* they bring Catholic rituals and doctrines to mind. In Bosch's Philadelphia *Adoration,* they are associated with the Mass, in which Christ's body is symbolically eaten, or the worship of the physical remains of the saints. The elaborate triple ciborium offered by the kneeling king, and the golden monstrance in the hands of the black Magus, are both used to hold the Eucharistic wafer. The reliquary, which is held by the king who faces the viewer, is a container for the bones of the saints. The decorations on the sleeve of the black Magus which illustrate the fall of manna, correspond with the other symbols, for this biblical event was seen by conventional Christians as a prefiguration of the eating of the Eucharistic bread.

Bosch's true feelings towards these Catholic rituals and doctrines are not expressed overtly here. Instead, they are revealed in subtle and ambiguous ways. In a conventional religious painting, for example, the bare-branched tree next to the wall at the lower left, could be interpreted as a premonition of Christ's future sacrifice. Here, however, it is much more likely to symbolize the spiritual death which, from a Cathar viewpoint, would be implicit in the conventional notion of Christ's incarnation. This interpretation is supported by the imagery in Bosch's later works. In his mature paintings, bare trees are used as unambiguous symbols of Satan and his world of evil.

In addition to this, the artist might also be making an oblique reference to the incarnation in his colour scheme. As Tolnay has pointed out, the clothing worn by three of the five people in the scene is coloured pink. Tolnay associates this predominant colour with hope and spring, but it has a different connotation in many of Bosch's other works.[29] In the left wing of *Garden of Earthly Delights* (Plate 22) and in

Figure 11. Bosch, the Philadelphia *Adoration of the Magi*.

the Venice *St Jerome Praying* (Plate 66), for example, pink is used as the symbolic colour of the material world.

In the painting at Philadelphia, the two shepherds are isolated in a dark enclosure of their own, and the Magi, Madonna and Child form an integrated group. All these figures are separated from the true image of hope: the star, the rays of which can be seen above the roof of the stable. This is because their worship of an incarnated Christ is misguided, and they do not have a true understanding of the real nature of the Saviour. Like the kings in the Prado *Adoration of the Magi,* they are deluded. Bosch expresses these ideas mildly and very subtly in this early work, presumably because he did not yet know how many oddities he could introduce into his paintings without arousing suspicion.

In later works, after he had discovered how unsuspecting his patrons actually were, Bosch's ambiguities became less subtle, and his real feelings towards established Christianity and the cult of Our Lady were revealed much more forcefully. The symbols in his later works make it plain that he took a dualistic view of the Madonna which was not at all conventional. This reflects the ideas of the Cathars, who contrasted their own image of the Virgin Mary (the Saviour's mother only in appearance) with the Madonna of the Roman Church. Because the latter had given birth to a physical baby, they saw her as impure and unholy. Scandella, the heretical miller of the sixteenth century, made the same contrasts, and even described the earthly Madonna as a whore.[30] Similar negative views of Mary in her role as earthly mother are found in the paintings of Bosch.

Some of the symbols in Bosch's works express his views of the conventional Madonna and the cult of Our Lady with a surprising frankness. One of the most common of these is his image of the swan. In Bosch's iconography, this bird is repeatedly used as a symbol of depravity. This is not what one would expect in a member of a confraternity whose alternative name was the Brotherhood of the Swan. The confraternity identified itself with the swan because it associated this bird, with its purity and grace, with the Madonna. On its coat of arms, a swan was depicted above a lily.[31] This flower, as is well-known, was a traditional symbol of the Virgin's purity. But in Bosch's works, the symbolism is changed around. Instead of employing the swan as an image of spotless virginity, he turns it into a symbol of drunkenness and prostitution.

This negative image of the swan appears in many of Bosch's works. The tavern/brothels in his paintings, for example, are identified more than once by a white swan on a flag or signboard. We see one example of this in the background of the central panel of the Prado *Adoration of the Magi,* where a couple stands arm in arm, looking at a tavern whose sign is decorated with a white swan (Plate 13). The pigeons which fly in and out of the attic of this building identify it as a brothel. We know this because, as Bax has pointed out, the Netherlanders of the fifteenth century referred to a house of ill repute as a place which had pigeons in its loft. The same tavern/brothel, characterized by the same pigeons and swan on a signboard, appears again in Bosch's so-called *'Prodigal Son'* at Rotterdam (Plate 58). Bax has shown that the swan could be an image of immorality, as well as an image of purity during the Middle Ages.[32] But surely it is unlikely that a devoted member of the Brotherhood of the Swan would have gone against his confraternity's traditional symbolism, and chosen to depict the group's namesake as a symbol of depravity. One wonders again how Bosch could have managed to flout conventions so blatantly without being noticed. The answer, as before, seems to be that his contemporaries did not take his 'drolleries' seriously enough to realize what they really meant.

Bosch's condemnation of the Brotherhood of the Swan's cult of the Virgin is expressed again, even more overtly, in the small scene on the right of the brothel in the Prado *Adoration of the Magi.* This surprisingly unsubtle vignette shows a man walking along a path, leading an ape mounted on an ass. Artists of Bosch's day sometimes depicted an ape as a symbol of Eve's sin, which contrasted with the purity of the Virgin Mary. In Bosch's painting, however, the ape is not a contrast to the Virgin, but a participant in the traditional story of the Nativity. What it really seems to be is an insulting mockery of Mary herself, led on the traditional donkey into Bethlehem or Egypt.

Bosch's strange version of the 'Holy Family' passes by an idol on a column, which is located on their right, at the top of a small mound. The idol, like the ape and donkey, parodies traditional Netherlandish depictions of the Flight into Egypt. In the conventional versions of this scene, pagan idols are shown falling to the ground as the Holy Family moves past them. In Bosch's work, however, the traditional images have, as usual, been altered. In his depiction, the idol does not fall, but remains firmly on its pillar. This is because the family which passes it is not holy. The ape and ass, led by the Joseph figure, will not topple the religion which the idol represents, for they are themselves part of the statue's world. As they make their way through a landscape of sin, war and corruption, the idol actually helps them to find their destination. It points to a town (Bethlehem, Jerusalem, Egypt, or all three), whose buildings are strange and misshapen. The message, it would seem, is that the traditionally described route of the Holy Family is the route of Satan, and that it leads to a realm of unwholesome corruption.

Another small but unusual feature of Bosch's idol is the crescent moon, attached to the statue's head by a tall, thin stick. The crescent, which appears frequently in Bosch's works, is an important key to many of his hidden meanings. Its immediate associations are with the Islamic infidel, but its significance goes further than this. In the fifteenth and sixteenth centuries, as Bax has pointed out, the crescent moon was identified particularly with the Turks, who were a great threat to the Christian West. Westerners reacted to this threat by thinking of the Turks as the servants of Lucifer, and as a result, the Turks came to be associated with the devil himself. This connection was reinforced by the fact that the Turks came from Asia Minor, where Babylon, the supposed domain of the devil, was located. By Bosch's day, these images were well established, and the Turkish crescent moon, with or without a star, had become a well-known symbol of Satan.[33]

If the crescent moon was an established symbol of the devil, Bosch must have used it as a sign that the idol in his Prado *Adoration of the Magi* belonged to a Satanic religion. This, in Bosch's world, would be established Christianity. At the same time, however, Bosch's idol also brings paganism and Islam to mind. This would not be out of keeping with Cathar views, for, according to the Cathars, all of these religions were false and unholy faiths which had been introduced by the Prince of the World in order to further his aims. The Cathars believed that before Satan had appeared to humanity as Jehovah, he had been known as Baal or Jove.[34] Bosch's idol, with its crescent moon, would seem therefore to be a kind of composite image, identified with all of the infidel religions for which Satan was responsible.

The Joseph figure who leads the ape and donkey past this very unholy idol appears to be a doltish peasant. He contrasts with the Joseph who sits drying swaddling clothes in the centre of the left wing of the triptych (see Plate 3). In this scene, Joseph looks isolated and unhappy, as though he is trapped in a world of sin and does not know how to escape. Like the deserted sheep in the right wing of the triptych, he is an image of ordinary humanity, lost in Satan's world, and led astray by Satan's religion. The fact that Joseph is given an apparently different character when he travels with the ape in the central panel is also relevant to Bosch's message. These two images of Joseph are probably meant to represent two aspects of the human soul caught in the world of darkness. The one who leads the donkey stupidly and doltishly cooperates with Satan's religion, while the isolated one realizes unhappily but helplessly that he is trapped. These two sides of ordinary human nature are also depicted in other works by Bosch, and will be looked at again in later chapters.

Bosch's painting of the *Marriage at Cana* at Rotterdam (Plate 60) is another work which uses images such as the swan and the crescent to make subtle criticisms of the Church and the Brotherhood of Our Lady. This very odd version of a well-known Biblical event was discussed earlier, as an example of a subversive picture which was bought by conventional Christians. In it, a swan is one of two dishes which are served to a group of corrupt revellers at a feast. Some scholars suggest that the banquet which they attend could be a depiction of one of the confraternity's ceremonial 'swan feasts.' Bosch is known to have participated in these feasts himself, but his painting does not give the impression that he thought very highly of them.[35] The swan has connotations of corruption and sin in Bosch's other works, and here, where it is served as an edible dish, it is probably a symbol of hypocrisy as well. As Tolnay points out, the ancient Flemish metaphor which contrasts the swan's white feathers (its stainless exterior) with its dark flesh (its hidden evil interior) could have been on Bosch's mind when he depicted this bird as a form of food.[36] The corrupt and hypocritical group which will eat the swan is contrasted with a self-contained group of holy figures who hold themselves separate from the rest of the people at the feast. This second group will be discussed in Chapter 8, when the painting is looked at in more detail.

The second dish which is served to the depraved revellers at the feast at Cana is the head of a boar. As we saw in Chapter 1, medieval heretics identified this animal with the Pope. Bosch has made his real views of both the swan and the boar explicit by decorating them with small, but unambiguous gold crescent moons. One crescent is painted on the boar's forehead and the other can be seen on the breast of the swan (Plate 61). By placing this fifteenth century image of the devil on the two symbolic forms of food, Bosch is telling us subtly but clearly that he sees both the Pope and the Brotherhood of the Swan as demonic. When the members of Bosch's Brotherhood ingest this demonic spiritual food, they will literally make the devil part of themselves.

Bosch was clearly able to express his real feelings about his confraternity's rituals and ceremonies in paint without getting into trouble, for as far as we know, none of his contemporaries ever criticized this painting. But he could not reveal his opinions in any other way. Outwardly, he had no choice but to participate in the very ceremonies he despised, and to pretend that he approved of them. He must have felt unclean and hypocritical himself, when he joined in the feasts and rituals which he so clearly loathed. The group to which he was really drawn was the second one at the feast at Cana, conducting its own holy private ceremony in the midst of the depraved banquet. But his membership of this second group had to be kept secret.

As we will see later, Bosch was very much a mystic. But, as many of his symbols show, he could also express anger and unhappiness. He seems to have combined the two poles of light and darkness within himself, and could even be called a living personification of the dualism of his own religion. Bosch was able to depict the light as well or better than any painter who has ever lived. And yet, few painters have ever represented the world's darker side with as much skill and intensity.

Like Bosch, the Cathars of earlier periods were also known for their dualism, as well as their anti-clericalism and dislike of Church dogma. Nevertheless, it appears that not all of them felt as intensely about these subjects as Bosch did. In fact, during the periods when they were comparatively free from persecution, the Cathars had coexisted well with the ordinary Christians. Their priests had converted people, but never by force or violence. Instead, they had practised the love and humanity recommended in the Gospels.[37] By Bosch's day, however, few of these priests remained, for the Inquisition's attacks on the Cathars had been going on for more than two centuries, and the heresy was well on its way to extinction. Bosch's anger and his hostile feelings towards mainstream Christianity and the other 'faiths of Jehovah' may not be attractive characteristics, but they can at least be understood if we see them as his reaction to centuries of violence and persecution.

3. Satan and the Entrapment of the Soul

The Cathars, or 'Modern Manicheans,' as they were called by the Inquisitors, were preoccupied with the Prince of the World and the evil nature of his realm. This Manichean dualism was central to the beliefs of all of them, but they did not all agree fully on questions of cosmology and mythology. Like all religious believers (and, for that matter, all political theorists), they tended to split up into factions. The· two main forms of Catharism — the Absolute and the Mitigated — have already been discussed in the Introduction. The Bulgarian Bogomils, the Bosnian Patarenes, and many of the Patarenes of Lombardy were Mitigated Cathars, and Bosch's iconography always corresponds with their point of view.

Written clues to Bosch's symbolism

Mitigated beliefs, along with others which correspond with the iconography of Bosch, can be found in a number of surviving texts. These writings, which will be looked at in more detail as we go along, include the records of the Inquisition and a few surviving Cathar books. The most important of these is probably the eleventh century work known as the Cathar *Secret Book,* which we met with earlier in the Introduction. The copy of this book in Vienna, which is bound together with a contemporary New Testament (Figure 12), contains twelve particularly interesting glosses which also help to explain some of the baffling mysteries in Bosch's works. The glosses were added to the manuscript in the twelfth century, perhaps by the Italian Cathar who translated the text into Latin. The Cathar *Vision of Isaiah,* mentioned above in Chapter 2, is another text which is particularly important for an understanding of Bosch's iconography. This early

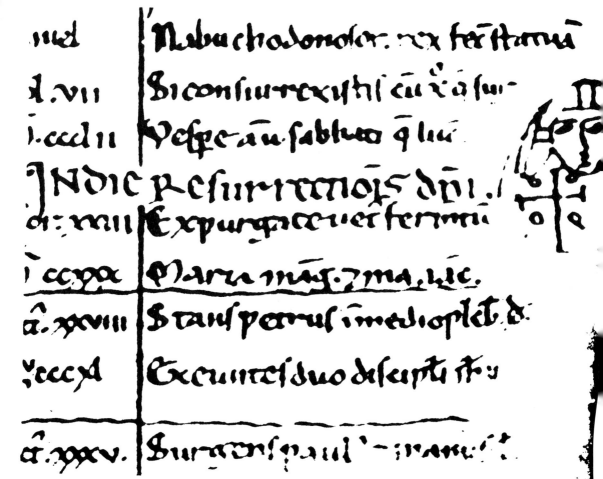

Figure 12. Head of Jesus and cross of light. Marginal drawing in brown and red ink from the *Interrogatio Johannes (Cathar Secret Book)*, twelfth century.

Gnostic apocryphal work was adapted for Bogomil use sometime in the twelfth century, and reached Western Europe by the early thirteenth century. According to Ivanov, it was probably written in one of the many monasteries in the Osogovo mountains of ex-Yugoslavian Macedonia. Perhaps, as Ivanov suggests, this monastery was St Joachim Osogovo, which is still extant today (see Figure 13).[1]

Further useful clues to an understanding of Bosch can be found in Manichean literature, especially a group of Christianized fourth century Coptic Manichean psalms, which came on to the market in Cairo in 1930. These, along with several other Manichean texts, were discovered by local people at the ancient site of Medinet Medi, in Egypt's Fayum Oasis. All that can be seen there today is a half-buried temple (Figure 14). This was begun by the pharoahs in the eighteenth century BC. It

96

1. *Mass of St. Gregory:* outer wings of the Prado *Adoration of the Magi* tryptich.

2. (Opposite) Central panel of the Prado *Adoration of the Magi*.

3. Left wing of the Prado *Adoration of the Magi*.

4. Right wing of the Prado *Adoration of Magi*.

5. (Opposite) Stable area: detail, central panel of the Prado *Adoration of the Magi.*

6.-9. (Above) Details of the Prado *Adoration of the Magi.*

6. (Top left) Gift and helmet.   7. (Top right) Man with wounded leg.

8. (Lower left) False heaven with owl.   9. (Lower right) Boars and wolf.

10. (Opposite above) Giorgione (c.1477-1510), *Sunset Landscape.*
11. (Opposite below) Leonardo da Vinci (c.1452-1519), *Adoration of the Magi.*
12. (Above) Giorgione, *The Three Philosophers* (detail).

13. (Top) Landscape with inn and donkey: detail, central panel of the Prado *Adoration of the Magi*.
14. (Lower) *The Conjurer*.   15. (Opposite) *The Ship of Foo*

16. Central panel of *The Haywain* tryptich.

17. *Eden:* left wing of *The Haywain*.   18. *Hell:* right wing of *The Haywain*.

(Opposite) Fall of the rebel angels, creation of Eve and fountain: detail, left wing of *The Haywain*.
20. *Creation of the World*: outer wings of the *Garden of Earthly Delights* tryptich.

21. Central panel of the *Garden of Earthly Delights*.

22. *Eden:* left wing of the *Garden of Earthly Delights.*
23. *Hell:* right wing of the *Garden of Earthly Delights.*

24. (Top left) Stone gate and egg with birds: detail, left wing of the *Garden of Earthly Delights*.

25. (Top right) Palm tree and monsters entering cave: detail, left wing of the *Garden of Earthly Delights*.

26. (Lower left) Souls entering egg shell: detail, central panel of the *Garden of Earthly Delights*.

27. (Lower right) *Ceremonial Meal of the Manichean Elect*, detail, miniature from an eighth/ninth century manuscript from Turfan.

Figure 13. Monastery churches of St Joakim Osogovo, Macedonia, founded in the twelfth century. The *Cathar Vision of Isaiah* might have been written here.

Figure 14. View of the Temple of Medinet Medi in Fayum Oasis, Egypt. Founded in the eighteenth century BC, extended in the Greco-Roman period, and site of an important Manichean find.

was extended during the Greco-Roman period, in conjunction with the growing local settlement of Narmouthis, and at that time, it seems to have been used by people of various religions. The psalms had probably been written in Syria in about 340 AD, and brought to Egypt soon after by Manichean missionaries.[2] Bosch could not have seen them, needless to say, but their connections with his images can be explained by the Christianized Manichean and/or Messalian traditions that helped to form Catharism. The Messalians were active in Syria during the fourth century. They could have picked up Manichean ideas there, and included them in literature which was later passed on to the Cathars.[3]

Bosch's omnipresent owl

All Cathars, whether they were Absolute or Mitigated, believed that Satan and the creator god Jehovah were a single entity, and that this evil deity was omnipresent in his kingdom, the material world. As they saw it, Jehovah/Satan used his realm of death and darkness as a snare for souls. If Bosch was a Cathar, then the Prince of the World would certainly have played an important part in his depictions of the earth. But does this actually happen? Bosch's earth is overrun by devils, but where is their leader, Satan? In fact, though Bosch only rarely depicts Jehovah, and never paints Satan overtly, he frequently represents the evil deity in a symbolic form. As many art historians have noticed, there is one particular recurrent image which is present in nearly every picture that Bosch has produced. This omnipresent creature is the owl.

The owl, in the Middle Ages, was usually thought of as either a symbol of the devil, or an image of the Jews, who, it was believed, valued darkness more than light.[4] If the owl had wisdom, it was the wisdom of darkness, witches and the occult. The owl was seen in this way because it is a bird of night which hunts in the shadows. It watches its prey unseen, and its aim is to catch and ingest its unsuspecting victims. A bird associated with these images is a highly suitable symbol for the Cathar Prince of the World, who lurks in the realm of darkness, plotting to trap humanity there forever.

Figure 15. Bosch, *The Hearing Forest and the Seeing Field*. Drawing in pen and bistre.

The owls in Bosch's paintings always stare attentively at the viewer, or at the foolish or evil activities of humanity. The observant nature of this bird is made particularly explicit in the drawing by Bosch at Berlin called *The Hearing Forest and the Seeing Field* (Figure 15). Here, a large owl looks out at the viewer from a hollow tree. Its attentive watchfulness is echoed by the eyes that are embedded in the ground all around it, and the ears which grow among the trees in the background. In this drawing the earth itself is identified with the staring and listening owl, and the owl's plot to trap and 'eat' the unwary is symbolized by the cock moving towards the wily fox at the base of the tree.[5]

Bosch's owls are usually smaller and more hidden than the one in the drawing at Berlin. Typically, they peer out at the world from dark gaps or holes. We find one lurking in the shadowy false heaven above the stable in the Prado *Adoration of the Magi,* for example, presiding over the 'Pope' and his evil entourage in the 'Synagogue of Satan.' (Plate 8, see also p. 56.) An owl can also be seen in the *Marriage at Cana* (Plate 60), observing the corrupt feast from behind a pillar. Another one watches the antics that go on in the *Ship of Fools* at the Louvre (Plate 15) from a tree tied to the mast of the boat. Yet another hides in the magician's basket in the painting of the *Conjurer* at Saint-Germain-en-Laye (Plate 14). In this work, the magician and his accomplice trick and rob a group of gullible fools, symbolically treating them as the Church treats its congregation (see also Chapter 6). The owl, it seems, is never absent where human beings are succumbing to the temptations of the world and its evil ruler. We see it again, observing the lovers on top of the *Haywain* (Plate 16), and crouching menacingly over the wanderer in the so-called *Prodigal Son* at Rotterdam (Plate 58). It also watches the taunting of Christ in the *Ecce Homo* at Frankfurt am Main (Plate 39). Here, as in many other works by Bosch, one has to look carefully, in order to see it peering out from a dark window in the wall near to Christ.

Satan and the creation of the world

Bosch does not often represent Jehovah/Satan in human form. One of the few times when he is shown in this way is in the creation scene, on the outer wings of the *Garden of Earthly Delights* triptych at the Prado

(Plate 20, see also Figure 20). Here, as in the other paintings where he is given a human shape, Jehovah is identified with the high clergy. In this case, he wears the tiara of a Pope. This is traditional enough, but in Bosch's world, it is not a positive attribute. The creator also holds a book, presumably the Old Testament. Sitting in the upper left-hand corner of the picture in a small gap in the clouds, he is small, unobtrusive, and almost hidden. He is similar in these ways to Bosch's owls, and like them, he presides over his realm. This is the newly formed earth, which floats below him in the midst of a dark and cloudy ether. Bosch depicts the earth as a flat-topped hemisphere, covered by a transparent firmament. This image corresponds strikingly with the Cathar model of the universe (see Map 2).

This creation scene may not seem at first to conflict with Church doctrine, but its oddities reveal hidden heretical ideas. The difference between this image and a more conventional one painted by Hugo van der Goes in 1478/80 is striking (Figure 16). Hugo was a pious Christian who had a tendency to melancholia or depression. He is known to have been worried about damnation and the devil. Nevertheless, in his depiction of the universe, the Holy Trinity dominates the scene. The huge figures of the Trinity are surrounded by heavenly brightness, and the small crystalline globe of the earth, which rests on God's throne at the feet of Christ, is hardly noticeable. In Hugo's depiction it is shown as a flat plate, surrounded by transparent spheres that reflect the light of heaven. There are no devils or symbols of evil, though the glowing spheres are dark compared with the brightness they reflect.

Hugo's painting shows an earth which is vastly inferior to the Trinity, but is very much in its realm, and under its domination. The assumptions behind Bosch's vision are very different. In his case, the deity who presides over the world is small, and separated from the higher realms of brightness. The light which shines on the earth's crystal sphere does not emanate from the direction of the creator, and the world itself is basically corrupt and unsound. This is shown by the eccentric spiky plants which grow on its surface.

The Latin inscription above the earth, which is taken from the Old Testament, can be translated as:

> For he spoke and it was;
> he commanded, and it stood firm. (Psalm 33:9)

This quotation identifies the creator with the Word. In Christian teaching this is Jesus, the Logos. And yet, strangely, it is not Jesus who presides over the earth, but the small and dark image of Jehovah. This oddity, as well as all the others, implies secret and subversive ideas. Bosch's creation scene corresponds much better with Cathar beliefs than with Church doctrines. According to the Cathar *Secret Book*, the deity who shaped the world of matter was actually the eldest son of the God of Light, who had once held a high position in his Father's realm. He had fallen from the spiritual world because of his rebelliousness and jealousy of his Father. After his descent, Satan had attempted to imitate the true God by setting up a throne of his own above the clouds, and commanding his angels to reorganize the earth and sky (already created by God the Father) into their present form.[6] His earth, like the one depicted by Bosch, was evil from the time it was first constructed.

The entrapment of the fallen angels

According to the *Secret Book* and the Inquisition records, Satan persuaded a large group of angels to join him in his rebellion. When they fell, these angels became either demons or human souls, depending on the degree of their rebelliousness and sinfulness.[7] Bosch depicts their descent in the background of the left wing of his *Haywain* triptych in Madrid (see Plates 17, 19). The rebel angels fall into the Garden of Eden, and are transformed as they tumble downwards. Some become insect-like devils, and others are turned into small birds. This original vision (the first of its kind in Western art) corresponds with the Cathar idea that there were two types of fallen angel. The most sinful ones, which turn into demons, merge into the earth and water of a world which is intrinsically evil. They are distinguished from the less sinful fallen angels, which turn into birds. The image of the soul as a small, quick-flying bird is an ancient and widespread metaphor which would also have been familiar to the medieval Cathars.[8] Unlike the demons, these ordinary human souls still have a potential for salvation.

When the fallen souls reached Eden, they became unable to resist the

Figure 16. Hugo van der Goes (c.1440–82), *The Trinity*, c.1479.

102

will of Satan. The *Secret Book* tells us that Eden, located on earth, was Satan's Garden. It had been planted by Satan himself, with the explicit aim of luring souls into incarnation.[9] It was seen as a place which had been evil from its first creation — a concept which accounts for the many small demons that are always scattered about in Bosch's Edens.

Once the angels were in Jehovah/Satan's power, he was able to put a key part of his plan into effect. This was the ensnarement of the fallen souls in physical bodies. According to the Cathar *Secret Book,* the creator made the bodies of Adam and Eve out of clay, and then ordered two angels (the collective souls of humanity) to enter these mortal forms.[10] Bosch depicts this physical creation scene in the back third of his *Haywain* Eden (Plate 19). Here the figure of Jehovah, dressed in red and wearing a bishop's mitre, creates the body of Eve in the midst of a shower of falling birds and demons.

The fountain of spiritual death

The creation of Eve in the *Haywain* takes place in front of a particularly odd and eccentric representation of the fountain of life. This fountain is described in Genesis 2:10 as a spring whose stream irrigates the Garden of Eden. Its four branches flow out of the Garden, and become the four great rivers of the world. The fountain of life, with its four streams, was always a central feature in medieval Christian depictions of the Garden of Eden. Its theological meaning was well worked out. As Lotte Brand Philip tells us in her discussion of Jan van Eyck's *Ghent Altarpiece:*

> The water in the fountain signifies the Redemption of mankind, which is accomplished through the Lamb's sacrifice. It is the Water of Life which the Church offers to her children.in the form of the Sacrament.[11]

This symbolism corresponds perfectly with the images in Jan van Eyck's Garden of Eden, but it has little connection with Bosch's version of the scene. Bosch's fountain is very different. It stands in a reddish pond that looks something like blood, and its shape is strangely anthropomorphic. It has a hat, hair and an eye. The more one looks at this fountain, the more obvious it becomes that its form is oddly similar to that of Jehovah. It is, in fact, a sinister looking parody of the creator himself. This is because the life it brings is the false life of Satan's world and Satan's religion. It is physical life, which, to the spirit, is the equivalent of death. Bosch's anthropomorphic fountain is thus the fountain of death, rather than life. It is the exact opposite of what one would find in a traditional Garden of Eden.

The same ideas about incarnation and the trapping of the soul are expressed even more strongly in the Eden wing of Bosch's *Garden of Earthly Delights* triptych (Plate 22). This unique and eccentric Eden has inspired numerous theories among art historians. Seen from the Cathar point of view, it represents Satan's Garden after the angels have already fallen. Glowing pearls and precious stones lie in a mound of mud below the pink fountain in the centre of the Garden (Figure 17). This is another version of Satan's fountain of physical life and spiritual death. The pearls and jewels at its base are depictions of human souls (the good fallen angels), which have come to rest in the mud of the material world. Cathars and Manicheans visualized these souls as particles of divine light, and thought that each one of them had a glowing inner kernel. The image of a pearl or jewel was frequently used by them as a symbol of either the soul or its kernel. The Coptic Manichean psalms, for example, speak of the jewels or treasure of 'the living ones.'[12] By this they mean the souls of people who are still spiritually alive, unlike those of the demons, which are beyond salvation.

The elaborate and delicate pink fountain which rests on the mound of mud is alluringly beautiful, but it is also fundamentally sinister. It is made up of complicated interwoven spires and traceries, with a crescent moon intersecting it near to the summit. Its substance is semi-vegetal, but it has also reminded some viewers of lobsters or crabs. Towards the bottom of this fountain, an owl, Bosch's symbol of Jehovah/Satan, stares pensively out from a hole in a round globe. The globe is a multi-layered symbol. It looks like an eye, from which the owl peers at his domain, and, at the same time, its round shape tells us that it is a symbol of the earth itself. This important 'eye' (whose symbolism will be discussed in more detail in Chapter 5) is located in the precise centre of Bosch's Eden. As Fraenger has pointed out, it is thus the focal point of the entire Garden.[13] Seen from the Cathar point of view, this

Figure 17. Bosch, fountain: detail, left wing of the *Garden of Earthly Delights*.

Figure 18. Gilded brass font, Cathedral of St-Jan, 's-Hertogenbosch, 1492.

shows that Jehovah/Satan dominates the entire earth, including the Garden of Eden.

As we saw earlier, the medieval Christians associated the fountain of life with redemption through the Eucharist. The fountain of spiritual death in the *Garden of Earthly Delights* is also identified in subtle ways with this sacrament. Its appearance brings the Eucharist to mind because, as Dixon has pointed out, it is similar in shape to a Gothic monstrance, the ritual vessel which holds the Communion wafer.[14] But this is not the fountain's only traditional Christian association. It also resembles a particular large Gothic baptismal font of gilded brass. Bosch would have known this font well, because it was located in the Cathedral of St Jan at 's-Hertogenbosch (Figure 18). The font was acquired by the Cathedral in 1492, and it is still there today. Bosch's paintings are all difficult to date, but most art historians believe that the *Garden of Delights* was executed around 1510. The artist would therefore have been very well acquainted with the font by the time that he parodied it in his painting.

The Cathars believed that Satan had devised the rite of baptism by water as an initiation into the Roman Church which taught his values, and set him up as a god.[15] It is therefore significant that the globe of Bosch's pink fountain, which is a key symbol of Satan and his world, is depicted in a parallel position to the baptismal basin of the 's-Hertogenbosch font. This basin, together with the lower part of its cover, forms a globular shape which is roughly similar to the one depicted by Bosch.

The upper part of the font's cover is decorated with many pinnacles and small statues. Bosch reproduces its general shape in his pink fountain. He does not copy any of the statues literally, but he hints at some of them in subtle ways. On the font, for example, an image of Jehovah, seated within a curtained niche, is located near to the top (Figure 19). This figure, which has clearly influenced the Jehovah on the outer panels of the *Garden of Earthly Delights* (see Figure 20), is placed in approximately the same position as the crescent moon on Bosch's fountain. As we saw in the last chapter, people in the fifteenth century viewed the crescent as a symbol of the devil. Its placement on Bosch's fountain is therefore an indication, subtle but nevertheless clear, that Jehovah and the devil do not have separate identities. Instead, they are a single entity: the evil ruler of the physical universe. This evil entity is symbolized again by the owl which peers out at its domain from the globe lower down on the fountain.

Bosch's globe, like the basin of the font, rests on symbolic images of fallen souls. In Bosch's painting, these are the glowing jewels of the Manichean tradition. In the conventional Christian version, the fallen souls are depicted as crippled and maimed figures. They represent the

Figure 19. Jehovah, detail of the 's-Hertogenbosch font (Figure 18).

Figure 20. Bosch, Jehovah: detail, outer
wings of the *Garden of Earthly Delights*.

sick at the pool of Bethesda, who wait symbolically for the purification
and salvation which baptism will bring.[16] The key difference between
these two images of the fallen is that, according to Church doctrine, the
soul of each newborn human being is freshly created in a condition of
original sin. The Cathars, in contrast, believed that all new-born humans had souls which had been trapped on the earth for thousands of
years. These souls were sullied, but their dormant spirituality could be
reawakened through the Cathar rite of spiritual baptism (see Chapters
7 and 8). As the Cathars saw it, spiritual baptism liberated the soul, but
the baptism with water caused it to become even more firmly entangled in the web of Satan.

The snare of the senses

The fallen souls which lie in the mud below Bosch's fountain are
presumably about to be ensnared by the religion of Jehovah/Satan. But
religion was not Satan's only means of binding the fallen souls to the
earth. According to the Cathars, he made use of another, even stronger
method of entrapment. This was the tempting beauty of the physical
world, and the almost irresistible pleasures which it offers. These
pleasures are first experienced by Adam and Eve, and in the middle
of the *Haywain* Eden panel, Bosch paints the two first parents eating
what the Cathar *Secret Book* calls the 'fruits of iniquity.'[17] These give

them a knowledge of the delights of the senses, and as a result they lose their purity and innocence, and become even more deeply enmeshed in the realm of physical life.

In the Eden of the *Garden of Earthly Delights*, Bosch expresses these same ideas in a more complicated and esoteric way. The Adam and Eve, who are depicted in the foreground of this panel, are on the verge of succumbing to the temptations of the world (Plate 22). They are separated from the fountain by a line of trees. Together with Jesus, who stands between them, they form an independent scene. The Saviour's part in these events will be discussed further in Chapter 5. What is relevant at this stage is the main theme of this vignette, and in fact the chief subject of the entire triptych. This is the destiny of Adam and Eve as the future parents of the human race on earth, and the reproduction and continual entrapment of souls which results from their attraction to the world and its delights. Adam sits in front of an eccentric depiction of the tree of sensual knowledge, an image which will be looked at more closely in Chapter 5. The consequences of eating its 'fruits' are made plain by the rabbit which sits on the ground, just behind Eve's left hand. This is a well-known symbol of the fecundity and reproduction which are the results of sensuality.

The numerous progeny of the two first parents (or, more accurately, the souls of their progeny) are depicted in the upper lefthand corner of Bosch's unusual version of Eden. Here, flocks of small birds fly in and out of holes and caves in a tall, rocky structure (Plate 24). Caves in the rock are ancient symbols of the womb and birth into the physical world. In front of the rocky construction, more birds push their way into a stone egg, another time-honoured symbol of birth. These birds, flying in and out of the rock, and entering the egg, are depictions of the souls of reincarnating human beings, leaving and re-entering the physical world and the physical body. The Cathars believed that human souls which had been caught by Satan in the wheel of birth and death would be condemned to return to the earth repeatedly. According to the Absolute Cathars, these souls could be reborn as animals, or even plants. The Mitigated Cathars, whose ideas correspond with those of Bosch, disagreed with this. As they saw it, human souls were always reincarnated in human bodies.[18] But, whatever their views on the details of reincarnation, all Cathars agreed that souls could only escape their entrapment if they were spiritually awakened. If they remained unenlightened, they would be caught permanently in the world at the time of the Last Judgment, and would share its terrible fate.[19] Satan's plot, begun with the entrapment of the fallen angels in the bodies of Adam and Eve, and continuing with their ensnarement by the pleasures of his earth and the duplicities of his religion, would end in permanent catastrophe for those who did not manage to make their escape.

As Beagle has pointed out, the central panel of the triptych (Plate 21) shows the same Garden and its environs, represented not in the past or the future, but in the present day. This is the world of pleasure which keeps the souls entrapped. Here the fountain of spiritual death is depicted unambiguously as a blue fountain of lust. It is surrounded by four fantastic pink and blue constructions. These echo the rocky structure in the left wing. They are clearly gates, which mark the boundaries of Eden. The traditional four rivers of paradise flow out from them, towards the rest of the earth. Small figures (the equivalent of the birds in the left wing) move in and out of the gates, and enter an eggshell to the left of the fountain (Plate 26). Bosch's depiction of this present day Eden reflects a gloss in the Cathar *Secret Book*, which tells us that Satan's paradise on earth is still in use today. Satan uses it to deceive men, who think, wrongly, that it is a good place.[20]

Satan's Eden, in other words, has now become an illusory paradise, in which souls destined for reincarnation spend a short period of time between lives. The Albigensian Cathars questioned by the Inquisition referred to this Eden on earth as 'the place of rest.'[21] In their cosmology, it was a temporary haven where souls could find peace and solace after the disturbed and restless early post-mortem period (for more on this, see Chapter 12). In Bosch's depiction of this place of illusory happiness, the souls are not actually resting, but they are undoubtedly enjoying themselves. His Eden is crowded with numerous lively little figures which climb, swim and perform acrobatics, as though in a paradise of dreams (see Plate 21 and Figure 48). No one looks upwards, aspiring to a higher, more spiritual paradise. All are happy to remain on earth. At this stage, the demons have taken on an attractive face. A number of small devils are scattered about, but all of them are playful and hedonistic, rather than menacing. Some appear in the alluring forms of mermaids with fish's tails. These demons tempt, rather than harm or attack the little human souls. The souls here have found a place where they can abandon themselves totally to pleasure. They are lulled into believing that all is well, and that incarnation is a thoroughly desirable condition.

The scenes in the foreground of the central panel again express ideas about lust and rebirth. Here, groups of slim and youthful naked figures, both black and white, crowd together on the land and in the water. The activities of these people are surprisingly erotic. Yet, as has often been observed, these hedonistic men and women continue to look childlike and innocent, whatever activities they indulge in. The reason for this is simple, although perhaps rather unexpected. These figures, like the ones in the background, are meant to be the souls of all the races of humankind. They are similar in appearance to the young, naked and innocent-looking souls represented in traditional medieval art. The difference is that they do not behave like traditional medieval souls. These go straight to purgatory, hell or heaven and do not frolic about lustfully after death, preparing to enter a new body in which they can enjoy all the pleasures of the flesh. The behaviour of Bosch's souls is more appropriate to the Cathar/Manichean tradition, in which the trapped soul, deeply identified with the body and its desires, is continually drawn back to the physical world.

Bosch's fruits, seeds and berries

The foreground of Bosch's central panel contains not only souls which are full of desire for physical pleasure, but also various shells, and round pearly fruits, seeds and berries. Scholars have interpreted these as symbols of sexuality, and this is no doubt correct on one level. But these objects have further meanings. Their symbolism, in this and other works by Bosch, becomes much more clear when we look at it from the point of view of the Cathars and Manicheans. In the Manichean tradition, the shell was used as a symbol of the physical body. The pearl within it, as we saw earlier, represented the soul, or, more accurately, the soul's kernel of light, a fragment of one of the original fallen angels. We find an example of these images in the Manichean book called the *Kephalaia*. Here, a raindrop (soul kernel) is described as falling from above into the sea (the Manichean symbol of the depths of matter), and forming there into a pearl within an oyster shell.[22]

The Manicheans and Cathars believed that the soul kernel or 'angel seed' could subdivide and reproduce itself, and that it did this with each new birth. In this way it became further and further entangled in matter.[23] This glowing spark of light, which Bosch depicts as a jewel or pearl in the left wing of his *Garden of Earthly Delights,* is therefore a key ingredient in human reproduction. One would expect to see it again in the central panel, where the souls are entering or preparing to enter new physical bodies. And in fact, it does appear. Jewels and pearls can be seen in the left foreground, for example, just below the tail of a mouse which is entering a glass tube. But most of the 'angel seeds' in this scene are shown in a different form. The majority of them, in this and other works by Bosch, are depicted as pearly seeds and berries, ingested by souls which can be shown as birds or small naked figures.

Bosch's reason for choosing seeds and berries as images of the 'angel seeds' has ancient, esoteric roots. The seeds bring to mind the grain of wheat in the mysteries of Eleusis, or the same image in John 12:23–25. This grain has to die in the physical world in order to be born into eternal life. The same idea is found in one of the Coptic Manichean Psalms.[24] It is also connected with the concepts which lay behind the ritual meals of the Manicheans. During these meals, the Elect ate foods which were believed to contain particles of light. These foods included melons and other glowing fruits, as well as bread made from grains of wheat. One of the ninth century Manichean miniatures found at the Turfan Oasis illustrates the Elect eating these foods (see Plate 27). The idea was that the Elect would ingest these, and amalgamate the light they contained into their own souls. When their bodies died, their souls, which now included this light, would be liberated from the realm of matter.[25]

All the Cathars (priests as well as followers) shared a ritual in which bread was broken and eaten, but this ceremony does not seem to have had the same significance as the Manichean one.[26] Nevertheless, the ideas behind the Manichean ritual lived on. They can be seen in Bosch's paintings, where the light particles of the human soul are depicted as glowing fruits and seeds. They are ingested by Bosch's birds and human figures, but in this case, the sparks will become trapped within the ordinary souls. They will not be liberated until these people manage to break free from the world of Satan.

In the *Garden of Earthly Delights,* Bosch treats the theme of the soul and its kernel of light in an imaginative and fanciful way. Some souls have their kernels on their heads; others grasp them, and so on. The glowing seeds and berries are often coloured, implying corruption. Some are red and inflamed with passion, and others are blue, indicating satiation. Shell-like body images are also found in abundance in Bosch's garden. Like the 'angel seeds,' the bodies are treated in a playful and fanciful way. Many of them are depicted as hollow fruits and fragile rinds, of varying colour and type. The concept of the plant shell as an image of the body again shows a resemblance to Manichean literature. A Coptic Manichean psalm, for example, tells us:

> Do not be like the pomegranate
> whose rind is gay outside;
> its rind is gay outside, but
> its inside is full of ashes.[27]

Bosch comes especially close to Manichean metaphors in his depiction of a large mussel or oyster shell, carried on a man's back. The legs of a naked couple protrude from the opening of the shell, along with three pearls scattered about in the vicinity of their reproductive organs. This image seems to be a kind of visual pun, in which the 'angel seed's' other title of 'sperm' is interpreted literally.

The circle of animals

Between Eden in the background, and the world of souls and bodies in the foreground of the central panel, Bosch depicts a revolving wheel of hedonistic, lascivious males. They ride on various animals around a pond filled with seductive females. Riding was a metaphor for the sexual act in Bosch's time, as it still is today.[28] But the image has further nuances of meaning beyond this. The round pool that the riders encircle is filled with women, and is in itself an anatomical female symbol. It is the sort of image that could surface in dreams. Perhaps Bosch drew it out of his own subconscious, and used it here as a symbol of birth and the sexual act. His feelings towards it are obvious. It is an object of desire in the central panel of the triptych, but in the left wing (Plate 22), where it is located in front of the first parents, it is a habitation of demons. In the right wing (Plate 23), the round pond (in the lower right) has become a cess pool, used by devils and unhappy souls.

The attitudes to sex that Bosch reveals here will not appeal to many people in the modern world. In the post-Freudian era, he can look like an ideal candidate for psychoanalysis. But we should remember that his attitudes were very typical of Manicheism and Catharism, and correspond with their views on reproduction and the sexual act. From the Cathar point of view, sex was the main cause of the soul's entrapment in the physical world. The revolving circle of riders in Bosch's painting is therefore more than just a symbol of the sin of lust. It is also an apt metaphor for the wheel of birth and death. The Manicheans spoke of this wheel, and identified it with the zodiac which lifts souls up to higher levels, and then plunges them down again to earth and another body.[29] A circle of animals is an ancient metaphor for the zodiac, which was also known in Bosch's Holland.[30] Bosch's circle can thus be seen on several levels. It is a lascivious dance, a female sexual symbol, and a wheel of birth and death associated with the zodiac.

4. The Final Destiny
of Trapped Souls

The hedonistic souls in the central panel of the *Garden of Earthly Delights* are enjoying themselves enormously, but, as Bosch makes plain in the 'hell' panel of the triptych, their enjoyment is shortsighted. If the little souls do not recognize their situation in time, they will find themselves trapped on the earth forever, and they will discover too late that their garden of illusion is destined in the end to become a place of unmitigated suffering.

The ultimate fate of the earth

In the right wing of the *Garden of Earthly Delights* (Plate 23), Bosch depicts the world (including Satan's Garden of Eden) as it will be after the destinies of all the souls have been fixed forever. Here, the beautiful landscape of the left and central panels has become an eternal realm of torture and agony. The wheel of birth and death has disappeared from the scene, along with the chance of escaping from Satan's grasp. A description in the Cathar *Secret Book* tells us that at the Last Judgment, a shadowy darkness and a 'gehenna of fire' will come out from the depths of the earth and consume all the lower parts of the earth up to the air of the firmament.[1] The scenes in the upper part of Bosch's panel, which somehow manage to be both beautiful and horrific, show the darkened earth and the myriads of souls that are still on it, consumed by the fire that will be part of their final destiny.

The real nature of Bosch's post-Last Judgment world is summed up in the haunting white monster located in the centre of the right wing. Its position in the composition is parallel with Satan's fountains of physical life in the other two wings. This is the same 'fountain' which was so tempting in the other two panels, but it is now revealed in its true form, as a triumphant image of spiritual death, associated with

Satan. Its hollow body suggests broken eggs, bare wood and bleached bone, all symbols of the barrenness and emptiness of the physical world. The Satanic monster dominates its hellish realm, and it looks back pensively towards the souls inside its body. For these souls, as well as all the others in the scene, the pleasures of the earth have now been transformed into torments, enacted in the company of hostile demons.

The fountains in the left and central panels stand in water, but in the right panel of the triptych, the monster's hollow, bare-branched legs stand in boats embedded in ice. The water, which once played such an important part in the world of temptations, has now become frozen and hard. The monster's legs which stand in it are images of the tree of death. Similar trees appear as masts in Bosch's painting of the *Ship of Fools* in the Louvre (Plate 15), and his various prints of the same subject. These ships, in which souls succumb to the temptations of the world, float on water. They are unstable, but their lack of fixedness implies the possibility of change. In the world after the Last Judgment, the water has solidified into ice. This means that the instability has gone, but it also shows that all possibilities of change have been lost along with it.

Bosch's Satanic monster, standing in a a frozen lake, is reminiscent of Dante's Satan, locked in ice at the very centre of the earth *(Inferno, Canto XXXIV)*. This fixedness and solidity represents matter at its furthest point away from the world of light and the spirit. The glowing 'angel seeds,' where they remain, have also been frozen. They have lost their spiritual core, and are distorted into hard, metallic objects such as shields, helmets or metal emblems. They are now irredeemably part of the material world.

The resurrection and Last Judgment

The images in the right wing of the *Garden of Earthly Delights* show the earth as it will be after the Last Judgment has taken place. Bosch also depicted the cataclysmic events which predeeded this stage in numerous other works. Some of his visions of the Last Judgment and the terrible changes which will coincide with it survive only as prints or fragments. Others, such as the examples at Bruges (Plates 28, 30-32) and Vienna are still complete, though the left inner wing of the Vienna painting is damaged and repainted later by another hand. All of the *Last Judgment*'s, however, have one significant feature in common. This is the lack of distinction between the right sides, or wings, which traditionally depict hell, and the central panels which traditionally represent the world at the time of the Judgment and resurrection of the dead. Bosch's hell is unique in that it is not located below the earth. Instead, it is a continuation of it. This corresponds with the Cathar idea that earth itself is hell.[2] In Bosch's *Last Judgment*'s, the world and the inferno form a single dark landscape, with fires shooting out from the ground and up into the sky (see Plate 30, for example). These images show a clear resemblance to the descriptions of the Last Judgment in the Cathar *Secret Book* which were quoted earlier.

A few of the figures in the *Last Judgment*'s by or after Bosch are rescued at the last moment by angels (see Chapter 11 and Figure 37). Most of his characters, however, find that they have to remain on earth. Some of them (located, for example, in the middle grounds of the central panels of the triptychs) can appear at first to be rising up out of the ground as though they are being resurrected. Looked at objectively, however, it is clear that these people are not emerging, but struggling. They are caught in a muddy quicksand that drags them down into the fabric of the world, rather than up, out of it. Sometimes all that can be seen of them is a pair of legs. Examples of this odd 'resurrection' can be found in all of Bosch's *Last Judgment*'s, including the triptych at Bruges (see Plate 28). These images correspond with the Cathar and Manichean view that there will be no resurrection of the physical body. At the time of the Last Judgment, the saved will experience a spiritual resurrection, and the damned souls will remain trapped in the realm of Satan.[3] They will share its inescapable fate of fire and total separation from the light.

Apart from the upper right roundel of the Madrid *Tabletop of the Seven Deadly Sins* (Plate 36), which (as we will see in Chapter 5) is certainly not by Bosch, there is only one extant *Last Judgment* by our artist in which the 'resurrection' scene seems at first to be near to the conventional type. This is the fragment of a *Last Judgment* at Munich (Plate 29). Here, some of the people are enmeshed in the mire, as in Bosch's other versions of the scene, but others are standing up, halfway out of their graves. One could view them as rising upwards. Their tombstones and shrouds are also similar to those found in many conventional depictions of the final resurrection. Nevertheless, from the point of view of the Cathars, these attributes could have a very different symbolism. As they saw it, the physical world is the realm of spiritual death, and the fate of the damned is to be permanently intermingled with this world. In the Cathar interpretation, the graves and winding sheets of Bosch's lost souls are therefore likely to be symbols of their irrevocable entrapment in the realm of death.

The unfortunate men and women in Bosch's Munich *Last Judgment* seem cold, and appear to be in a state of great misery and depression. Some of them gaze upwards. We do not know what they are looking at, as most of the panel has been destroyed, but perhaps they are staring hopelessly at higher levels now beyond their reach. This idea would fit with the descriptions in the Cathar *Secret Book* and the Manichean writings from Turfan, which were quoted in the Introduction. These talk of the deities and the saved who walk above the firmament, looking down on the sinners suffering on the earth below. Presumably these sinners also looked back up at them. Bosch might well have had images such as these in mind when he painted his unhappy, gazing figures.

Bosch's sinners, left behind in the hell-on-earth depicted in the panel at Munich, suffer total despair as they finally understand their condition and future fate. They appear to have just awakened, but it seems that their awakening is a psychological one, rather than a physical resurrection. One of them clutches at his bishop's mitre, as though realizing that it has been the instrument of his doom. Other figures cover their reproductive organs, finally aware that it was lust that led to their present condition. For them, the cycle of physical death and rebirth, with its illusory pleasures, is over. They have lost their opportunity of salvation, and must now share the fate of Satan and his material realm.

5. The Saviour in Satan's World

The spirit and the soul

Cathars believed that, as a result of their immersion in matter, the souls of ordinary humans had forgotten their true origins, and had become 'drunk' or 'asleep.' This is the state of mind of the souls which move unthinkingly towards their doom in the *Garden of Earthly Delights.* Such souls need to be awakened again, so that they can remember their real natures and understand their condition. Awakening is the first step in the soul's rescue, and the beginning of true knowledge or 'gnosis.'

In Cathar and Manichean literature the soul's rescue is performed by a Saviour. This Saviour may appear to be a separate entity, but he is actually the soul's own spirit. He descends from the world of light into the darkness of matter, in order to help the fallen soul. The Cathars and Manicheans believed that the fallen souls or angels had once been united with their spirits, but had become separated from them when they fell into the physical realm. Once on earth, the angel or soul identified itself with the desires and emotions of the body, and became fully involved with the world and its pleasures. The spirit, though it could become temporarily ensnared or eclipsed, remained essentially detached and uncorrupted.[1]

This Cathar distinction between soul and spirit has its origins in the prehistoric period, as we saw in the Introduction. It was later incorporated into the Old and New Testaments, where the soul is called the *nefesh* or *psyche,* and the spirit the *ruach* or *pneuma.* This doctrine continued to be accepted during the Early Christian era. It was espoused by the influential third century writer Origen of Alexandria, among others. In 553, however, the Second Council of Constantinople condemned Origen and deleted this doctrine from the accepted canon. The idea that human beings had divine spirits, and could become divine themselves if their souls were reunited with these spirits, was presumably considered unacceptable because it diminished the unique status of Christ. It would also have conflicted with the Church's doctrine of salvation through grace. Nevertheless, this esoteric doctrine is of such major importance that it was never eliminated completely, even within the established Church. It was hinted at in the writings of the medieval Italian Christian mystics Arnold of Brescia and Joachim de Fiore, for example. In the Islamic world, it was stated fairly openly by the philosopher Averroes of Cordoba. And it was also accepted by the Jewish Kabbalists, who refined and elaborated on the original Biblical concepts.[2]

In the Gnostic tradition, the idea of the separation and eventual reunion of the soul and its spirit were expressed openly from the beginning. They are written about in a particularly poignant way in a beautiful poem called the *Hymn of the Pearl*. This is one of the three hymns which make up the *Acts of Thomas*. These *Acts* were known during the Middle Ages, and were also discovered among the Gnostic Gospels at Nag Hammadi in Egypt. They and the other *Thomas* Gospels are the only writings in that find which are directly connected with Manicheism. The *Acts of Thomas* were probably written in Mesopotamia in about 200 AD, and, according to many scholars, they had an important influence on Mani's ideas.[3] The concepts expressed in all of the three hymns also help to explain Bosch's iconography. The *Hymn of the Pearl*, which is relevant to the ideas we are looking at in this chapter, describes the descent of the Saviour into the physical world on a mission to save the fallen 'pearl,' or soul. The Saviour himself succumbs temporarily to 'drunkenness' and 'sleep,' which are metaphors for spiritual forgetfulness. Finally, however, he succeeds in rescuing the pearl and returning with it to his true home.

The Manicheans and Cathars thought of the Saviour as the collective spirit, as well as each individual's own, personal spirit.[4] In Manicheism, the Saviour could be personified as either Mani or Jesus, but in Catharism (probably for reasons of prudence, as said in the Introduction), Jesus was the only personification of the Saviour. As we have already seen, the Cathars viewed Jesus as a messenger of the light, whose mission on earth was the rescue of mankind, either individually or collectively.

The trees of life and death

Bosch's various depictions of Jesus take on an altered meaning when seen from the Cathar point of view. In the Eden panel of the *Garden of Earthly Delights* (Plate 22), for example, the figure of Jesus who stands between Adam and Eve can be understood as the Saviour (collective spirit) warning Adam (the newly fallen collective soul) about the perils of seduction. This story, well-known in Manichean literature, is called the Awakening of Adam. A similar Cathar concept is referred to in an Italian anti-Cathar polemic of 1235 named the *Liber Supra Stella*.[5] The Manichean versions of the story are much more specific and detailed than this single surviving Cathar example, however. They give us an idea of what might have existed in some of the lost Cathar books. One of them describes the events as follows:

> ... Jesus the Luminous approached Adam the Innocent and woke him from the sleep of death [ignorance] in order that he might be delivered from the [two?] great [?] spirit[s] .... And he woke him and took hold of him and shook him; and he drove away from him the seductive demon [Greed or Lust] and bound away from him the great female Archon [Concupiscence]. Then Adam examined himself and recognized what he was. And he [Jesus] showed him the Fathers in the Height, and His own self [Jesus/the Light] thrown ... into the teeth of leopards and into the teeth of elephants, and swallowed by the voracious and devoured by the gluttons and eaten by dogs, and mixed and imprisoned in all that exists and bound by the pollution of darkness. And ... He [Jesus] raised him [Adam] up and made him eat of the Tree of Life. And then Adam looked and wept; and he raised his voice mightily ... and said 'Woe, woe! to the fashioner of my body and to the binder of my soul, and to the rebels who have enslaved me.'[6]

The voracious animals in the Eden panel of the *Garden of Earthly Delights* (for example, the cat catching a mouselike monster in the lower

121

left, or the lion eating a deer in the upper right) illustrate the idea of the light fragments which are ingested and trapped in matter. They need to be rescued, but the process is a slow one. The first step, from the point of view of humanity, is the awakening, which is achieved by 'eating' the fruits of the tree of life.

Looking at Bosch's Eden, with its symbols of evil, one wonders where this tree of life can be. In fact, the answer is simple. Jesus, the Saviour and teacher, is himself identified with the tree of life from which Adam eats. This idea is found in both Manicheism and Catharism. The Coptic Manichean psalms state it explicitly, and a work by an anonymous early thirteenth century Cathar known as the *'Manichean' Treatise* hints at it subtly but clearly.[7] The 'eating' of its fruits is a metaphor for the communication of the knowledge which leads to salvation. When Adam 'ate,' his eyes were opened briefly to the realization that he was an immortal spirit, to whom physical life was spiritual death. But his awakening did not last long. He soon forgot Christ's warning, gave in to his desires, and (as we saw in Chapter 3) ate a different sort of food: the 'fruits of iniquity.' Adam was not abandoned because of this weakness, however. He was destined to have many other chances of enlightenment before the time of the Last Judgment. As long as his soul was spiritually alive, the Saviour would always be available to awaken and rescue it.

According to a gloss in the *Secret Book,* the Satanic plant that Eden's 'iniquitous' fruits grow on is a vine.[8] And in Bosch's eccentric image of Eden, a vine is in fact represented behind Adam, twining up a fleshy looking tree. Its fruits produce the wine which the Manicheans called 'the bile of the Prince of Darkness.' This wine causes intoxication and spiritual forgetfulness.[9] Those who drink it forget their true nature, and become enmeshed in the realm of Satan.

The vine of iniquity is a form of the Manichean tree of darkness. This symbolic plant is an important subject in Gnostic and Manichean literature. It is described there as the tree of death, bitterness and evil. Unlike the tree of life, which is identified with the Saviour, the tree of death belongs to Satan and his realm: the physical world. The Coptic Manichean psalms refer to 'the root of the bitter tree,' for example.[10] They associate the bitterness and darkness of this tree with incarnation on earth in a physical body. The psalms talk of 'the body of death,' or describe the body as 'the creature of the darkness.'[11]

Figure 21. Figures worshipping the Tree of Life, which rises out of the firmament. Manichean wall painting, Turfan Oasis, *circa* ninth century AD.

One of the Gnostic Gospels from Nag Hammadi also describes the tree of death:

> ... its fruit is sin;
> its seed is desire.
> It grows from darkness;
> those who taste it receive Amente [hell]
> as their dwelling,
> and darkness is their habitation.[12]

The trees of life and death, so important in the literature of the Manichean tradition, are also depicted in some of the surviving Manichean wall paintings and manuscripts. All of these date from the ninth century, and come from the Turfan Oasis in Central Asia. A painting of the tree of life has been found in a cave at Bäzäklik in the Turfan region, for example (Figure 21). This shows a group of Manichean believers praying in front of a large triple-trunked tree. The tree rises out of a round base which represents the earth's firmament (see Map 2 and Chapters 10 and 11). The three trunks are probably symbols of Mani, Jesus and Buddha, viewed in Turfan (where Buddhism was beginning to merge with Manicheism) as the three routes to Paradise.[13] The flowers and fruits of Paradise hang from the branches of this Manichean tree of life. Other cave paintings in the same area, which have only been discovered recently and are not yet published, apparently depict the tree of death as well as the tree of life.[14] There is no doubt that these two symbolic trees and the conflict between them, were key images for the Manicheans and their successors.

The importance of the two conflicting Manichean trees is reflected in the iconography of Bosch. Bosch depicts the tree of life as Jesus in his *Garden of Earthly Delights,* as we have already seen. In other works, which we will look at in later chapters, he represents Jesus as a tree or cosmic cross. In the *Garden of Earthly Delights,* however, it is not the tree of life but the tree of death which dominates the scene. In the Eden panel, this negative tree is given an especially great emphasis. It is represented not just once, but several times, and in several different forms. This vision of a variety of evil trees, all associated in one way or another with Satan, corresponds with certain Manichean writings, which tell us that 'The tree of death is divided into a great number of trees. War and cruelty are in them; they are strangers to peace, filled with absolute wickedness, and never bear good fruit.'[15]

The vine of iniquity, winding up the fleshy tree behind Adam, is Bosch's most obvious image of the tree of death. But there are others which come into focus, once we look at the panel from the Cathar/Manichean point of view. The pink fountain, with its vegetal spires and its associations with Satan and his religion is a second example. A third one can be seen in the middleground of the panel. Here the tree of death is depicted as a palm, which is located to the right of the pink fountain (Plate 25). In traditional Christian art, the palm, like the fountain, is a symbol of eternal life. In Bosch's hands, the meaning of both of these images is reversed, and the palm becomes a tree of spiritual death, associated with the transient and illusory life of the physical body. Bosch's palm literally grows out of darkness, for its roots are planted in a rock, directly over the entrance to a cave. The cave is an ancient symbol of the womb and physical birth. When one enters its shadowy mouth, one goes into what, from the point of view of the spirit, is the realm of darkness and death.

A serpent, parallel in meaning and position to the vine of iniquity, is wound around Bosch's palm of death. As one might expect in the works of Bosch (and particularly this one), it is different from the serpents which are traditionally depicted in the Garden of Eden. This reptile, when looked at closely, is revealed to be hanging upsidedown. The thin end of its tail is wound around the upper part of the tree trunk, and its head, with an eye clearly visible, points directly towards the entrance of the cave. A crowd of loathsome reptilian monsters emerges from the water at the left, and moves to join it at the cave. These, surely, must be the demonic fallen angels, headed towards incarnation. There is no possibility that they represent fiery salamanders, or lizards sacred to Apollo and the light, as Fraenger suggests.[16] (Fraenger's book contains many important insights, but one cannot help feeling that this suggestion would have caused Bosch, austere as he must have been, to laugh.)

The Prince of the World is such a dominant force in Bosch's Garden of Eden that even the figure of Jesus in the foreground of the scene appears to have a double identity. On the one hand, this figure can be seen as the Saviour and the tree of life, issuing a warning and holding Eve away from Adam. On the other hand, he could also be Satan, introducing or even marrying the first couple. This second identity is hinted at by a certain oddness in the face of the Jesus figure. Its peculiar redness and distortion, which are presumably original and deliberate, have been commented on by several writers. The redness has even been explained by alchemical symbolism.[17] The *Secret Book* tells us that after Satan had fallen and become the Prince of the World and the corrupter of souls, his face changed. It lost its radiance, and became the colour of red hot iron. This change has implications of passion and lust, and could explain the flushed face of the 'Jesus' figure in Bosch's panel.

A Cathar description of the way in which Satan introduced the two first parents to the pleasures of the flesh could also help to explain the symbolism behind Bosch's 'marriage' scene. According to the Cathar *Secret Book,* the Prince of the World appeared to Eve in the garden, taking the form of a serpent or (if we go by the gloss in the Vienna copy) a beautiful young man. He then proceeded to inflame Eve with

125

desire like a glowing oven. He sated his lust on her, and afterwards he caused Adam to be filled with desire. From this time onwards, Adam and Eve were consumed with lust, and they produced children of the devil and the serpent.[18]

The idea that the figure placed by Bosch between Adam and Eve might actually be a double image of Jesus and Satan (two sides of the coin, so to speak) may sound strange. Nevertheless this concept is hinted at in the doctrines of the Mitigated Cathars. On the cosmic level, these heretics saw Satan as the elder son of God the Father, and Jesus as the younger son. They believed that Jesus took Satan's place in the Land of Light after his fall, but that he was also present on earth, waiting to help humankind. They saw the two brothers, dark and light, as two creations or aspects of the Father. Although brothers, they were unrelenting enemies who made the earth their battleground.

These dramatic cosmic images were also valid on the individual, personal level. Cathars as far apart in time as the Bogomils of the late eleventh century and Domenico Scandella, the sixteenth century heretical miller from the Fruili, believed that each human being harbours an evil spirit as well as a good one.[19] The two spirits struggle against each other, just as Satan and Jesus do on the cosmic level, and ultimately each person must choose between them. In Bosch's paintings, Jesus and Satan can usually be understood on a personal as well as a cosmic level, and humanity's choice between them is always an underlying theme. The double image in the *Garden of Earthly Delights,* in which Jesus discourages earthly desires while Satan promotes them, is a good example of this.

The reflected eye of God

The double image discussed above is unusual. In other paintings by Bosch, Satan and Jesus are depicted individually or as two contrasting figures. In these scenes, Bosch always depicts Satan as small, half hidden and watchful, while Jesus, in contrast, is in plain view, waiting for humankind to recognize him and take up his offer of help. Sometimes the figure of Jesus is located outside the world, but in many of Bosch's works, he stands patiently in the very centre of Satan's realm.

One of Bosch's most interesting and unusual visions, which puts particular stress on the presence of Jesus in Satan's dominions, can be seen in Berlin. This panel (Plate 33) is on the reverse side of Bosch's *St John on Patmos*. It depicts the world as a double circle like an eye. As in other works by Bosch, the circle of earth floats in the midst of a demon-ridden sea or ether. The swarming, diaphanous devils in this matrix show us that the entire material universe is the realm of Satan. Satan's dominions are not entirely without light, however, for Jesus is present in the inner part of the circle, as well as the outer one. The story of his Passion is depicted in the outer ring ('iris') of the eye. These depictions of the suffering Saviour, which symbolize the spirit's descent into matter, will be discussed in more detail later in this chapter.

In the inner circle ('pupil') of the eye at Berlin, a giant pelican shelters a group of five tiny human beings. This appears at first to be a traditional Christian image of Christ as the pelican which feeds its young with its own blood, but in fact, the pelican is not plucking at its breast, but leaning over a group of souls which need its help. The real significance of the scene is nearer to the Cathar story of the pelican than the conventional one. The Cathars did not believe that Christ had literally shed his blood for mankind, but they did see this bird as a symbol of Christ. According to a parable told by a Cathar preacher to a clerk in the Languedoc in 1306, a pelican who normally followed the sun went to the earth, where he hid his brightness. By this ruse, he was able to protect and deliver his little ones from the beast which wanted to mutilate and kill them. The beast, of course, is a metaphor for Satan, and the pelican represents Christ. Christ hides his true brightness by taking on a human appearance.[20]

Bosch's vision of the Saviour's self-sacrificing mission in a Satanic eye, which floats in a black, demon-ridden matrix, is highly unusual. Where did this strange image come from? It seems diametrically opposed to the traditional Christian view of nature as the mirror or reflection of God's great plan (see Introduction). Instead, Bosch's Satanic earth is surrounded by demons, and entirely cut off from God the Father and his heaven. There is no hint that this place is the creation of a benign deity. In the centre of this fundamentally diabolical universe, the Saviour attempts to rescue humanity from the eternal and unchangeable darkness.

The ideas behind Bosch's concept of the eye are precisely the opposite of the Church doctrines. Their real meaning is elucidated by a metaphor in the Gnostic *Apocryphon of John*, or *Secret Book According to John*. This Gnostic gospel, which should not be confused with the Cathar *Secret Book*, is not Manichean. Nevertheless, some of its concepts could have reached the Messalians, and been passed on by them to the Cathars and Bosch. The gospel uses the metaphor of the eye as one of its models of the creation. The relevant part is very brief; less than a sentence. All it says is 'For it is this that gazes at its own self in its light *around* it ....' This image could easily be overlooked, but its significance is elucidated by Layton. As he explains it, the gospel compares the Godhead, or first principle to 'a solitary *eye*, floating in a luminous reflective medium. Its only function is to look, and all it has to see is itself. The reflection that it sees, however, is the second principle.'[21] In other words, the physical universe, or 'second principle,' is the mirror image of God's eye.

In conventional Christian imagery, this mirror image would be positive, but in the Gnostic tradition, it is the opposite. As Bosch depicts it, the reflection becomes the spiritual reverse of the original, just as right becomes left in a mirror. The reflection is demonic rather than holy: the province of Satan and his followers. It floats in a sea of darkness, which swarms with diaphanous demons. This sea of devils is the reversed image of the angelic light which surrounds the Godhead. In the painting at Berlin, the demonic 'eye' is contrasted with the circle which St John gazes at on the other side of the panel. Unlike the earth, John's heavenly circle is golden, and the spiritual (rather than the physical) Virgin Mary sits in the middle of it, holding a child or soul. This holy vision will be discussed further in Chapter 12.

The contrast between Bosch's demonic earth and the angelic one of the medieval Christians becomes particularly clear if we compare Bosch's dark circle with a fifteenth century French miniature from the British Library (Plate 34). The miniature depicts God the Great Architect, creating the world. Here, the creator stands on top of a grassy circular earth, holding his compass and surrounded by the elements of water, air and fire. When we look closely at the elements of air and fire, we can see that they are composed entirely of angels. A world of difference separates this image from Bosch's vision. Bosch would not have disputed the concept of a Godhead surrounded by angels, but for him the deity who formed the earth was Satanic and aided by demons. The true God and the angelic beings around him could never have been identified with the elements of the visible world. As Bosch saw it, any spiritual angels which chose to enter Satan's material universe were strangers. They went to the alien land not because they wanted to be there, but in order to help save the 'good' fallen angels which had become entrapped in Satan's world.

The Madrid Tabletop

Another representation of the eye of God, reflected as a Satanic world full of misguided actions, is depicted on Bosch's *Tabletop of the Seven Deadly Sins* at Madrid (Plate 36). Gibson compares this painting with medieval writings that describe the reflections of human sin in the eye of God or Christ.[22] His interpretation explains the painting's Christian level of meaning well, but as we will see, even the outwardly conventional *Tabletop* holds a secret heretical message. In this work, Bosch has again depicted the figure of Jesus in the centre of the picture, standing in his sarcophagus in the pupil of a circular eye. The iris of the eye is made up of seven vignettes which depict the sins, rather than the Passion, as at Berlin. The Madrid eye floats in a dark matrix, flecked with small dots and dashes. These hint at demons, even though they do not actually depict them.

The Madrid eye, as we see it today, is surrounded by four roundels that illustrate the so-called Four Last Things (Death, the Last Judgment, Heaven and Hell). These four roundels lack Bosch's usual oddities and eccentricities, and express sincere and traditional Christian beliefs. In the roundel on the upper left, for example, several members of the clergy are shown as positive and helpful. Using the crucifix and the Church rites, they assist the dying man as he passes into the next world. If this scene had really been designed by Bosch, it would be unique and completely out of character. Again, in the roundel on the upper right, the resurrection of the flesh is depicted in a traditional rather than an eccentric way. Here figures rise out of the hard ground, rather than sinking into the mire. This resurrection is different from all the others in Bosch's works.

The reason for this uncharacteristically conventional piety is simple. Plainly, Bosch had no part in either the execution or the design of any of the four roundels. The painting style and some of the images in these four traditional scenes show his influence, but as several authors have pointed out, the hand which was responsible for them was obviously not his. The figures in all four roundels are coarse and wooden. They are clearly the work of another artist. As Justi says, they must be by a follower of Bosch, rather than the master himself.[23] Originally, Bosch's Madrid *Tabletop* must have depicted a single Satanic eye, floating without the roundels in a sea of darkness.

But when were the roundels added to this scene? We do not know the answer to this question, but it is clear that the painting has a complex history. Even the 'eye' itself could be a copy rather than an original. In the main scenes, which show the seven deadly sins, the figures are nearer to Bosch's style than in the roundels, but they too are rather coarse. Scholars once believed that these scenes were executed at the beginning of Bosch's career, but this idea is now out of favour because some of the costumes date from the 1490's or later.[24] Perhaps, like the *Marriage at Cana* in Rotterdam, the *Tabletop* was a mature work, reproduced in Bosch's studio (see Chapter 2). The painting which survives today was in the collection of Philip II of Spain by 1560, but another version was once located in Antwerp. A *Seven Deadly Sins* by Hieronymus Bosch is mentioned in the inventory of Margaretha Boghe, a resident of that city, in 1574/75.[25] Perhaps the painting at Antwerp was the original by the artist's hand.

Philip II took such a special interest in his version of Bosch's painting that he kept it on the wall of his bedroom in the Escorial.[26] He did not use it as a table, but its design indicates that it (or its original) was meant to be seen from all sides. This is because the only way that one can view each of the seven deadly sins from the correct viewpoint is by walking around the circle. The inscriptions on the painting are the right way up if one stands in front of the figure of Jesus, and by the time Philip had acquired the work, the roundels, whose figures have the same orientation as Jesus, had been added to the panel. These additions made the composition more suited to a wall painting than it had been before.

Philip must have used his tabletop-turned-wall-painting for his own private meditations, for, with the addition of the later roundels, it appears to exemplify traditional Christian ideas of sin and punishment. The written inscriptions, which will be discussed soon, seem at first to reinforce this message. From the Cathar point of view, however, the original floating eye, with its scenes of sin, would have presented a rather different message. The Cathars would have seen the sins as examples of the low level to which humanity has fallen. Looked at in this way, the stress in Bosch's painting would not be on guilt or blame, but on weakness, imprisonment in the world of matter, and forgetfulness of the spirit. Like the Passion in the iris at Berlin, this eye would have represented the evil effects of Satan's realm.

The Saviour who looks out from the pupil of the *Tabletop* eye also takes on a new significance when seen from the Cathar point of view. For the heretics, this figure is an emissary from the realm of light, a stranger who has descended into the heart of Satan's dominions. In the Cathar/Manichean tradition, his wounds and sarcophagus are not reminders of his atonement for the sins of humanity. Instead, they represent his immolation in the world of death and darkness, and the opportunity of salvation that this provides. He does not offer vicarious atonement, but he does give each soul a chance to save itself through his influence. Like the pelican in the Cathar story, he is identified with the spiritual sun. This is revealed by the circle of golden, sunlike rays which surrounds him as he looks out from the centre of the earth (see Plate 36). Bosch's Saviour thus extends his radiance to the ignorant and uninterested sinners in the everyday world at the periphery of the circle.

The Latin inscription in the golden ring beneath the Saviour translates as 'Beware, Beware, God sees.' These words apparently refer to the watch that Jesus keeps on sinners. But, seen from the Cathar point of view, they have a different meaning. In Catharism, the Saviour is on earth to help humanity. He is not an angry or accusing figure. The words painted below Jesus are therefore not a warning of his fierceness or revenge. Instead, they are spoken by the Saviour himself. They tell the viewer that a different 'god' is looking at humanity, and they warn mankind to beware of this false deity's calculating and dangerous watchfulness.

The second, dangerous deity is also represented on Bosch's panel, but it is not easy to spot. One has to look closely to see a half-hidden owl, the bird of night and Bosch's symbol of Jehovah/Satan, staring out at the sinners in the *Gluttony* scene. It is only just visible in a shadowy niche above the door (Plate 37). Its association with gluttony is not a coincidence either, for Satan and his world of matter trap and 'eat' the soul. The hat with the arrow through it, which hangs on the wall near to the niche, is reminiscent of the hunt. It confirms the image of the owl as a creature which captures and kills its prey. The bird of darkness is located almost directly behind the luminous figure of Jesus, and can be interpreted as his dark counterpart. The two contrasting images are another example of Bosch's depictions of the good and evil deities between which mankind must choose.

The two banderols, which are painted above and below the eye, are also very relevant to the meaning of the scene. Their printed inscriptions appear at first to be conventionally Christian, but they are actually further evidence of Bosch's dualism, and they illuminate the true significance of the *Tabletop*. The Latin words on the banderol above the circular 'eye' translate as:

> They are a nation that lacks good counsel,
> devoid of understanding.
> If only they had the wisdom to understand this
> and give thought to their end! (Deut.32:28f)

This quotation seems to be spoken by someone who is concerned with the well-being of the sinners. Presumably Bosch intended these words to be those of Jesus.

The second banderol is located at the bottom of the picture, beneath the circular 'eye.' The speaker of its words is unambiguous, for the quotation is taken from a speech given by Jehovah in the Bible:

> I will hide my face from them ...
> let me see what their end will be. (Deut.32:20)

Even if we did not know the Biblical source of this quotation, it would still be plain that these words are not spoken by Jesus. How could they be, when Jesus does not hide his face? Instead, he faces the viewer directly. It is not Jesus, but the owl in the Gluttony scene who hides and watches mankind's progress towards an unhappy end. These very significant words of Jehovah's are also relevant to many other works by Bosch, for an owl hiding and watching mankind's sinfulness can be found in nearly every painting the artist produced.

The composition of the Gluttony scene is paralleled fairly closely in the adjoining vignette which depicts the sin of Sloth (Plate 38). In this scene, a nun enters a room, holding out a rosary to a man sleeping in a chair in front of the fire. These images seem to depict a person who is too lazy to attend to his Christian devotions. But, as so often in Bosch's works, the underlying meaning is different from the one on the surface. As always, Bosch reveals his hidden message through subtle images and symbols which look like eccentric or amusing details. Is it expected, for example, for a nun to wear a red gown under her conventional black robe? What order has a habit such as this? This oddity can be dismissed as an unimportant example of Bosch's eccentricities. Or, more accurately, it can be seen as a sign that the light-footed young 'nun' is actually a temptress. She enters the room from the left, in a parallel position to the housewife who brings in the food in the Gluttony scene. She too is offering a source of temptation. Her face is beautiful, and she holds out a rosary made of glowing red beads. These look remarkably similar to the fruits and berries in many of Bosch's other works, including the ones in the *Garden of Earthly Delights* and the Madrid *Tabletop*'s scene of Lust. Like the fruits, the red beads can be seen as images of the glowing soul, corrupted by lust and destined for rebirth on the earth. Seen from the Cathar point of view, Bosch's 'nun,' with her prayer book and rosary, is not an image of virtue. Instead, she represents Satan's tempting trap of lust, promoted by the Church with its Biblical injunction to reproduce and multiply.

The implications of the nun in the Sloth scene are made more explicit by the objects in the niche above the sleeping man's head. These include a jug (a female sexual symbol) and a crossbow (a male symbol, or a reference to the hunt of the soul). The two spindles which protrude from the jug are traditional symbols of continuing death and rebirth on earth, and hint at the recurrent entrapment of the soul in the material world (see also Chapter 7). The man who sleeps in his chair is too slothful to struggle against his entrapment, but, even more importantly, he is 'asleep' in the Gnostic sense. He is drugged by matter, and unaware of the figure of Jesus who stands waiting to rescue him.

The sleeping man is spiritually drugged, but he is an ordinary human being, whose soul is still alive. He has not yet lost his chance to choose between the worlds of Jesus and Satan. This choice is indicated by the location of the shining pearl (his soul) which lies in a niche inside the fireplace. Above it, a round golden plate with a candle in front of it hangs on the chimney-breast. The plate and candle are symbols in miniature of Jesus surrounded by the spiritual sun. The placement of the pearl between the holy images above and the red flames of the fire in the grate below is significant, for the heat and light of the fire belong to the world of Satan, with all its passions and desires.

The same images of a plate and candle above a fire, with a pearl (red in this case) set in the fireplace between them, can be seen through the doorway of the vignette which depicts the sin of Vanity (Plate 36). In the main scene, a woman gazes at her reflection in a round mirror. She stands in a room which is lit from the left by a double window with an orange resting on the sill below it. These images all bring Jan van Eyck's *Arnolfini Marriage Portrait* of 1434 to mind. Van Eyck's well-known painting contains a similar window with oranges below it, as well as a round mirror which reflects the people in the room. In van Eyck's painting, however, all of the imagery is holy. His mirror and the figures within it are surrounded by decorations which depict the Passion of Jesus. These are traditional Christian representations of Christ's atonement for original sin, and they show that the figures within the mirror are pious and will be saved.[27] Bosch's mirror is very different. It is held up — literally supported — by a demon, whose headdress mimics that of the woman. This is another of Bosch's images of the world controlled by Satanic forces. The woman whose face is reflected in the mirror is trapped (at least temporarily) within it.

The mirror in the Vanity scene, and the round 'eye' of the *Tabletop* itself are symbols of Satan's world. Circular tables, which again represent the earth, can also be seen in three of the other vignettes (Plate 36). Each of these is significant to the particular sin in the scene. In the depiction of Gluttony, for example, there is a round table covered with food. There is also a plain wooden table on the left side of the Anger scene, which has presumably been overturned in a scuffle. And an elaborately decorated circular table is placed on the left side of the scene of Lust. A round plate on its surface contains the red fruits which were mentioned earlier. These three tables echo the shape of the 'eye,' and all of them represent the temptations and corruption of the physical world.

The recurrence of round shapes which are positive (the circular 'sun' around the Saviour) or negative (the tables, eye and mirror) in the Madrid *Tabletop* are important. They are images which would have reminded the heretical viewer of the most central ceremony of the Cathar religion. As Stein Schneider says, Bosch's *Tabletop* seems to be related in some way to the *Descum*, or round table which was used during the Latin Ritual of the Consolamentum, or Cathar Spiritual Baptism.[28] The Provençal Ritual of this initiation ceremony calls the same table a *desc* or *discus*. According to Duvernoy, this piece of furniture was made up of a circular platter supported on legs, and was the same kind of table which is still used in the Muslim world.[29]

The platters on the Muslim tables are usually made of polished bronze, or even gold. If the Cathar tables were the same, then their circular tops would have symbolized Jesus as the spiritual sun. But Bosch's *Tabletop*, with its positive and negative circles, is clearly different from this. It contains images of the demonic world of Satan, as well as depictions of the spiritual sun identified with the Saviour. It contrasts the two sorts of circle and points out the condition of unbaptized humanity. With the help of the Saviour and the Consolamentum, the trapped soul can be liberated from the world of sin and darkness, and will then be able to enter the world of purity and light. These ideas are expressed in both versions of the Ritual. According to the Latin version, Christ came 'to cleanse the filth of God's souls that have been soiled by contact with evil spirits.' The Provençal Ritual talks of St John's First Epistle, with its injunction to:

> love not the world, nor the things which are in the
> world .... For all that is in the world is the concupiscence of
> the flesh, and the concupiscence of the eyes, and the pride
> of life, which is not of the Father ...[30]

Bosch's painting contains numerous references to the Consolamentum, then, and it also seems that it once functioned as a table. Does this mean that it was originally meant to be used in the ceremony of spiritual baptism? Stein Schneider believes that this was the case, but his theory is open to doubts. For one thing, we don't know whether

Figure 22. Upper half of a tapestry after a lost painting of the *Haywain* by Bosch (Plate 35).

the round tables used in the Cathar baptism ever had dualistic images on them. As well as this, Bosch's *Tabletop* is actually rectangular rather than round, and it is probably a copy rather than an original. But whatever its original function might have been, there is no doubt that the *Tabletop* contains images which would have reminded the Cathar viewer of both the meaning and the furniture of the Consolamentum. As we will see in later chapters, the iconography of several other works by Bosch support the idea of the table's symbolism and possible use.

The hidden meanings in the Haywain

Whatever the original use of Bosch's *Tabletop* might have been, there is no doubt that in Bosch's works, the circle represents the world. On the reverse of the Berlin *St John* and the Madrid *Tabletop*, Bosch places Jesus in the very centre of this circle. Jesus is not confined to the world, however, for his real function is as a channel, which leads the soul away from the earth into the realm of the spirit. It is therefore not surprising that, in some of Bosch's works, Jesus is represented literally

Figure 23. Figure 22 reversed, with cosmic cross on left, as it would have been in the lost *Haywain* painting.

as a route of escape, which stretches upwards towards the heavens. An example of this can be seen in a little known tapestry, located at the Royal Palace in Madrid (Plate 35). This tapestry reproduces a lost painting which was a variation of Bosch's well-known triptych, the *Haywain*.[31] It has a different format than the triptych, but the basic ideas that it expresses are the same.

In the *Haywain Tapestry*, the world resembles the circles at Madrid and Berlin in shape, but it is not an eye, and Jesus is not in its centre. Instead, the Saviour is represented symbolically as a large, jewelled cross, which points upwards towards the unseen spiritual realms beyond the physical universe. As will be shown later (see Chapter 10 and Map 2), this cosmic cross is an anthropomorphic image which was well-known to the Manicheans and Cathars. It emerges from the upper right side of the earth in the tapestry, but, since tapestries reverse the scenes from which they are copied, it would have been on the left side of the original painting. The left is the place where we should expect it, for it is the side from which souls traditionally ascend to heaven in medieval Last Judgments (Figures 22, 23).

The cross in the *Haywain Tapestry* represents the Cathar image of the Saviour as the route of escape from a hellish world. It is not the only cross in the scene, however. If we look carefully, we can see another cross, much smaller, and surrounded by a flock of dark birds. This second cross is the cross of the crucifixion, identified by the Cathars with the spirit's sacrificial 'death' and immolation in the realm of matter. It is located within the circle of the earth, at the top of a hill to the left of the symbolic Saviour. Armies fight on the hills below this dark, earthly cross, and in front of them, crowds of human beings enter into the foreground from behind tall rocks. These rocks are simplified versions of the fantastic gates, which led from Eden into the world of incarnation in the *Garden of Earthly Delights.*

The brown foreground, which occupies most of the circle in the *Haywain Tapestry,* is crowded with men, women and demons. This scene is dominated by a large haywain. Three devils sit on top of this cart, handing out hay to the people below. The hay which they all so desperately crave is a well-known symbol of worldly goods. Not one person, either here or in the rest of the earth, shows any glimmer of awareness of the jewelled cross of salvation which points away from the devil-ridden world. All are busy with their earthly interests and pursuits, encouraged and helped by the many demons which mingle with the crowds.

The circular world in the *Haywain Tapestry* is surrounded by monstrous devils and strange, spiky fish, which cavort in a large body of water. This setting is less generalized than the surroundings of the 'eye' at Berlin. Here, the demons are not spread out evenly around the earth, but are in a concrete space, where the world rests on waters, and has a second sky surrounding its firmament. This scene is a kind of crystallization of the demonic matrix or sea. It corresponds with the Cathar map of the physical universe, a cosmology which was a dualistic version of the Biblical one (see Map 2). The reference to an earth which floats on waters in Genesis I is well-known. Related Cathar images can be found in the *Secret Book* and a Bogomil work called *The Sea of Tiberias.* These are discussed by Ivanov in his book on Bogomil literature.[32]

The spiritual cross in Bosch's tapestry, decorated with luminous jewels and reaching upwards towards the heavens, is balanced, on what was originally the right (hell) side of the painting, by a large sea monster. The monster's head emerges out of the waters on which the world floats. Its huge, fiery maw spits smoke, and clouds of dark birds surround it. The sea monster is an ancient image of the earth, hades, and/or hell. It is found in myths from many countries and periods, and it is a common feature in medieval Last Judgments. It swallows souls, and entraps them in the darkness of the realm of Satan. In Bosch's tapestry, it represents the antithesis to the cosmic cross: the lowest abyss to which souls can descend.

By the late Middle Ages, the early Biblical cosmology was no longer taken literally. The educated people of Bosch's day now visualized the earth as the centre of a series of concentric, transparent planetary spheres (see Map 3). Since all scholars agree that Bosch was an educated man, we must assume that he knew about the more modern cosmology. He must have chosen consciously to depict the earlier Biblical one in his *Haywain Tapestry*. But he did not depict it literally, for his scene is not fully in accord with Genesis either. The Bible certainly gives no indication that either the earth or the waters below it are Satanic and riddled with devils. There is only one view of the universe which corresponds fully with the one in Bosch's tapestry. This is the one which was held by the Cathars.

Bosch's painted triptych of the *Haywain*, which is also at Madrid (Plates 16–18), is less odd and heretical than the tapestry version. Nevertheless, it expresses the same basic ideas. In its central panel, a crowd of people, from the highest to the lowest levels of society, also follow a hay wagon. As in the tapestry, they struggle and fight for its contents, totally unaware of the Saviour (an image of the passage between the earthly and heavenly worlds), who stands above them with arms outstretched. But, with the probable exception of the haughty noblemen and the upper clergy who follow the haywain on horseback, all of these people are weak and ignorant, rather than evil. They are the ordinary deluded members of the human race. Like the lovers on top of the haywain, each of them has access to an angel as well as a devil. Nevertheless, they all continue to pursue the pleasures, desires, greeds and violence of Satan's world heedless of their predicament. They have forgotten the spiritual realms from which they came, and their spirits, represented by the figure of Jesus, are wounded and ignored.

In both versions of the *Haywain*, the cart moves towards the side of hell. In the painted triptych, however, its destination is more clearly delineated. Here, the cart, along with the struggling and greedy procession which follows it, moves inexorably into the right wing of the triptych, with its tortures and fiery sky. This hell scene is a continuation of the earth, and reveals the real nature of Satan's realm. As we will see in Chapter 12, the basic underlying character of the world becomes obvious to the souls which suffer in a literal hell-on-earth between lives.

The misguided struggling crowds in both versions of the *Haywain* are remarkably similar to the people described in one of the fourth century Coptic Manichean psalms, written eleven hundred years before Bosch was born:

> The world whence I am come is
> all full of evil, envy, hatred and strife.
> They all kill one another, they destroy their flesh
> with the sword.
> There is creation, conception and creation ...
> They are prostrated,
> They lie on their faces,
> their faces are not turned to the Land of [Light].
> They increase greatly in evil ...
> ... lift up your eyes to the Land of Light;
> you shall see the friend of the righteous standing
> beyond the world ....[33]

Bosch's depictions of the Passion of Christ

The Jesus who is represented in Bosch's *Tabletop* and *Haywain* does not force himself on the ordinary, erring human souls which are trapped in Satan's world. Nevertheless, as we have seen, he is always available to help those who can recognize him. In Bosch's depictions of the Passion, however, ordinary, everyday people do not appear. In these works, Jesus is surrounded not by simple misguided human beings, but by monsters in human form which are totally alien to him and his message. These odd and eccentric figures are not just the products of Bosch's wild imagination. They have a meaning which is relevant to the thinking of the Cathars and Manicheans. According to the theology of these two very closely related religions, the historical Jesus had only appeared to suffer the Passion, because, lacking a real physical body, he could not have been physically harmed. Nevertheless, the Manicheans used the sufferings of Jesus as a paradigm for the sufferings of the light, or spirit which is trapped by Satan in a hostile and alien material world.[34] It is this Manichean metaphor, which was no doubt taken up by the Cathars, that Bosch is illustrating in his odd and eccentric Passion scenes.

The depiction of the tormentors of Christ as ugly beings was not in itself new or original. It can be found in a number of Netherlandish woodcarvings, paintings and drawings of the fifteenth and sixteenth centuries. But in Bosch's works, these figures become much more wild, grotesque and fantastic, and they exhibit a more extreme and uncontrolled bestiality. These jeering or peering creatures show great variations of clothing and facial features, but all of them are barbaric and outlandish. Their strange clothes and antics are not those of ordinary human beings. This is because they are demons in human form, whose Satanic natures are revealed by their monstrous outward appearances. Like the wild followers of the 'Pope,' who burst out of the stable door in the Prado *Adoration of the Magi*, they are the forces of darkness which surround and attack the light when it appears on earth. The Manicheans and Cathars often referred to these demons as beasts, vultures or wolves.

The bestiality, sadism, hypocritical smiles and mocking interest of the demons which attack the Saviour in Bosch's paintings correspond almost exactly with the images in one of the Coptic Manichean Psalms:

> An image of
> Light was revealed
> in the dwelling place of the beasts ...
> they grovelled ... they bent their knees,
> they worshipped him ....
> The demons were saying this with their mouth,
> yet planning evil nevertheless in their heart:
> Come, let us cast him into the stocks
> let us set a fetter on him ...
> and put him in the world and secure him ...
> that he may not return ....[35]

141

In the comparatively simple Passion scenes of traditional Christian art the tormentors of Christ include only Jews and Roman soldiers. Bosch's persecution scenes, in contrast, contain figures with many identities. In the *Ecce Homo* at Frankfurt (Plate 39), for example, Christ stands on a platform, jeered at by a motley crowd. The wild group includes not only a man in red wearing a pointed Jewish hat, but also a clerical figure in green and white, who stands behind the Jew, holding a sharp, metallic cross. In the distance, other figures crowd into a building which flies a flag decorated with an Islamic crescent.

In several of Bosch's Passion scenes, the figures are large, half-length, and seen at close range. This, as several authors have pointed out, is an influence of Italy, and particularly of Leonardo. It is a further indication that Bosch travelled to Venice. The two versions of the *Crowning of Thorns* at London and in the Escorial (Plates 40, 41) are examples of this sort of Passion scene. In these works, as Tolnay puts it, the persecutors surround the Saviour 'like a pack of wild beasts.'[36] Jesus stands patiently in the midst of the sadistic group, looking outwards at the viewer. The figures which surround him are again varied. They include not only members of the established religions, but also representatives of the military or political power of the state. In the *Crowning with Thorns* at the Escorial, for example, one of the figures wears a badge decorated with a Habsburg double eagle.[37] As the Cathars saw it, rich and powerful secular figures such as these were followers of Satan, and promoters of his aims.[38]

A detailed interpretation of the version of the *Crowning with Thorns* at the London National Gallery is made by Foster and Tudor-Craig. Although these two authors do not see Bosch as a heretic, much of their analysis of the painting corresponds well with Cathar views. According to their book, *The Secret Life of Paintings*, this picture has several layers of meaning. On one of its levels, the figure of Jesus is a symbol of the human spirit, and the four persecutors which surround and seek to entrap him represent the four temperaments or humours of the body.[39] The Cathars thought of the physical body as demonic, and Bosch could well have had this imagery in mind as one of his layers of symbolism.

On another level of symbolism, as Foster and Tudor-Craig point out, Bosch's figure of Jesus in the National Gallery is surrounded by religious and military figures. According to this interpretation, the man on the upper left with the mailed fist is a soldier, while the man on the lower left with the star and crescent on his headdress is a Muslim, and the one on the lower right is a Jew. The fourth persecutor, located above the Jew in the upper righthand corner of the painting, is a Christian cleric, and it is he who is the most interesting of all from our point of view. According to Foster and Tudor-Craig, the oak leaves and acorns in this man's hat associate him in some way with the della Rovere Popes, who used this symbol as their family coat of arms. Tudor-Craig also suggests in her 1987 BBC television programme, which is associated with the book, that this same man's spiked collar could identify him with the Dominicans. These friars were called the 'dogs of god' as a pun on their name, and because they wore black and white habits.[40]

Again, though Tudor-Craig does not mean it in this way, her interpretation makes perfect sense if Bosch is seen as an underground Cathar heretic. The 'Dominican' tormentor wears a pensive expression which some viewers see as sympathetic, but his evil nature is confirmed not only by his vicious spiked collar, but also by the odd metal disk with a metallic pearl in its centre that he wears on his shoulder. This motif, which is also found on medieval suits of armour, is frequently worn by the demonic figures in Bosch's paintings. Bosch uses it as a symbol of the soul kernel, solidified and trapped in matter to the point where it is beyond redemption.

The uncontrolled demonic antics of Bosch's wild and vicious figures reach a crescendo in the *Carrying of the Cross* at Ghent (Plate 42). Here, Bosch's expression of Satanic madness is so effective that he really does seem to be verging on insanity himself. In this disturbed work, Christ and the good thief in the upper right are hardly able to breathe in what the Manichean writings often describe as the 'poison,' 'stink' and 'pollution' of Satan's world. The barbaric creatures express their hostility overtly. There is only one exception: the figure of St Veronica in the lower left. Scholars normally associate Veronica with the two other positive figures in the picture: Christ and the good thief. But Bosch may not have taken this point of view. In his Passion scene on the right outer wing of the Lisbon *St Antony*, Veronica appears to be included among the jeering tormentors. Bosch may well be representing her in the same way in the panel at Ghent. In this version, Veronica's head can be seen as one half of a double-faced image. Her other 'face' is that of a snarling man with a red hat and a white moustache. His side of the twin image looks towards Jesus, while Veronica's side looks in the other direction. Veronica, whose name means the 'True Icon,' holds a cloth on which the unhappy face of Jesus is imprinted. It is very likely that, in the world of Bosch, her cloth represents the false Church image or 'icon' of Christ. Seen from this point of view, Veronica's slight smirk and demure downcast eyes give her a look of hypocritical piety. She could personify the falsely pious face of Satan's Church. The snarling man who is her other face could personify its viciousness and Satanic hatred of the truth.

The demonic tormentors' wild attacks on Jesus in all of Bosch's Passion scenes are cosmic events. But, at the same time, the individual identities of some of the sadistic figures in these paintings tell us that this drama of darkness and light is also acted out on a human level in the everyday world. What we are most likely seeing in all of these works, and most especially the one at Ghent, is the expression of Bosch's terrible agony as he watched the extinguishing of Catharism by what he would have seen as the forces of darkness. From the Cathar point of view, the Church hierarchy, with its false beliefs and its hatred of the religion which transmitted the light and the real message of Jesus, would, in persecuting the Cathars, have been attacking the Saviour himself. These concepts would apply not just to the ill-treatment of the Cathars, but to any occasions where the forces of darkness, manifesting through apparently human figures, attack the forces of light.

6. Bosch's Depictions of the Saints

Up to this point, we have looked at some of the ways in which the two brothers, Jesus and Satan, interact with the ordinary humans and the demons in human form. But in the Cathar religion, this is not the full story. The Cathars believed that some human beings could become more than ordinary, and achieve a state of mind in which they were no longer disturbed by the temptations of the earth.

Variations among Bosch's saints

One might expect that Bosch is representing people of this sort in his numerous depictions of the saints. After all, saints are supposed to be holy figures, successful in their fight against Satan and his devils. But are all of Bosch's saints really equally successful? In fact, a close look at the way Bosch portrays them shows that they are not all alike. Some are oblivious to Satan's temptations, which Bosch represents symbolically by strange disfigured animals and plants. Others, however, seem to be overwhelmed by them, and are even part of their world. These less successful saints are represented by Bosch as men who are longing to achieve union with God, but are prevented from achieving their aims by their misguided adherence to the religion of the devil. Bosch associates these saints with the demonic distorted natural forms which symbolize their sinfulness. He also surrounds them with negative allusions to the Old Testament or the established Christian faith. These negative religious images are particularly difficult to explain when Bosch is seen as a traditional Christian who reveres the saints.

Bosch's opinion of all of the religions which worship Jehovah is in fact hostile to an extent that may seem shocking. His attitudes reflect the views of the Cathars, who believed that all of the established religions had been invented by Satan to further his aims. According to Cathar theology in the Balkans and Europe, the saints who accepted the Roman or Greek Orthodox faiths were in fact not truly holy figures. How could they have been, when they had gone along with what were seen as the false views of the religion of Satan? They had revered the cross of the Crucifixion and had accepted the Old Testament. It was also believed that these saints had been involved with demons, which had performed their miracles for them when they were on earth, and continued to do so through their relics.[1]

Monasticism and the Lisbon St Anthony

The misguided saint whom Bosch depicts most often is St Anthony Abbot. Anthony was an Egyptian who was not directly associated with either of the two established Christian faiths, but was well-known as the founder of monasticism. Bosch dresses him in monastic habits which vary from painting to painting, and does not associate him with any particular order. In Bosch's works, St Anthony appears to be used as a general symbol of the traditional monk or friar. This does not make him a positive figure, from Bosch's point of view. It is therefore not surprising that the devils which traditionally torment the saint are sometimes intimately associated with him and his way of life. Even when this is not the case, there is no sign that Anthony has defeated them and no evidence that he is going to do so.

The *Temptation of St Anthony* triptych at Lisbon is an especially good example of Bosch's approach to this particular saint. The symbolism is very complicated and much has been written about it. It is generally agreed that it is full of allusions to witchcraft and devils. This is certainly true, but there is more to the painting than this. The devils, witches and other negative symbols have further layers of meaning that associate them with Judaism, traditional Christianity and monasticism.

Images of monasticism and the Inquisition

The images on the closed wings of the Lisbon triptych (Plates 43, 44) depict the evils performed by Satan and those who support his violent religion. In the backgrounds of these two pictures, the cosmic attack of evil upon good is taking place. Here Jesus, the personification of the light, is tormented and attacked in the realm of Satan by various demons in human form. In the foregrounds, similar events are repeated on the human level. In these scenes, misguided and evil clerics are attacking the human beings who have attempted to listen to the word of Jesus.

The left outer wing of the triptych (Plate 43) depicts the arrest of Jesus. In the foreground of this scene, St Peter, traditionally identified with the Pope, holds a knife in the air, preparing to cut off the ear of Malchus, the servant of the Jewish high priest. Since the Cathars would have seen the Jewish High Priest as another image of the Pope (the Church of Rome was termed by them 'the Synagogue of Satan'), it follows that St Peter is here attacking his own servant. In other words, his victim is a member of the clergy; most likely St Anthony himself. Bosch depicts the 'Pope's servant' as a pilgrim, whose staff and lantern have been knocked to the ground during the violent attack. He has been thwarted in his religious quest, and after St Peter has cut off his ear, he will also be prevented from hearing the word, or real message of Jesus.

In the Gospel story, Jesus soon heals the servant's ear. In Bosch's depiction, however, the Saviour is literally on his knees. He is unable to help Malchus at this stage, and the unfortunate pilgrim must remain a victim of the Church, at least for a while. Nevertheless, there are indications in the scene that someone else has just recently managed to escape from the realm of Satan. This escapee, who is not shown in person, is the young man in the linen cloth (Mark 14:51f). More will be said of the symbols connected with his story in Chapter 12.

On the right outer wing of the Lisbon St Anthony (Plate 44), it is Cathars who are suffering the attacks of the Church. The two talkative members of the monastic fraternity, one sitting on the left and the other standing on the right, are undoubtedly Franciscans. They give their unwelcome attentions to two captives. Seen from the conventional Christian point of view, these captives are the two thieves who were crucified with Christ. They, and similar figures who are harangued by friars in Bosch's other paintings of the Passion, have sometimes been interpreted as anachronisms which show the Roman sacrament of confession. This, however, is only the outer layer of their meaning. Bosch was clearly an educated and complicated man. He did not put in these scenes just because he was stupid, or as a joke. He intended them to have an underlying meaning. The real message here, hidden below the superficial level, refers to events that were very relevant to his own life. What we are actually seeing here is an image of two Cathars who have fallen into the clutches of the Inquisition.

It is particularly interesting that the two friars on the closed right wing of the Lisbon *St Anthony* are both Franciscans. The Dominicans had been the original persecutors of the Cathars, but by Bosch's day, it was mainly the Franciscans who were at work in Venice, Bosnia and the Dalmatian Coast.[2] In Bosch's depiction, the standing thief who is tied by an executioner and simultaneously harangued by a persistent Franciscan friar, has one slipper and one bare foot. This might be an image of slipshodness, indicating that he is the bad thief. He could represent a Cathar who weakens under pressure. The other thief (the good one) sits gloomily in the clutches of a second friar. He is approached from the right by a menacing executioner who holds a rope and wears flames on his hat. Could this be a reference to the burnings which awaited the Cathar priests and the most fervent Cathar believers? This would seem to be the best explanation for this otherwise baffling symbol.

Images of Satan's religions

In the central panel of the Lisbon *St Anthony* (Plate 45), Bosch again reveals his hostility towards monks, clerics and Catholism in general. His negative attitude towards Judaism, the religion which preceded Christianity, is also made plain. It is expressed in an only lightly disguised form on the odd decorated pillar located on the right side of the panel. This structure is broken at the top, and a barren dead tree grows out of it. The pillar is an ancient and well-known esoteric symbol, associated with the trees of life and death. When it is shown as unbroken and aspiring upwards towards heaven, it is identified with Christ and salvation. (This positive image will be looked at in more detail in Chapter 10.) When it is broken, however, it takes on a different meaning, and is associated with Satan and death.[3] In Bosch's version, the pillar is clearly another image of the tree of death. As we saw in Chapter 5, this important Cathar/Manichean symbol reappears several times in Bosch's *Garden of Earthly Delights*. The bare branches which grow out of its broken top in the Lisbon *St Anthony* emphasise its barrenness, and the scenes which decorate it reveal its connection with the religions that Satan uses to trap people in his world.

The images on the pillar or tree of death are taken mainly from Jehovah/Satan's book, the Old Testament. These are arranged in horizontal bands (Plate 48). An owl whose breast feathers, in this illustration, look almost like the white beard of the conventional Jehovah, peers out from a hole on the left side of the pink band halfway up the pillar. The hole is located just behind an ape or pig which sits on a raised platform. The hybrid ape/pig is presumably meant to be a depiction of the Jews' image of their god. It is receiving offerings and sacrifices from a crowd of adoring worshippers. A man wearing a pointed Jewish hat kneels at the front of the crowd and holds up a swan. The swan, as we have already seen, is a symbol of corruption, idolatry and hypocrisy in Bosch's works. A bull and a lamb, traditional Old Testament offerings, are also presented to the 'deity.' The Cathars believed that Jehovah/Satan had helped the Hebrews to escape from Egypt and reach the Promised Land, so that they would adore him like a god and sacrifice animals to him.[4] Sacrifices were particularly abhorrent to Cathars, as they believed in non-violence, and viewed the taking of any human or animal life as a sin.[5]

In the scene at the top level of the pillar, the Children of Israel dance wildly below a calf, which is raised to about the same height as Moses. Moses himself, receiving the Law from the hand of Jehovah, is not portrayed in quite the usual way. If one looks closely at his traditional horns, it becomes apparent that they have taken on the crescent shapes normally associated with devils. He even seems — quite clearly — to have a tail. The Cathars saw Moses as the dupe of Jehovah/Satan. According to their *Secret Book*, Satan announced his divinity to Moses, and ordained him to give the Law to the Hebrews.[6]

The lowest scene on Bosch's pillar shows two more of the Children of Israel, now in Canaan, carrying a huge bunch of grapes back from Eshkol (Num.13:17–29). These fruits are similar to the ones shown in the *Garden of Earthly Delights.* They represent lust, and a compliance with Satan's injunction to reproduce and multiply. The images in the thin band just below this scene reinforce this message. Here, a stag is chased by a man and a dog (see also Figure 40). The chase takes place among brambles or tree branches, which entangle the pursuers as well as the pursued. Deer and stags are Biblical symbols of the soul (Psalm 42). In the Gnostic tradition, they represent the soul caught in the cycle of birth and death.[7] It is this Gnostic meaning that illuminates their significance in Bosch's iconography. His stag hunt is clearly a depiction of the demonic pursuit of the wandering soul, rather than a scene of everyday life, as it would be in ordinary medieval art. It is similar to the stag hunts that can be found on Bosnian tombstones (see Chapter 12). Bosch's hunt among the branches is thus not just decoration. It is an image of the soul's continuing enmeshment in Satan's forest of desire and reincarnation.

The bottom of Satan's pillar rests in a muddy lake inhabited by demons. The features of many of these devils correspond with Bosch's Gnostic message that physical birth is equated with spiritual death. For example, the demonic monk reading a book has a horrible rotting corpse-like body. The devil-mother, who rides a rat to the right of the pillar, is composed largely of a barren, bone-like dead tree, and holds a swaddled dead baby. Bax and others have suggested that this woman, like the blue-cloaked female demon in the right wing, is a kind of negative Virgin Mary. This odd concept can be explained if we see her as a Cathar image of the physical, earthly Mary. Near her, a devilish nobleman rides a mount, whose jug-like body is clearly a female sexual symbol associated with lust and reproduction. In other parts of the muddy lake, one can see images of demonic babies, creatures trapped in cages, and, on the left, a phallic monster wearing clogs and dipping his head in the unclean water. All of these are further expressions of Bosch's negative attitudes towards sex and parenthood. We are being told through symbols that the pleasures of the flesh lead to the continuing entrapment of the soul in the deadly and demonic realm of Satan, and that the Church, which encourges humanity to increase and multiply, is an integral part of this world.

The Old Testament pillar, which rises out of the muddy lake, is attached to the edge of a cave-like building. St Anthony kneels against the wall of the building's forecourt, surrounded by a crowd of demons. According to the Golden Legend, St Anthony went twice to a cave, hole, pit or tomb, where he was attacked and beaten by devils. In the tradition of the Cathars and their Gnostic predecessors, the pit symbolizes the earth, and the tomb symbolizes the physical body. St Anthony, in other words, has descended into the realm of Satan. In

Bosch's version of the scene, the cave-like building is dilapidated. This is symbolic of its spiritual impoverishment. It represents not only Satan's world, but also his Church — the religion with which he keeps souls entrapped. It is attached to the Old Testament pillar because, as in traditional Christian iconography, it represents the new order which has grown out of the old one.

The living Jesus and the dead Jesus

Deep within the the interior of the building, as though deep within the earth, two figures of Jesus are depicted. One is the lifeless traditional Christian image of Christ, crucified on a cross. The other is the Living Jesus, the image of the individual's own inner divine light or divine double. The image of the Living Jesus is found in the Gnostic/Manichean *Book of Thomas*.[8] This second Jesus holds up his hand in blessing, apparently telling the viewer that there is still hope of spiritual life and salvation. But spiritual salvation can only be achieved if people understand the true message of the Jesus who is alive, and are not taken in by the false religion of Satan, with its deceptive dead image of Christ.

In front of the doorway of Bosch's shadowy building, a beam of light pierces through a hole in the wall. This beam is thin and not easily visible, but it is a message of hope. It corresponds with another episode in the legend of St Anthony, in which Jesus appears in a column of light and disperses all of the devils which have been tormenting the holy man. Seen from the Cathar point of view, this light beam represents the message of enlightenment that all of the Christian Gnostics believed Jesus had brought into the world. If St Anthony can manage to see it, the devils which cavort all around him will disperse. But does he? It would seem not. The saint kneels and gives his own version of Christ's gesture of blessing, but he does not look at the ray of light. He is closely surrounded by creatures which are acting out a demonic Mass, and there is no sign that he will be able to vanquish them. As Hamburger has pointed out in his article of 1984, Bosch's painting *The Conjurer* (Plate 14) is also a parody of the Mass, in which the Eucharist is identified with evil charlatans and their magic tricks.

St Anthony and the Church

Bosch's identification of St Anthony with 'religious' sorcery, lust, and entrapment in Satan's world are found in all parts of the Lisbon triptych. Space will not allow an analysis of all of them, but some particularly interesting ones are found in the left wing of the triptych (see Plate 46). Here, in the upper half of the panel, St Anthony prays for help as the demons take him for a wild ride in the air. Below him, Bosch has depicted a building which is formed partly by a giant kneeling in an obscene position. The giant has a wounded left thigh, a symbol of lust, and the barren branches of Satan's tree of death grow from his legs. The hut which he helps to form is a brothel, with a woman peering out from its window. This structure reveals that Anthony himself is impure, for, as many scholars plausibly believe, it is likely to be the saint's own hut. A group of four demons in clerical dress make their way towards its obscene doorway. Presumably they are about to pay a visit to its inhabitants.

To the left of the hut, a demonic fish, encased in an scorpion-like shell with a cathedral tower on top, is shown eating a smaller fish. The fish is a well-known symbol of Christianity, and, according to Bax, the scorpion is an image of hypocrisy, treachery and Judaism.[9] The tower and the scorpion shell clearly associate the large fish with the Church, or 'Synagogue of Satan.' The metal disk on its side is a symbol of spiritual death (see Chapters 4 and 5). This menacing creature swallows the smaller fish with the help of a demon holding on to a rope. Its victim could be a misguided Christian believer, perhaps another image of St Anthony, who is ingested and trapped in Satan's world because of his acceptance of Satan's religion.

The association of St Anthony and his devils with the Roman faith and the realm of Satan is reinforced by the demon below the bridge, at the bottom of the left wing. This wicked devil appears to be involved in some sort of plot, for he holds a piece of paper and is about to receive a letter. As Beagle has pointed out, he has the features of Pope Alexander VI who reigned between 1492–1503, and was identified by many with the Antichrist.[10] This same association of Pope and Antichrist is found in Bosch's Prado *Adoration of the Magi*, as we saw in Chapter 1. Near to the demonic 'Pope,' a large heron stands on its egg, eating its newly hatched children. The fact that the body of this bird is identical with the 'Pope's' skullcap reveals the underlying symbolism. Clearly this is another comment on the Church of Rome.

A group of four men walks along a bridge over the head of Bosch's demonic Pope figure. One of them is presumably St Anthony again, now fainting and exhausted from his encounters with the demons. The other three men support him, and help him back to his obscene hut. This hut will not be much of a refuge from the demons, but one of the saint's three supporters does seem to offer a thread of hope. This is the man in red. Unlike St Anthony and the other two assistants, this fourth man does not wear monastic robes. He is another of Bosch's 'pilgrim' figures and is therefore meant to represent a sincere seeker (see Chapter 7 for more on this). He does not look happy, but unlike the other three men, he does not bow his head. Perhaps he is present in the scene as an indication that someone who is not connected with the Church can offer the help and support that the tormented saint so desperately needs.

In Bosch's paintings, every detail is significant, and the two ships in the upper lefthand corner of the left wing of the Lisbon *St Anthony* are no exception. These vessels, which contrast with each other, can be seen as parallels to the spiritual states of the figures on the bridge. One of the ships has a billowing white sail. This sound ship contrasts with a sinking one, whose sail is muddy looking and half submerged. The ailing ship represents the spiritual condition of St Anthony and his fellow monks, while the healthy one can be identified with the nonclerical seeker. As in so many of Bosch's works, the viewer is given a choice between symbols of dark and light; salvation and spiritual death.

Bosch's St Jerome at Ghent

Another tormented saint whom Bosch depicts in a less than positive way is St Jerome. Bosch also associates this hermit, supporter of monasticism, translator of the Bible, and Doctor of the Church, with the Roman faith and all its evils. Like St Anthony, Jerome is a man who appears to long for union with God, but who is prevented from achieving his aim by his identification with the religion devised by Satan.

This message comes across strongly in Bosch's painting of *St Jerome at Prayer* in Ghent (Plate 49). In this work, Jerome lies prostrate in the wilderness or 'desert' (a Manichean metaphor for the earth).[11] Bosch represents this 'desert' as a dark and muddy swamp, separated from a brighter, more peaceful landscape beyond. Jerome, surrounded by darkness, prays and clutches a crucifix. His swamp contains many of Bosch's recurrent images of Satan and his corrupt religion. An owl sits near to a tit on a dead tree stump at Jerome's right, for example. This symbol of weakness confronted by the Prince of the World is also found in Bosch's painting of the peddler at Rotterdam (see Chapter 7). The lower lefthand corner of the painting at Ghent is particularly dark and shadowy, but when one looks closely at the original, it is possible to make out the figure of a cock walking innocently towards a fox which pretends to be asleep. This is a metaphor of the soul fooled by Satan, who lies quietly, patiently waiting for an opportunity to trap and eat the unwary. As we have seen, it is also used by Bosch in his drawing of *The Hearing Forest and the Seeing Field.* A Mosaic Tablet of the Law, located above St Jerome's head, is yet another image which has a subtly negative significance. On the one hand it identifies Jerome with the laws of Jehovah/Satan, the Old Testament God. On the other hand, it resembles a tombstone, and can be seen as a reminder of the spiritual death associated with Satan's realm and religion.

Bosch's panel at Ghent also contains some of the symbols of the physical body that are found in the *Garden of Earthly Delights.* One of these, a large hollow plant shell, is half sunk in the muddy lake next to the saint. The shell is broken and pierced with a barren twig. It hints at the saint's corruption, and his inability to escape the desires of the body which are associated with spiritual death. Jerome also lies in a 'cave' which resembles a large mussel shell, another symbol of his entrapment in the physical body. The stone with which he traditionally beat his breast lies beneath his elbow, and doubles as a pearl within the mussel or oyster shell. As we have seen, the pearl was a Manichean symbol of the soul's glowing kernel of light. In Jerome's case, however, it is depicted as an opaque, grey stone, used for the misguided Catholic practice of self-mortification. This metaphor indicates that Jerome's soul, trapped within his body, is sullied and impure.

St John the Baptist

There is one saint, also represented by Bosch, who, in the view of most Cathars, did not even aspire to a world beyond that of Satan. This demon in human form is, perhaps surprisingly, John the Baptist. Many Cathars believed that this key Biblical figure was a close accomplice of Jehovah/Satan. The *Secret Book*, for example, tells us that the Baptist was an incarnation of Satan's angel the Prophet Elijah, sent by the Prince of the World to counteract the mission of Christ.[12] He introduced baptism with water, which the Cathars saw as an initiation into the religion of the devil. Water was the element that was most closely identified with darkness and demons in the Cathar tradition, and immersion in it was seen as a symbol of immersion in the physical world.[13] Baptism with water thus led the initiate into spiritual death rather than spiritual rebirth.

Bosch's St John the Baptist, depicted in a painting in Madrid (Plate 50), is an enigmatic figure. He reclines on the ground between a giant plant which half obscures his body, and a lamb to which he points. The plant bears large hollow fruits, which emit pearly seeds that are eaten by birds. The imagery here is again similar to that in the *Garden of Earthly Delights*. The plant is a version of the tree of death, and a symbol of incarnation, Satan's means of entrapping the soul in the physical world. Seen from the Cathar point of view, this plant is a reference to the Baptist's collusion with Satan's plans to ensnare men.

The lamb to which the Baptist points is traditionally a symbol of Christ, but on the Cathar level of meaning, the message is different. Bosch's lamb would represent the lost sheep or ordinary Christian believer, whose misguided faith ensnares him in Satan's world. This lamb is very similar to the one on the right wing of the Prado *Adoration of the Magi*. Both lie next to a large rock (the Church of Rome) from which a bare branch (another image of Satan's tree of death) emerges. The Baptist could well be pointing to the lamb to indicate his cooperation with Satan in the attempt to capture it.

The landscape around the Baptist should be the wilderness, if one goes by the Gospels. It does contain some odd rock formations, but it is neither a desert nor a swamp. Instead, it is green and lush. It resembles Bosch's depictions of the earthly Eden. Like them, it contains a rocky 'gate,' and is dotted about with small animals (some of them monsters) and oddly formed plants. The Baptist lies in this deceptively tempting 'paradise,' curled around the tree of death and the rock of the Church, and focussing his thoughts on the lamb below him.

Saints and the Last Judgment

Bosch's negative attitudes towards the saints whom he associates with Roman Christianity could also explain an unusual aspect of his visions of the Last Judgment. Unlike the other painters of his time, Bosch includes very few saints in these scenes. In his *Last Judgment* triptych at Bruges (Plate 30), for example, Bosch surrounds the figure of Christ with four trumpet-blowing angels, and fourteen men kneeling in prayer. Presumably these last are the twelve Apostles, together with two other unidentified holy figures. The hoards of saints which appear in the Last Judgment scenes of Bosch's contemporaries are absent. Since many of the traditional Christian saints were seen by the Cathars as sinful followers of an unholy religion, it is not surprising that Bosch does not include them among the companions of Christ at the Last Judgment.

7. Cathar Priests and Hearers

The Cathar Elect

There is one saint in Bosch's works who, unlike the others, seems to be entirely untouched by the earth and its temptations. This is John the Evangelist, the favourite Apostle of Christ. Bosch depicts the Evangelist in the painting located in Berlin (Plate 51). In this work, John looks upwards at his heavenly visions, untroubled by the demons at his feet. The earth to which he is so serenely immune is represented on the other side of the painting. It is shown as a round Satanic eye, the reflection in reverse of the eye of God (see Chapter 5 and Plate 33). This image of the Evangelist as a person whose soul and spirit are untroubled by any earthly desires corresponds with the Cathar view of this particular saint. The Cathars saw him as the most holy of the Apostles. Like Jesus, he was believed to be human in appearance only. He was really an angel of God, and had a body that was not made of ordinary human flesh.[1]

John's lack of interest in the demons, which represent the pull of the earth, is also the chief characteristic of a person who has attained what the Gnostics of the early AD period called 'gnosis.' A person who has reached this spiritual level has a genuine understanding and acceptance of the contrast between the two realms, and a personal knowledge of the God of Light and his spiritual world. This knowledge, when it is fully assimilated, frees the human soul from any attachment to the material realm.

The concept of gnosis did not die out with the religions of the Ancient World. It (or its medieval equivalent) was also attained by the Cathar priests, who were called the Perfects or the Elect. These were the men and women who managed to become immune to earthly desires. Such a state was very difficult to achieve, and the Perfects did not reach it by learning alone. The Cathars believed that the soul

157

needed more than mere information, if it was to be freed entirely from the powerful pull of the material realm. As they understood it, such a radical transformation could only occur when the soul, or fallen angel, had reunited with the spirit it had left behind at the time of its fall to earth. They believed they brought this reunion about through their baptism by fire and the Holy Spirit. This ritual, as we saw in Chapter 5, was also known as the Consolamentum. According to the Cathars, it united the soul with the collective Holy Spirit, as well as with its own, individual spirit.

Jesus's own baptism by fire and the Holy Spirit was seen by the Cathars as a prototype of their Consolamentum. The spiritual baptism of the Saviour had occurred soon after his baptism by water in the Jordan. Most Cathars saw the water baptism as an initiation into Satan's religion and Satan's realm. They probably interpreted Jesus's submission to it as a symbol of his brief period of entrapment by matter. But in the case of the Saviour, its effects did not last long, and were soon overruled by the spiritual baptism.

At Pentecost, after the mission of the historical Jesus had ended, the Apostles experienced the same liberation from the pull of the earth. They too went through a fiery transformation, during which they received the Holy Spirit. Afterwards they were able to touch others and pass the Spirit on to them. The Cathars believed that their Consolamentum conferred the same abilities. There are strong indications that the Manicheans, the Messalians, and possibly the Paulicans, also had a rite of spiritual baptism (see Chapter 8). In any case, the Cathars believed that there had been a continual chain of baptisms which had passed the Holy Spirit from the Apostles on to the Elect members of the religions which had preceded their own. The initiates of these religions had then passed the Spirit on to the Cathars, just as the Cathars continued to pass it on to their own initiates.[2]

The Cathar Ritual of baptism included the laying on of hands, and the placing of a copy of the Gospels on the postulant's head. The ceremony ended with the Act of Peace, during which the males embraced and kissed each other. The women also kissed each other, the Gospels, or the shoulder or elbow of a man.[3] Once baptized, the neophyte was on earth, but no longer of it. From now on, he or she had to follow strict and unbreakable rules of purity, including food restrictions, no sexual contact, no lying and no taking of oaths. Only a few women and men were permitted to have the spiritual baptism during their lifetimes and become priests. These were the ones whose souls were seen as having been less corrupt to start with. The more ordinary members of the faith would not have been able to keep to the taxing rules of purity, and therefore had to wait for baptism until they were on their deathbeds. The people who were allowed to become Cathar priests had various duties, including helping and advising the ordinary Cathar believers, healing the sick, imparting the main Cathar doctrines, and administering the spiritual baptism.

Bosch depicts a spiritual teacher of this type in an unexpected place: the central panel of the *Garden of Earthly Delights*. This man can be seen in the lower lefthand corner, surrounded by a small group of listeners (Plate 52). As Beagle says, he is meant as a contrast to the three figures which emerge from a cave in the lower righthand corner of the painting (Plate 53). Most scholars believe that these three figures represent Adam, Eve, and a descendant. Eve is ensnared in the physical body and the physical world, and Adam is about to join her. Entrapment and reproduction are symbolized by the glass tube — an alchemical symbol of the body — which covers Eve. The tube is ornamented with breast-like circles. This scene is paralleled by the glass cage at the left, with its two birds, symbolic of souls. One bird is already in the cage, and the other teeters on the brink. The spiritual teacher on the left side of the panel who, unlike Adam and Eve, has achieved liberation, points up and away from the garden of lust and procreation. But even the few people who are aware of his words seem bemused and not quite able to understand the message he is trying to impart.

Bosch's painting of the *Stone Operation* in Madrid (Plate 54), is another variation on this same theme. This work probably depicts an initiated Cathar priestess. Many authors believe that this woman (who stands on the right with a book on her head) is a nun, but in fact her robe, headdress and purse are more typical of an older middle-class wife. In the fifteenth century Netherlands, such women swathed their heads and necks in a manner very similar to that of Bosch's figure. They were conservative, and continued with this custom until late in the century.[4] In Catharism's early days, before the persecutions had made special dress too risky, the male and female Perfects had been recognizable by their dark robes. After this time, they reverted to ordinary clothes with a special cord hidden underneath them.[5]

Because of these changes, Bosch had to use symbols, rather than special dress to identify his Perfects. And in the *Stone Operation,* he shows that the middle-aged woman is a Cathar priestess by the book on her head, and the hand which she points towards her elbow. These images would have reminded the Cathar viewer of the ceremony of spiritual baptism. The woman also leans on a round table, which, together with its base, looks something like a mushroom. Its shape and its odd vegetal associations show that it is a symbol of Satan's world. As we saw in Chapter 5, a round platter on legs, as seen today in the Muslim world, was used in the Consolamentum ceremony. When the top of this table was made of polished metal, it would have represented Christ as the spiritual sun, but in some cases, the tabletop might have been painted with negative images symbolic of the evils of the earth.

The *Stone Operation,* then, contains several images which are connected in some way with the Cathar spiritual baptism. The same general conclusion is reached by Stein Schneider, but he understands the details of the scene in a somewhat different way. The painting does not depict the Ritual itself, given by the woman and the man in black, and contrasted with spiritual 'castration' by the Church of Rome, as in Stein Schneider's interpretation.[6] Instead, it is a more subtle example of Bosch's recurrent theme of religious choice. The woman offers the Cathar spiritual baptism, but the fool who is allowing himself to be operated on pays no attention to her. Instead, he has chosen to submit to the ministrations of two quack doctors, who are both identified with the Roman clergy.

The tonsured man on the right wears a black robe which could well be a monastic habit. The quack who is actually performing the operation is more ambiguous in his dress. His dark cowl could belong to a friar, but his pink robe seems to be secular. The metal funnel on his head is particularly difficult to understand. This symbol is not found in the art of Bosch's era, but according to Bax, its inability to retain liquids caused it to be used as a folk metaphor for wastefulness, intemperance, unreliability, unscrupulousness, deceit and the like.[7] Bosch's funnel hat probably shows that the quack doctor has some or all of these characteristics, but in Bosch's paintings, symbols usually have several layers of meaning. The chances are that his funnel is more than just a comment on the quack's character. Most likely, it also has

28. Souls struggling in the mire: detail, central panel of the Bruges *Last Judgment* tryptich.

29. Unhappy souls: the Munich *Last Judgment* (fragment).

30. (Opposite) Central panel of the Bruges *Last Judgment* tryptich.

31. (Left) *Terrestrial Paradise of the Third Heaven*: left wing of the Bruges *Last Judgment*.

32. (Right) *Hell on Earth*: right wing of the Bruges *Last Judgment*.

33. (Opposite) Demonic 'Eye' with Passion and Pelican: reverse of the *St John on Patmos*.

34. *God the Great Architect:* miniature from a fifteenth century French manuscript.

35. Tapestry after a lost painting of the *Haywain*.

36. Tabletop of the *Seven Deadly Sins*.
37. (Opposite top) *Gluttony:* detail, the *Seven Deadly Sins*.
38. (Opposite lower) *Sloth:* detail, the *Seven Deadly Sins*.

gula

accidia

39. Frankfurt *Ecce Homo*.

40. Escorial *Crowning with Thorns*, with demonic scenes surrounding the tondo.

41. London *Crowning with Thorns*.

42. Ghent *Carrying of the Cross*.

Arrest of Christ: left outer wing of the Lisbon *St Anthony.*

44. *Carrying of the Cross:* right outer wing of the Lisbon *St Anthony.*

45. Central panel of the Lisbon *St Anthony*.

46. Left wing of the Lisbon *St Anthony*.   47. Right wing of the Lisbon *St Anthony*.

48. Satan's pillar: detail, central panel of the Lisbon *St Anthony*.

49. Ghent *St Jerome Praying*.

50. *St John the Baptist in the Wilderness.*

a religious significance. The connection with religion is hinted at by the arrangement of the figures. The quack, on the far left of the composition, is balanced on the other side by the Cathar priestess. Both figures wear symbolic objects on their heads. In the Cathar rite of baptism by fire and the spirit, a copy of the Gospels was placed on the initiate's head. In the baptismal ceremony of the Church, water is poured over the head of the person who is being admitted into the Church. Bosch's Cathar priestess wears a book on her head, and his charlatan wears a funnel, an object which is used for pouring water. The quack is not dressed as a priest, but he could still have helped in the performance of a baptism. The Christian baptism by water did not have to be administered by an ordained priest, and lay baptisms were fairly common during the Middle Ages.[8]

Baptismal water could not literally be poured through the funnel on the man's head, because it is upside-down. But if it was the right way up it would not work nearly as well as a piece of headgear, and, in any case, it is meant as a symbol. What it represents (or, more accurately, confirms) is the fool's decision to accept established Christianity rather than Catharism. Its association with Roman ritual is further amplified by the jug on the quack's belt and the silver vessel in the friar's hand. The former could hold baptismal water, and the latter Communion wine. This interpretation is supported by the use of the funnel hat in other works by Bosch. Five out of the eight figures which wear this headgear are either clerical demons, or devils which talk to or assist Satanic churchmen. The other three are fools or witches.[9] In the central panel of the Lisbon *St Anthony*, for example, a funnel hat is worn by a bestial devil who shouts into the ear of the demon monk with the book, spectacles and gruesome rotting body. In the left wing of the same triptych, we find it again on the head of the monster on skates who brings a letter to the demonic 'Pope.'

The inscription which surrounds Bosch's *Stone Operation* reads 'Master, cut the stone out, my name is Lubbert Das.' In Dutch literature and folklore, the name 'Lubbert' was given to people known for their stupidity, and the operation itself was supposed literally to cut the stone of their folly out.[10] But in Bosch's version of the traditional scene, the meaning is, as usual, not traditional. What is cut out is something that conventional Christians, but not Cathars, would consider to be folly. Its extraction is identified with the exorcism which traditionally preceded the Roman baptism.[11] And in this case, what is being exorcized by the charlatan is something that the established Church has no place for. It is, in fact, the man's spiritual potential. This symbolic meaning is revealed by the way that Bosch depicts the 'stone.' In his version of the scene it is not a stone at all, but a flower. This oddity, which cannot be explained in conventional Christian terms, makes perfect sense when seen from the Cathar point of view. The flower resembles a lotus, whose opening is an ancient symbol of the development of spiritual awareness. The man's lotus is still closed, and, stupidly, he allows it to be cut out by the Church.

The Cathar priestess offers another choice, but she is totally ignored. She stares gloomily into space, depressed by the path which the fool is choosing to take.

The Hearers

'Lubbert Das' is depicted by Bosch as a simple member of the Church, who lives in a foolish world of illusions. He is very different from the ordinary believers in the Cathar religion, who, in contrast, are highly aware, but very troubled. These followers of the faith were known as Hearers (those who had heard the word). Bosch represents them as people whose spiritual awareness is still intact, but not yet in flower. They are constantly in danger of falling back into a state of spiritual forgetfulness. These Hearers will only receive the spiritual baptism when they are so near to death that they can no longer give in to their earthly desires. And even after death, they will not be fully secure. If their longings for earthly pleasures are powerful enough, they will overcome the effects of the baptism, and will draw the Hearers' souls back to another life in the physical body.

Bosch frequently represents the Cathar Hearers as pilgrims and wayfarers. They are shown as sincere seekers who genuinely long to achieve salvation, but who struggle with the temptations of the world because they are not yet free of their desires. On one level, as Gibson points out, these figures fit very well with the traditional Christian pilgrim who travels through a world full of temptations.[12] And yet, as always, Bosch includes symbols in his depictions of the pilgrims which are odd, eccentric and difficult to explain. These symbols correspond more closely with Cathar and Manichean concepts than with traditional Christian ideas.

Bosch's pilgrim figures always assume the same posture. They all walk with their backs and knees bent, holding staffs or poles. Their model, and the example for those who want to follow in his path, is the traditional Christian pilgrim, St James the Greater of Compostella. Bosch depicts this saint on the left outer wing of the *Last Judgment* at Vienna (Plate 56). St James was one of the Apostles who had received the spiritual baptism at Pentecost, and he is now genuinely immune to the temptations of the world. He looks at the viewer, rather than the symbols of sin and violence around him. He is is different in this way from all of the other wayfarers depicted by Bosch. Even Bosch's St Christopher, who is represented in the pilgrim pose in Bosch's panel at Rotterdam (Plate 55), is torn between the burden of Jesus which he carries on his back, and the dead and bloody fish, which is attached to his staff. The child on his back is the Living Jesus, and the fish can be seen as the false, dead image of Christ offered by the Church.

Bosch's best known pilgrim figures are the so-called 'Prodigal Son' at Rotterdam (Plate 58), and the wayfarer on the external panels of the *Haywain* triptych (Plate 59). These two suffering and isolated men, who wander unhappily through scenes of violence, corruption and lust, are aware that they are not, or should not be of this world. And yet, at the same time, they are troubled in their attempts to resist its pull. In both paintings, the wayfarers are depicted as peddlers. This could be Bosch's way of emphasising their lack of a permanent home in the world. They are strangers in Satan's realm, even though they are also attracted by it.

The peddler at Rotterdam is walking away from an inn, but he looks backwards over his shoulder at the same time as he moves forwards. The inn which he finds so tempting is obviously a place of sin and corruption. Its swan signboard, its pigeons in the loft, its jug, and its women all show that it is a house of prostitution. It also a place of drunkenness and intoxication. Symbols of drink include the leaking barrel and the man who urinates at the side of the wall.

Bosch's inn can be interpreted as a conventional Christian image of temptation, but it corresponds even more closely with a metaphor in the Manichean-related *Hymn of the Pearl*. In this poem, the Saviour who has come to rescue the fallen soul goes to stay in a similar inn.

Symbolically, this is a temporary dwelling, which represents the earth.[13] Like the tavern/brothel in the painting at Rotterdam, it is a place where corruption and drunkenness are rife. In Bosch's painting, the peddler has the rather unhappy choice between joining the people in this inn, or walking alone as a stranger. In the *Hymn of the Pearl*, the Saviour is in the same position. As long as he remains unsullied by the corruption of the inn, he experiences the same isolation as Bosch's wayfarer. He describes his condition of separateness when he says:

> Since I was one and kept to myself
> I was a stranger to my fellow
> dwellers in the inn.[14]

The peddler's susceptibility to the inebriation at the inn is made plain by several symbols. One of the most obvious is the tit above his head. According to Bax, this bird is a symbol of both drunkenness and wavering weakness.[15] The tit is menaced by a particularly fierce and predatory owl, and does not look as though it has much chance of resisting the owl's advances. This stress on intoxication is particularly relevant to the Cathar meaning of Bosch's painting, for as we saw earlier, the Gnostics and Manicheans used drunkenness and sleep as metaphors for the soul's forgetfulness of its true nature. A Manichean call to the soul from one of the ninth century writings found at the Turfan Oasis between 1902 and 1907 illustrates this concept:

> My soul, O most splendid one,
> ... whither hast thou gone?
> Return again,
> Awake, soul of splendor,
> from the slumber of drunkenness
> into which thou hast fallen ...[16]

The Saviour in the *Hymn of the Pearl* resists the drunkenness which he finds in the inn for awhile, but even he is unable to hold out indefinitely. He finally eats and drinks the heavy 'nourishment' of the world, and lapses into a state of sleep. He soon awakens again, but the soul or pearl which he has come to rescue is, like Bosch's peddler, more helpless and entrapped. This is because the soul is more deeply involved than the spirit with the earth and the physical body.

The physical body in which the soul is entrapped is often called an 'impure garment' in Gnostic and Manichean literature.[17] This same concept is also hinted at in Bosch's painting, where the peddler's ragged and unkempt clothes symbolize the corruption of his body. The wanderer's bandaged left leg is also significant from the Cathar point of view. It indicates that he is wounded. As we saw in Chapter 1, the wound means that he is subject to sin, and its location on the left foot or leg identifies his sin as lust. The wayfarer is not shown as unredeemably wicked, however. A truly evil nature is represented in Bosch's works by a visible open, festering wound. Bosch depicts leg wounds of this sort on the Satanic white monster in the *Garden of Earthly Delights* and the 'Pope' figure in the central panel of the Prado *Adoration of the Magi*. The dual nature of the Hearer, which contains both darkness and light, is also symbolized by the black and white plumage of the two magpies in the painting. One of these is trapped in a cage next to the door of the inn, and the other stands on a bar of the gate in front of the peddler.

The Hearers in both of Bosch's paintings are grey haired men, whose journey through physical life is nearing its end. The wayfarer in the Rotterdam panel walks towards the gate with its uncaged magpie, while the peddler in the *Haywain* approaches a bridge. Both of these images symbolize the transition to the afterworld, and the possibility of life and freedom which it can bring. It is interesting that, in the *Haywain,* dismembered animal bones are painted on the *peddler's* side of the bridge, and that dark, menacing birds (demonic souls) alight on them. This is a way of showing that life in the physical realm is not the true life. From the spiritual point of view, it is the realm of death, and is beset by demons. The long staffs of bone which are held by both wayfarers probably express the same image of the world through which the two men are travelling.

The temptations of Bosch's Hearers are particularly dangerous because these wayfarers are nearing the ends of their physical lives. If they die 'drunk' and full of fleshly desires, their longings will draw their souls back again into the morass of physical life. The unhappy fate of souls which succumb to lust is shown by the locations of the trapped or enclosed birds in both paintings. In the example at

Rotterdam, the caged magpie hanging from the wall of the inn is next to the lovers in the doorway, and looks directly at them. Similarly, in the *Haywain* panels, a birdhouse is nailed to a tree above a man who plays the bagpipe for two hedonistic dancers.

The spindle in the hat held out by the Hearer in the panel at Rotterdam is a traditional symbol of the weaving of the thread of physical life. Only one small strand remains on it, and as Wertheim Aymès says, this is probably a sign that the peddler has very little time left on earth. Alternatively, in the interpretation of Stein Schneider, the spindle itself is an image of continuing death and rebirth, which implies reincarnation.[18] Perhaps Bosch is expressing both ideas. In any case, the gallows on the hill behind the gate and spindle warns us that the pilgrim will suffer spiritual death if his desires lead to his rebirth in the physical world. In the *Haywain* panels, the same danger is suggested by the crack, implying the possibility of breakage, on the stone bridge which the wayfarer is about to cross. Even the stone gateposts in the painting at Rotterdam repeat the message. Close examination reveals that one of these is cracked and crumbling, while the other is firm and unblemished. This contrast symbolizes the peddler's choice between salvation in the world of light, and rebirth into hell (the Cathar name for the earth).

The two Hearers are tempted by Satan's world, and, as Cathars, they are also persecuted by it. This is hinted at in both works by the fierce dog, wearing the same spiked collar as the 'Dominican' in the National Gallery *Crowning with Thorns*, which barks at the peddlers' feet and staffs. This demonic animal is an image of the Church Inquisitors who threaten and torment the Cathar believers as they travel through the world of matter. The same message is repeated in the left background of the *Haywain* panels, where a meek and unresisting man is tied to a tree by brigands. This scene has a clear resemblance to Bosch's depiction of the thief (standing to the right of the picture) on the exterior of the Lisbon *St Anthony* (see Chapter 6). Like the latter, it represents an unfortunate Cathar heretic submitting to the persecutions of the demonic members of the Church hierarchy. The lot of the Hearer is difficult in more than one way. It is not surprising that Bosch's pilgrims look troubled as they travel through the world.

8. The Union of Soul and Spirit

The spiritual marriage

As said earlier, the ordinary Cathar Hearer would not have been given the spiritual baptism until the time of death, while the less corrupt future priest was able to have it during his or her lifetime. The Cathar baptism achieved liberation from the pull of the earth and the attainment of spiritual wholeness by purifying the initiate's soul, and reuniting it with the spirit it had left behind at its fall. This reunion of soul and spirit was often called a 'spiritual marriage' by the Cathars and their predecessors. The initiate or protagonist in the ceremony was traditionally called the 'bride.' These ideas are found in the Inquisition Records.[1] They can also be seen in the Coptic Manichean Psalms,[2] and the *Acts of Thomas,* which contain a hymn where the soul is described as uniting with wisdom during a nuptual banquet.[3] In the Messalian tradition, baptism is also spoken of as a marriage, with the soul as the 'earthly bride,' and the spirit as the 'heavenly bridegroom.'[4]

Some of the symbols in Bosch's *Marriage at Cana* in Rotterdam (see Plate 60) have already been discussed in Chapter 2. But further layers of its meaning can be revealed if one sees the central ceremony in this painting as a depiction of a Cathar 'spiritual marriage.' When the picture's symbols are analysed, they show a contrast between the heresy and corruption of Satan's realm, and the spirituality of a genuine religious ritual. The figures which sit on the righthand side of the feast table are the ones who actually make up the bridal party. There are six of them, beginning on the left with a young man who appears to ignore the whispers of an envoy of the world. The members of this group sit isolated in their own independent realm. They are participating in a solemn ceremony, and pay no attention to the worldly feast that surrounds them.[5]

The six celebrants of this private rite all sit more or less facing a seventh figure. This seventh person is small, youthful and unidentified in gender. Nevertheless, it is clearly very important. It faces the bride, with its back to the viewer. It holds a chalice in its right hand, and raises its left hand in some sort of ceremonial greeting. It wears a garland and a brocaded robe, and stands next to an empty throne.

This small but richly dressed child is extremely difficult to explain in terms of traditional Christian theology. What is its significance, and why is it so little and young? Looked at from the point of view of Catharism, its meaning becomes more clear. The Cathar and Manichean records tell us repeatedly that the fallen angels or souls left their attributes of garland (or crown), robe and throne behind in the Land of Light when they descended to earth. These attributes would only be regained by the souls after they had reunited once again with their spirits.[6] The way to achieve this reunion was through the spiritual baptism or marriage. It therefore follows that, while Bosch's bride represents the initiate, the small and youthful figure which has re-acquired its attributes of robe, garland and throne represents her newly baptized soul. In medieval depictions of death and dying, the soul is often shown as a child which is separated from the adult body. In Bosch's painting, the bride is not on her deathbed, but her newly saved soul is a key player in the events, and is therefore depicted as a separate figure.

If the bride is the initiate, and the child is her soul, which figure is her bridegroom or spirit? In Cathar and Manichean symbolism, the spirit is usually identified with Jesus. It is surely significant, then, that in Bosch's unconventional depiction of the *Marriage at Cana*, it is Jesus who sits beneath the bridal canopy. The circular golden platter in front of him is a reminder of his identification with the spiritual sun, and also brings the round tabletop used in the Consolamentum ceremony to mind (see Chapter 5).

The wine of the spirit

In Bosch's eccentric and esoteric version of the *Marriage at Cana* story, Jesus directs his blessing not at the traditional water jars, but at the golden chalice held by the soul. This chalice is the vessel of 'quickening' or living water which, in the Manichean vision, would be placed

in the hand of the robed and crowned saved soul.[7] Jesus is in the act
of changing what the Coptic Manichean Psalms call the 'cold water' of
the bride's earthly nature, into the living water or fiery wine of her
new spiritual nature. This is the wine made from the vine or tree of life
with which Jesus was identified. The Manicheans described it as 'the
new wine,' which was 'sweet honey, burning pepper ...'[8] In other
words, it is the fiery spiritual energy, which transforms the initiate, and
reunites her soul with her spirit.

These Manichean metaphors correspond with what we know about
the Cathar baptism, and show that the Cathar initiation was a
continuation of the Manichean one. The Manichean images of the cold,
earthly 'water,' which is transformed by the spirit into fiery, living
'wine,' also tell us obliquely about the real nature of this baptism. This
probably involved a radical transformation of the initiate's energies. Its
implications will be looked at in more detail in the Appendix (see
p.243).

Bosch's identification of the biblical Marriage at Cana with the
Cathar spiritual baptism is not mentioned specifically in any of the
Cathar/Manichean writings or Inquisition records, but it is hinted at
by a Mitigated Cathar bishop called Nazarius. Nazarius, who lived in
Northern Italy during the thirteenth century, is quoted as saying that
the Italian Cathars interpreted all the biblical references to marriage in
a spiritual sense.[9] No further details are given about this, but an illustration of the *Marriage at Cana* from a fifteenth century Bosnian Cathar
manuscript known as the *Missal of Duke Hrvoj of Split* (Figure 24) could
have the same symbolism as Bosch's version of the scene.[10] There are
far fewer details in the Bosnian illustration than in Bosch's painting,
but the double meaning is suggested by the dove in flight on the
round golden platter next to Jesus. This bird, a symbol of the spirit,
hints that the scene is really a Cathar baptism.

The feast of Satan

In the illustration of the *Marriage at Cana* in the Bosnian manuscript
(Figure 24), the holy figures are placed on the left. It is possible
(though not certain) that the two figures on the right, separated
from the others by a large knife, are worldly outsiders who do not

Figure 24. *The Marriage at Cana* with symbolic dove. Miniature from the *Missal of Duke Hrvoj of Split*, *c*.1407.

participate in the ceremony. In Bosch's depiction of the scene, the seven holy figures who drink the wine of the spirit are clearly contrasted with the corrupt people in the room. These evil men and women drink a different sort of wine. Their wine is the wine of spiritual forgetfulness. It is Satan's wine, made from the vine of sensual knowledge (see Chapter 5). The lust of the men and women who drink it is indicated by the lewdly smiling bagpipe player, whose music entertains the guests. In Bosch's day, bagpipe music was associated with revelry and lasciviousness, and the instruments themselves were well-known phallic symbols.[11] For the Cathars, lust, which led to the procreation of children, was Satan's greatest trap. The bagpipe player's connection with Satan is revealed by a crescent moon which decorates a medallion on his sleeve (Plate 61).

The two main dishes which are served to the corrupt members of the feast are a swan and the head of a boar. Like the bagpipe player, these creatures are ornamented with crescent moons that associate them with Satan. Both animals are also identified with established Christianity, as we saw in Chapters 1 and 2. The swan and boar spit golden flames as they are carried in on golden salvers, images which contrast with the round platter in front of Jesus. According to a document at Bologna referred to by Iris Origo, the *plat de résistance* at elaborate and expensive medieval banquets was sometimes a peacock which had cotton wool soaked in acquavitae put in its mouth. This was set alight, with the result that the bird appeared to spit fire.[12] In Bosch's depiction, these flames are the fires of Satan. They show that the food is both important and corrupt. The fire-spitting also has connotations of magic and luxury, two characteristics which Bosch frequently associates with the Church.

The crescent moons and flame-spitting are not very obvious, and cannot be seen from a distance. Nevertheless, they must have been included in Bosch's original version of this scene, for they put across an important message. They tell us that the food and music at Satan's feast are dangerous spiritual poisons. Like the wine of Satan, they are drugs which cause the soul to forget its origins in the Land of Light. The men and women who partake of these drugs have become hopelessly entangled in the snares of the Prince of the World. They are so enmeshed in Satan's trap that they are no longer aware that anything else exists. The Cathar spiritual marriage is therefore able to take place literally in their midst, without their noticing it or realizing what is happening.

At the back of the room in which Satan's followers enjoy their unholy feast, a man holding a rod stands within a small, separated area. The vaulted roof in this section, and the pillars in front of it, are reminiscent of the apse of a cathedral. An owl peers out from behind the pillar on the right, as a sign that Jehovah/Satan is present, and watching the various events. Above him, a stone cupid-demon stands on top of the lefthand pillar, shooting arrows at a devil. The demon at which it shoots disappears into a hole above the righthand pillar. This small scene might seem like an amusing drollery, but even these minor

171

events have a meaning. The cupid has associations with paganism, one of the religions of Prince of the World, and the demon at which its arrows of lust and reproduction are aimed is a corrupt soul. The hole into which it crawls is the dark realm of Satan. These scenes, which echo the unholy nature of the participants in Satan's feast, take place on the columns in front of the apse. Their location shows that they are identified with traditional Christianity as well as paganism.

According to Bax, the man holding the rod inside of the apse is the steward of the feast mentioned in the Biblical account of the Marriage at Cana. In Bax's interpretation, he stands by a sideboard, directing the servants with his staff.[13] This identity is no doubt accurate when the painting is seen as an eccentric but conventionally pious work. But, like so many of Bosch's images, the steward has a double meaning. Looked at from the Cathar point of view, this master of ceremonies, who directs Satan's infidel feast from within an apse, is a priest of the Roman Church. The sideboard, seen from this viewpoint, becomes an altar which has three shelves. These contain a miscellaneous group of objects, many of which have religious associations. We see, for example, a crescent which represents both Satan and the infidel on the right side of the top shelf. On the left side of the middle shelf, two figures dance below a pointed Jewish hat. Various Christian images can also be seen. One of these is a tall half-hidden cross, mounted on a yellowish triangular base, which is located in the centre of the bottom shelf. The other Christian images are a pelican on the bottom shelf at the left, and, on the middle shelf, a figure bent by the weight of a world topped by a cross.

The altar or sideboard in Bosch's painting also contains many jugs and vessels which could hold fluids of some sort. These are likely to be associated with one of the central subjects of the painting: the transformation of liquids which symbolize spiritual energies. In the main scene, Jesus changes the earthly water into spiritual wine. In the apse, the priest is also performing a transformation with what can be interpreted as a magician's rod. His magical act has some connection with Church rites and the wine of Satan. Most likely it is associated in some way with the Eucharistic transformation of the wine on the altar into the blood of Christ.

The contrast between Satan's world and that of Jesus, and the dualistic symbolism that lies behind the images in the *Marriage at Cana*

and all of Bosch's other works, is expressed poignantly in the following
Coptic Manichean Psalm:

> Come, my Lord Jesus, the Saviour of souls, who hast
> saved me from the drunkenness and Error of the world
> ... thou hast driven away from me
> the oblivion of Error ...
> I have distinguished this pair of trees
> and this pair of kingdoms ...
> the bitter fountain and the holy essence of God.
> The Light I have distinguished from the Darkness,
> life from death,
> Christ and the church I have distinguished
> from the deceit of the world.
> I have known my soul and this body that lies upon it,
> that they are enemies to each other
> before the creations ...
> The body of death indeed and the soul
> are never in accord.[14]

9. Noah's Ark and the Two Baptisms

Bosch's *Marriage at Cana*, with its parallel but separate 'feasts,' contrasts the Cathar baptism of fire and the Holy Spirit with the Church and its corrupt rituals. The same contrasts, expressed though different symbols, are made in Bosch's *Flood* panels at Rotterdam (Plates 62–65). These rectangular panels, which are painted in grisaille on both sides, are thought to be the surviving wings of a triptych whose central panel has now disappeared.

The demons and Noah's Flood

There is no way of guessing what the subject matter of the central panel of this work might have been. We can't even be sure that the 'wings' really were part of a triptych. What we do know is that Bosch has covered one side of the panels with depictions of a dark, gloomy and hellish world, dominated by Satan and his evil fallen angels (Plates 62, 63). The landscape on one of these 'wings' swarms with devils, which fill the sky, and populate the entire surface of the earth. Satanic fires burn ominously on the horizon. The scene on the second 'wing' depicts Noah's ark after the Flood, with the animals emerging two by two into a grim and colourless landscape, filled with the bloated bodies of the drowned.

Noah and his family, still on the ark, are outlandishly dressed, and some wear medieval Jewish hats. Such outfits are always a sign of evil in Bosch's works. They are found in the crowds which torment Christ, for example, and among the wicked and worldly guests in the *Marriage at Cana*. Clearly, the people on Noah's ark belong to Satan, and are not saved in the spiritual sense. Instead, they illustrate the Cathar interpretation of Old Testament story of Noah, as described in the Latin

Ritual of the Consolamentum. According to this version of the Ritual, 'It is ... found in the Old Testament that those who went out from that ark and their descendants committed many and most shameful misdeeds, and ... that they killed each other.' The Ritual then points out the contrast between the 'eight souls ... saved by water' (a pre-figuration of the water baptism) in Noah's Old Testament ark, and true salvation in the ark of the New Testament. Those who enter this second ark can find genuine life, through the baptism of fire and the Holy Spirit.[1]

The reverse sides of Bosch's *Flood* panels complement these ideas, by illustrating the drama of the collective human soul which falls into Satan's world, but eventually manages to find spiritual salvation and make its escape through the Cathar spiritual baptism. This story is told in four roundels, which have puzzled art historians for many years. The author who has written about them most fully is Irma Wittrock. She interprets them from a conventionally Christian point of view, and the result, as she herself says, is that her understanding of their iconography is incomplete. From the Cathar viewpoint, however, the two sides of the wings at Rotterdam show a clear relationship, pointing out the contrast between the Old Testament and baptism of water, and the New Testament and baptism of fire.

The fall of the soul

The first episode of the drama (the soul's fall) is depicted in the upper roundel of what is usually called the right wing (Plate 65a). Here Bosch shows a man who is stripped and beaten by devils. This image is seen by Wittrock as a partial illustration of the Parable of the Good Samaritan (Luke 10:30–37).[2] Bosch's depiction does indeed correspond with this Parable, but what it illustrates is the esoteric interpretation of the story. This hidden, or inner meaning refers to the fall of the soul, and has nothing to do with the events on the physical road between Jerusalem and Jerico.

The esoteric interpretation of the Parable of the Good Samaritan was given special mention as an example of Cathar thinking by the Dominican friar Moneta.[3] Its origins are much more ancient, however. They go back to the early Mesopotamian mythology which influenced both the Manicheans and the orthodox Christian Syrian hymn writers of the fourth century.[4] A hymn by Balai, a follower of the Christian Syrian poet Ephrem, helps us to understand the symbolism:

> A man went down
> from Jerusalem,
> and robbers smote him
> and maltreated him mercilessly,
> and stripped him of his clothes,
> and left him like dead.
> Adam, however, was
> the man who was smitten
> by the Accuser
> And Death in Hades.
> But when Christ came,
> He saved him from Death.[5]

The message of this poem is exactly the same as the esoteric Cathar interpretation of the parable described by Moneta. Seen symbolically, it is Adam, the collective soul, who falls from heaven (Jerusalem). He is stripped of his clothes (robe or spiritual body) by robbers (demons). The Hades into which he falls is the earth. It is often described as a pit, or even a grave in Manichean or other Gnostic writings. It is therefore particularly interesting that in Bosch's roundel a shadowy gap that looks like a pit can be seen in front of the 'Adam' figure.

The domination of Satan

The second episode of the story is depicted in the lower roundel of what is assumed to be the left panel (Plate 64b). In the ancient Mesopotamian myth which influenced Manicheism, the collective soul (Tammuz) has fallen into the pit, and is cast down and imprisoned by his enemies. He may be drugged, or bitten by a poisonous serpent or dog.[6] He lies in the dust and cannot arise.[7] In Bosch's later version of the same story, the man or collective soul seems unable to get up from his position on the ground. He is dominated by the devil, who sits in a superior position on a horse above him, holding a staff which seems to be an emblem of power and evil. One is reminded here of an episode in the apocryphal Bogomil book of Adam and Eve. In this allegory, Adam is forced to make a pact with the Prince of the World. Satan owns the earth, and will only allow Adam to farm it if Adam and his descendants agree to become the devil's men. This pact traps the soul in Satan's cycle of reproduction and rebirth, symbolized by the birth and death of plants, and the seeds which the man sows in the earth. In Bosch's painting, it is the devil's horse which pulls the harrow, thus aiding and encouraging the planting of seeds in the furrows. According to the Bogomil book. the agricultural pact with Satan will continue unbroken until the coming of Jesus, when men will be given the chance to escape.[8]

Escape from Satan's trap

In the third episode, depicted in the upper roundel of the left panel (Plate 64a), a change has taken place. The Saviour has now arrived, making it possible for the fallen soul to escape from the power of the demon. This picture shows a man kneeling and praying for a woman, who is running out of a burning, devil-ridden house. The house is a Manichean symbol of the physical body, subject to the fires of passion and desire. This image can be found in the Coptic Manichean Psalms. For example:

> The care of my poor body has made me drunk
> in its drunkenness ...
> Its fire, its lust, they trick me daily ...
> Many are the labours that I suffered while I was in
> this dark house ...
> Be not far from me, O Physician that hast
> the medicines of life ...
> do thou heal me of the grievous wound of lawlessness ...[9]

The kneeling man in Bosch's painting, with his long robe and his shoulder-length untonsured hair, is presumably a Cathar priest or Perfect, who is able to pass on the Spirit. He prays for the salvation of another soul: the woman who flees from her imprisonment in matter and the body. She can now be rescued from the fires of Satan with the spiritual fire of the Cathar baptism. The Church baptism, in which material water is used to save Noah and his family from more material water, can only bring false physical life, and further bondage in the realm of Satan.

Departure from the Earth

The fourth episode of the drama of the soul on earth is depicted in the lower roundel of the right panel (Plate 65b). Here, a rescued soul prepares to leave the world for good. In the background of the tondo, an angel restores the robe (spiritual body of light) which the soul had left behind in the Land of Light at the time of its fall. This scene is a depiction of what the Cathars referred to the soul's 'ascension.' It is now reunited with its spiritual body, and it is ready to move upwards into the realm of Light.[10] The Cathars did not believe that the material body would ever be resurrected. According to their doctrines, it was discarded forever at death and it dissolved into its original elements.[11] Bosch illustrates this last idea by the half-submerged ship in the distance. This physical boat (the body) sinks back into the waters of the material world, much as Bosch's ships of fools might, if they were abandoned by their passengers (see also Chapter 11, including note 21).

In the foreground of the fourth roundel, the soul kneels reverently in front of a robed and haloed Saviour. This radiant figure is the being of light which comes to meet the saved soul at death.[12] It is the man's own spirit, identified in the Cathar/Manichean tradition with Jesus. The soul, robed in its body of light, and united with its spirit, is now ready to leave the darkness of earth behind forever. The time has come for it to ascend upwards to the Land of Light, far beyond the physical world.

10. The Route to the Empyrean

The saved soul in Bosch's fourth *Flood* roundel is about to ascend to a spiritual realm which contrasts with the physical one. But what is this realm like, and where, exactly, is it? Is it described by the Manicheans or Cathars, and is it represented in the works of Bosch? The answer to all of these questions is yes, but it is a qualified yes. We can never know everything about the Cathar and Manichean visions of the next world, because there are no sources, either written, painted, or carved on tombstones, that describe them in complete detail. Nevertheless, a number of partial descriptions, in both words and pictures, do still exist. None of these tell the full story of the future of the soul, but, when enough written and artistic fragments are pieced together, a fairly complete picture of the Cathar/Manichean afterworld begins to emerge. And, when we look at Bosch's paintings with this picture in mind, it gradually becomes apparent that he was aware of it too.

Jesus as the column of glory

If we begin our look at this afterworld by taking up the story of the saved soul in Bosch's fourth *Flood* roundel at Rotterdam (Plate 65b), we see that the soul has received its robe (i.e., that it has united with its spiritual body). We also see that it kneels in front of Jesus. Jesus, the being of light, is the soul's own spirit. But is there anything more here — any hint of the next step: the ascension upwards, away from the realm of matter? In fact, when this scene is looked at from the Cathar/Manichean point of view, it turns out that there is a strong yet subtle indication of the next step. The key to this is found in the luminous and upright figure of Jesus. Jesus, as we have already seen, was identified with the tree of life. This tree, or column, which reaches upwards to heaven, contrasts with Satan's broken tree and column of death. Instead of keeping the soul confined to the earth, it enables it to rise away from the realm of Satan. It is a route of ascent, which takes the soul through the cosmos to the Land of Light. The image of this route is found often in Manichean literature, and, as we will see soon, it is one of the most common symbols in the art of the Cathars. The Manicheans often referred to it as the column of glory. It was a symbol of Jesus, the Saviour, spirit, and tree of life, but at the same time, the Cathars and Manicheans seem to have envisioned it as a real channel, through which the saved souls literally moved.

The association of the column of glory with Jesus is made plain in the Coptic Manichean psalms. One of these psalms tells us, for example, that 'Jesus is the Perfect Man in the Pillar.'[1] Another of these psalms says graphically that:

> ... the Perfect Man is stretched out in the middle
> of the world that thou mayest walk in him
> and be taken to the Light.[2]

Yet another psalm talks of:

> The glorious Column
> which is the Perfect Man ...
> the baptism of Life.
> The place of the washing of souls.
> The harbour of them that are in the sea.[3]

Cathar tombstones: the anthropomorphic cross

These psalms are only a few examples of the many descriptions of the column of glory in Manichean literature. Surviving Cathar texts never speak overtly of the column, but they do refer to the related concept of the tree of life. It is therefore not a coincidence that the image of an anthropomorphic column, tree or cross, which leads to the light, is an important and recurrent subject on the tombstones of the Balkan Cathars. This image can be seen, depicted in several symbolic but unambiguous forms, on some of the medieval gravestones from Bosnia,

Herzegovina and parts of the Dalmatian Coast (see Map 5). These Balkan tombstones are known locally as 'stećci.'

The first stone memorials in Bosnia appeared suddenly and without explanation during the thirteenth century. Perhaps the techniques for making them were brought to what was then a rather wild and undeveloped land by thirteenth century refugees from the Inquisition in the Languedoc.[4] In any case, the earliest stećci were only small, plain stone slabs. They might originally have been decorated with painted ornaments, but no signs of paint survive today. The stećci developed gradually as time passed, and, by the fourteenth century, they had grown in size and complexity. In the fifteenth century, they burst into a proliferation of carved ornamentation, and during the sixteenth century, they were replaced by Muslim tombs.[5] Their dates correspond with the period when Catharism, known locally as the Bosnian Church, was the state religion (see Chapters 2 and 12 for more on this). Some of the stećci had inscriptions as well as carvings, and at least eight of these, which are discussed by Fine, show connections with the Bosnian Church and its doctrines.[6]

Most of the stećci are found in graveyards near to villages in Bosnia and Herzegovina. There are 3150 of these necropoli. Many tombstones have been destroyed over the years, but before the fighting which began in 1992, 69350 of them still survived intact. At the time of writing this book, it is impossible to find out how many of these tombstones have been damaged by the fighting. For this reason, all the stećci will be described as they were in the 1980s.

Of the 69350 surviving tombstones, only 7427 are decorated with carvings. Papasov suggests that the many undecorated ones were made for the ordinary Hearers, who had no right to pictures or ornaments because they had not had the spiritual baptism. This might have been the case, but as Papasov herself says later in her book, the Hearers did have the Consolamentum on their deathbeds.[7] It seems more likely that the carved stones were made for those who could pay, whether they were Hearers or Perfects. This is supported by Fine's account of the eight stećci with inscriptions. These include five which were unquestionably made for Perfects. Three of them (those of Petko Krstienin, Gost Mišljen and an unnamed cleric) are undecorated; the fourth (that of Ostoja Krstjanin) is sparsely decorated, and the fifth (the well-known stone of the wealthy gost Milutin from Humsko, now at Sarajevo) is elaborately decorated (see note 6). Perhaps the stećci which seem plain today were less expensively decorated with paint which has now been eroded by the elements.

The carved decorations on the ornamented stećci are as eccentric and puzzling as the symbols in Bosch's paintings. This is because they, too, use an iconography which is heretical rather than traditional. But once we see them as representations of the Cathar afterworld, their meanings become clearer, and their connection with Bosch's iconography becomes apparent. Most of these symbols will be discussed in Chapter 12, but there is one which is particularly relevant at this stage. This is the depiction of the mystical channel, or route to the light. It can be shown literally as a column, but more often it is represented in the form of an anthropomorphic cross.

Bosch might possibly have visited the Dalmatian Coast (it is not far from Venice, and was in Venetian territory), but even if he did not, he would still have been aware of the image of the cosmic cross and column of glory. This is because it was fundamental to the Manichean heritage. It would have been familiar to Cathars in any country. The Bosnian Cathars were able to represent this and other visions of the afterlife fairly openly on their stećci, because they were comparatively free from persecution. The Cathars of Western Europe would have been more limited, but it is possible that their tombstones expressed some of their ideas about the route to the light in a more simplified form. If they did, have any of them survived, and can any of them be identified?

We know that many Cathars (Patarenes) lived in Lombardy, but unfortunately, all the Northern Italian graveyards were ploughed under by Napoleon. As a result, very few medieval tombstones survive, and (as yet) no grave monuments with Cathar connections have been found in that area. In the Languedoc, however, the situation is different. During the middle decades of the twentieth century, tombstones which looked like anthropomorphic crosses were discovered by René Nelli and several other scholars in the part of the Languedoc called the Lauragais. We know that at least some of these date from the Cathar period, because a group of them were discovered in a cemetery belonging to the Château of Labarth, which had only been in use during the thirteenth century.[8] The Lauragais was a part of the Languedoc where heresy was particularly widespread.[9] It therefore seemed reason-

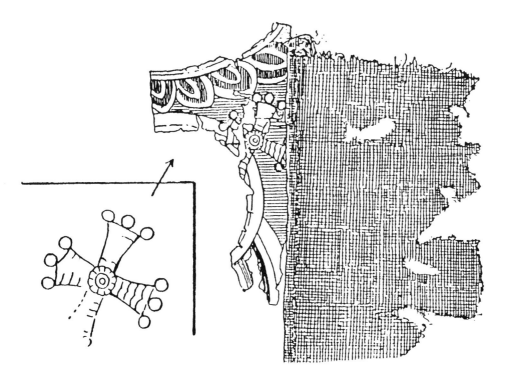

Figure 25. Manichean cross of light painted on silk, from Turfan, eighth century.

able at the time to suppose that the stele which appeared to be anthro-pomorphic crosses had been made for Cathars.

Typically, the monuments in the Languedoc were small columns, topped by a disc in which an equal-armed Greek cross was frequently inscribed. Some had 'arms,' but many did not. According to Nelli and Soloviev, the tombstones with arms represented the Cathar/Manichean cross of light — in other words, they were images of the Saviour, with arms outstretched and a radiant 'head' at the top.[10]

The image of a Saviour with a radiant sun-like head goes back a long way. Equal-armed crosses, which are images of the sun god whose light rays extend in four directions, can be traced back as far as Sumeria.[11] The same symbol was used later by Mani and his followers to represent the solar nature of the Saviour. For example, an eighth century equal-armed solar cross, painted on silk, was among the Manichean finds at Turfan (Figure 25).[12]

The established Christians also made use of this solar symbol from an early period. It is found frequently in Coptic art, for example, and can also be seen on a fourth century mosaic in the Vatican Grotte. Here, Christ is depicted as the sun god, with cruciform rays around his head. The medieval cruciform halo, which was used later by the Church to identify Christ or the Trinity, probably evolved from symbols such as this. But even though the established Church still used the image of the Greek cross, conventional Christians seem to have forgotten the original meaning of the symbol.

When the stele of the Languedoc were first discovered, people did not associate the inscribed Greek cross with conventional Christian tombstones. The stele with their 'arms' and 'solar heads' were therefore accepted by most people as Cathar images of the Saviour. But things are rarely as straightforward as they seem to be at first, and as so often happens, doubts have now crept in. Since the time of Nelli, the continuing search for medieval tombstones has led to the discovery of similar stele in many other parts of Europe. They are particularly prevalent in Catalonia and the Languedoc, where Cathars are known to have lived, but they are also found in other areas of France, Spain, Portugal and Germany. They are particularly prevalent in the British Isles, where they follow a long Celtic tradition.[13]

It is clear, then, that the tombstones with the inscribed Greek crosses were not exclusive to the Cathars. But this does not mean that no stele of this sort were ever made for the heretics. Equal-armed crosses are common decorations in Cathar manuscripts, and can be seen in works such as the *Secret Book* (Figure 12) and the *Missal of Duke Hrvoj of Split* (Figure 26). They were also used as decorations on everyday Cathar objects. The thirteenth or fourteenth century lead buttons and pectoral cross which were unearthed around the Cathar stronghold of Montségur in the Languedoc are examples of this (Figures 27 and 28). There is therefore every reason to suppose that these crosses were also used on the tombstones made for the European Cathars.

Probably the Cathars in areas such as the Languedoc, where heresy was widespread but more persecuted than it was in Bosnia, took the same approach to their tombstones as they did to the Scriptures. From their point of view, it was the *interpretation* of the images and symbols which counted. They could therefore have decorated their tombstones with Greek crosses that might have been either conventionally Christian or Cathar. There is no doubt that they would have found

186

Figure 26. Calendar miniature for January, with cross of light, *Missal of Duke Hrvoj of Split, c.1407.*

Figure 27. Lead buttons with crosses of light, found near the castle of Montségur. Thirteenth-fourteenth century.

Figure 28. Cathar pectoral crosses found near the castle of Montségur. Thirteenth-fourteenth century.

their own personal meaning in a column topped by a symbol of the radiant sun.

It is likely, then, that some anthropomorphic Cathar tombstones are intermingled among the conventional Christian ones, at least in the Languedoc. The Cathars, who believed that the physical body belonged to Satan anyway, did not object to burying their dead in church cemeteries. One incident which shows their attitudes occurred in the Languedoc in 1209, when Cathars wanted to inter a notorious heretic in the graveyard at Lordat, and the local church refused to allow them to do this.[14] There are no other records of similar objections, and it appears that most Cathars were buried in churchyards.

The real question, from our point of view, is whether any of the surviving examples in the Languedoc can be established definitely as Cathar stele. There are no names or identifications on these tombstones, so we can never be certain of any of them. Nevertheless, we can at least make guesses, based on the appearance of individual stele. It is possible that the examples which are the most anthropomorphic, or the ones whose 'heads' look the most radiant were made by Cathars.

188

Figure 29. Anthropomorphic cross tombstone with bent 'arms' and a 'head' in the form of a cross of light, rising from a block symbolizing the earth. Montmaur, Languedoc, twelfth or thirteenth century.

And among the many stele from the Lauragais, two come particularly near to expressing these ideas. One of them, which is outside the church at Montmaur, has part of its body embedded in a square stone which is probably a symbol of the earth, and arms which bend downwards. These give it a human look, and make the Greek cross which is inscribed in a circle at the top look particularly like a head (Figure 29). The other stela, which is now in the museum at Montferrand, has a sunburst head and outstretched arms (Figure 30). This sunburst image is known as a solar wheel, and its radiating spokes symbolize rays of light.[15] It is more unusual than the equal-armed cross, and has particular connections with the symbols on the tombstones of Bosnia.

The stela at Montferrand is similar, for example, to a Bosnian stećak from Simiova which was moved to the Museum at Sarajevo (Figure 31). Both are anthropomorphic crosses, and both have the same radiant sunburst heads. The inscription on the Bosnian monument is partially destroyed, and does not tell us much more than the name of

Figure 30. Anthropomorphic cross tombstone with inscribed sunburst 'head.' Montferrand, Languedoc, twelfth or thirteenth century.

Figure 31. Anthropomorphic cross tombstone from Simiova, with sunburst 'head,' and stars on the 'neck.' Sarajevo Museum, fifteenth century.

the deceased.[16] Nevertheless, as we will see soon, its symbols show that it is Cathar. These are more explicit than the ones on the anthropomorphic crosses of the Languedoc, for they reveal clearly that the monument is also identified with the column of glory.

Nelli and Soloviev did not connect the Cathar anthropomorphic cross with the Manichean image of the column, and as a result they ignored a very important aspect of the tombstones' significance. If we see the crosses of light as depictions of both the Saviour and the upward-leading passage to the Land of Light, it becomes obvious that they are channels or paths for the soul. The radiant 'heads' at their summits are not only the shining head of Jesus, but also, literally, the light at the end of the route or tunnel. Interestingly, these images have much in common with the descriptions given in recent first-hand accounts of near-death experiences.

The cross from Simiova is revealed as a column of glory which leads to the light when we look at the area above its outstretched arms. Here, two stars of different shapes have been carved in a line on the 'neck.' These are located on a path leading to the 'head' at the top. The stars show that the cross is an image of the Saviour as an anthropomorphic path, which the soul follows upwards through the heavens to the Land of Light (see Map 2).

Cathar crosses in the works of Bosch

The stela from Montmaur in the Languedoc has a Greek cross 'head' which is less unusual than the ones from Montferrand and Simiova. But, as said earlier, its particularly anthropomorphic 'body' indicates that it is Cathar. This combination of solar head and semi-human body give it a resemblance to an image in a drawing by Bosch called *The Death of the Miser* (Figure 32). The drawing is a study for a painting of the same subject (Figure 33), and is located in the Cabinet des Dessins at the Louvre. In it, Bosch depicts a dying man who is given a choice between a crucifix and a subtly drawn figure which stands in an arched space above the bed canopy. This semi-visible figure is topped by a Greek cross inscribed within a circle. It looks very much like an anthropomorphic tombstone, with a symbolically radiant head. An angel points up at this Cathar symbol, indicating the correct choice.

The anthropomorphic cross does not appear in the painted version of the scene, which is now in Washington D.C. Here, it has been replaced by a beam of light which is next to the crucifix. For the Cathars, as we have already seen, the crucifix was a hated image of the spirit immolated in Satan's world. It represented the dark conventional Christian image of Jesus, which contrasted with the radiant Cathar one.

Bosch also depicts an unusual cross, similar to a Bosnian example, in his *Haywain Tapestry* in the Royal Palace at Madrid (Plate 35, see also Figures 22, 23). In the tapestry, as we saw in Chapter 5, the cross of light is shown as a route of escape from a hellish world. This image of salvation rises out of the rim of the earth, and points upwards towards the higher levels of the cosmos. Its arms and shaft have rounded ends which are decorated with blue gems. Its triangular base is also covered with red and blue jewels.

Figure 32 (opposite). Bosch, preliminary drawing for *The Death of the Miser* including anthropomorphic cross with inscribed cross of light 'head.'

Figure 33 (right). Bosch, Washington painting of the *Death of the Miser*.

The cosmic cross in the *Haywain Tapestry* is very similar in design to some of the anthropomorphic stećci of Bosnia. One which is particularly close to Bosch's cross of light comes from Jela Šuma, and is now at the museum in Sarajevo (Figure 34). The Bosnian example has the same triangular base, and the same jewelled arms and 'head.' The spiralling tendrils which grow out from its base are not found on Bosch's cosmic cross, and their symbolism will be discussed in Chapter 12. Basically, both crosses are images of Jesus, the route of escape from the earth. They are identified with the tree of life, as well as the column of glory.

Bosch and the column of glory

Another dualistic picture which contains an image of the route of ascent, this time in the form of a crystalline column without arms, is Bosch's *St Jerome Praying* at Venice (Plate 66). This painting is the central panel of a triptych called the *Altarpiece of the Hermits*. In it, the saint kneels in front of a crucifix, which hangs from a barren tree. The tree emerges out of a ruined throne that is carved and painted with Old Testament scenes and images of lust and sin. From the Cathar point of view, this is the throne of Satan. Jerome worships at it because, as the Cathars saw it, he has a misguided affiliation with the Church. He faces to the right: the side of hell.

On the other side of the painting, facing left, a small praying figure rises weightlessly upwards through the stars in a glassy cylinder, in the direction of the moon and sun (Figure 35). This figure is surely a saved Cathar soul, moving away from the earth through the column of glory. The fact that this picture was located in Venice by or before 1521 indicates that Bosch painted it when he was there in about 1500. Its small but significant depiction of the soul's journey to the heavens through a column is more overtly Cathar than is usual in the works he executed in the Netherlands.

The small image of the column of glory in Bosch's Venetian *St Jerome* could well have been inspired, directly or indirectly, by the Cathar version of the *Vision of Isaiah*. As we saw in Chapter 2, this important piece of literature was still in existence in early sixteenth century Venice, and was probably owned by a local Cathar group. Like the

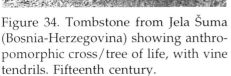

Figure 34. Tombstone from Jela Šuma (Bosnia-Herzegovina) showing anthropomorphic cross/tree of life, with vine tendrils. Fifteenth century.

Figure 35. Bosch, soul moving upwards through the column of glory: detail, *St Jerome* (Plate 66).

Cathars of the Middle Ages, they would have used this apocryphal book as a vehicle of meditation. Its text describes the Prophet Isaiah's visions of the seven heavens. The writer of the book pictured the heavens as a series of horizontal layers. They were not the same as the planetary spheres of Ptolemy and Dante, but represented a much more ancient view of the universe (see Maps 1, 2 and 3). As Isaiah passed through them, he saw things which were 'not of this world but of what is hidden from all flesh.'[17]

The book's descriptions of what Isaiah saw in these heavens are mystical and otherworldly, rather than concrete and specific. They appear to have induced states of mind in the Cathars which were similar to the near-death experiences recorded in recent literature. The adepts who had these visions could have described what they saw to Bosch. Alternatively, Bosch might have experienced the visions himself. Either way, there is no doubt that he depicts the soul's ascent more literally and mystically in his Venetian works than in any of his other paintings.

The column in Bosch's Venice *St Jerome* does not contain all the seven levels of the universe described in the *Vision of Isaiah,* but it is undoubtedly layered. It is divided into four distinct levels. These rest on a semi-circular pink base, an image of the material parts of the universe. The base has much in common with the lower part of the pink fountain in the *Garden of Earthly Delights.* It, too, has a hole in its centre, and a frog, symbolic of the slime of the realm of Satan, looks out from the hole. The first level of the column, which rises upwards from the top of the semi-circle, is still pink, but it changes its character about a fifth of the way up. The border between the pink, material level and the higher heavenly ones is marked by a circle of spiky branches. They resemble the branches in the hunt scene on Satan's column in the Lisbon *St Anthony* (see Figure 40). They are also reminiscent of the branches which make up the 'Pope' figure's crown of thorns in the Prado *Adoration of the Magi* (Plate 7). They symbolize the entanglements of the physical world, which the soul in the glassy column has finally managed to escape.

Above the tangled branches, the liberated soul moves upwards through a dark layer, dotted with 'stars' (probably the lesser angels; see Map 2). This second level is divided from the third one by an abrupt change from darkness to blue light. The blue band in the column must be the paradise of the third heaven, which will be discussed in Chapter 11 and is illustrated in Maps 1 and 2. Above it there is another layer, which contains a sparser number of stars, a crescent moon, and a bright, radiant sun. All of the heavenly bodies above the tangled branches belong to the spiritual levels of the universe. These stars, sun and moon are different from the lower, physical ones in the earth's firmament, for they are identified with angels, Jesus and the saved. According to the Inquisition records, the lower sun, moon and stars — which would be located in the pink part of Bosch's column — were identified by the Cathars with Satan and his demonic fallen angels. The discord of the fallen angels on the firmament, which is reflected on the earth below, is described in the Cathar *Vision of Isaiah.*[18]

The bright spiritual sun, which is only visible from the paradise of the third heaven, is metaphorically the shining 'head' of Jesus. It is the soul's final goal — a kind of portal, which leads to the Land of Light. Other Cathar images, which we will look at later, place this sun at the end of a special path that leads through the final three layers of the cosmos. This secret path is accessible only to the adepts and those who are fully purified. Bosch uses the sun as a sort of shorthand image of both the secret path and the Land of Light which is visible at its end.

Bosch's column of glory, which takes the soul upwards through the cosmos, ends suddenly and neatly in a flat top. When the structure is looked at as a whole, it can be seen as a pedestal with an empty space for a statue on top. The statue which once surmounted it is falling off, and is half way to the ground. It descends downwards between the flat top of the pillar and the foot of St Jerome. This statue is reminiscent of the pagan idols which fall from their columns in traditional Nether-landish depictions of the Flight into Egypt (see Chapter 2). Like them, it is overthrown by Christianity. But, as one might expect in a work by Bosch, the underlying significance of its overthrow is unconventional and heretical. Seen from the Cathar point of view, the 'idol' has been pushed off its pedestal by its own perverted form of Christianity. Its religion is false, for, like St Jerome, it is a saint honoured by the Church. The Cathars saw the veneration of the saints as a form of idolatry. This saint or 'idol' has no place in the realm of the saved. It tumbles back into Jehovah/Satan's world of matter because, at this stage of its development, this is where it belongs. The ladders on the pavement below it, interspersed with chevrons which point up and down, are also significant. They can be seen as a reference to the ordinary soul's rise and fall between lives.

Bosch represents these same concepts of ascent and descent, in a different form, in his four eschatological panels in the Doge's Palace at Venice. We do not know how these paintings were originally organ-ized, or whether they were once the right and left panels of a triptych. Many scholars have assumed that they were the wings of a lost *Last Judgment*, but this is unlikely. All four scenes, and particularly the two which deal with souls in torment, differ from the depictions of salva-tion and damnation on the wings of Bosch's known illustrations of the Last Judgment. These include the prints which copy his lost paintings of this theme, as well as the versions that are still extant. It is more likely, in view of their unique and particular characteristics, that the four panels at Venice are not Last Judgment scenes. Instead, they illustrate the soul's experiences immediately after death. Two of the panels show the saved, and the other two show the less enlightened souls, which, like the falling 'idol' in the Venice *St Jerome,* are destined to return to the earth. These less fortunate souls will be discussed in Chapter 12.

The column of glory of the Cathars and Manicheans is represented in a particularly striking and unforgettable way in the most famous of Bosch's four eschatological panels at Venice. This painting is usually called the *Ascent to the Empyrean*[19] (Plate 67). It is exceptional — even unique — in Western art. It reveals beyond doubt that Bosch was a mystic, and one who believed that at least some souls were destined to return to the spiritual world from which they had fallen. Like the *St Jerome,* it was probably painted in Venice, and probably inspired by mystical experiences induced by the Cathar *Vision of Isaiah.* In fact, its images of the ascent to the light show such an attunement with the otherworld journeys of the mystics that one wonders again whether Bosch himself used the *Vision of Isaiah* as a source of meditation. Could he really have produced such images if he had not had the experience himself? It seems unlikely.

In Bosch's visionary depiction of the final escape from Satan's world, a number of ecstatic souls, escorted by angels, rise upwards to an area beyond the clouds. They move towards a suspended tunnel that grows progressively brighter, and leads finally to the spiritual Land of Light. This channel appears to pass through five layers of the cosmos when it ought to pass through only three, but in spite of this aberration, it undoubtedly represents the final, secret path of the Cathar saved. It takes the purified souls through the highest and most rarefied levels of the universe, up to the entrance of the realm of light. It is this final path, together with the entrance at the end of it, that is so frequently shown as the mystical, sunlike 'head' of Jesus in Bosch's works and the tombstones of the Cathars. Two of the souls can be seen disappearing — almost dissolving — into the world of light beyond it. These souls are totally stripped of all ties with the world of matter. They have left the earth, with all its temptations, far behind.

The otherworldly figures which move towards the brightness seem to be almost without gender. Cathars followed the Gnostic and Manichean tradition in their belief that gender belonged to the flesh, and their idea that the soul's original and uncorrupted form, like that of Jesus, was semi-masculine or even neuter. According to various Bogomil and Cathar depositions, the saved souls would resume

Figure 36. Tombstone from Rogatika (Bosnia-Herzegovina) in shape of column of glory, with stars, moon and 'sun-tunnel.' Sarajevo Museum, fifteenth century.

their original immaterial bodies before ascending to the Land of Light.[20]

An image which may not at first look much like the tunnel in Bosch's *Ascent to the Empyrean,* but which actually has a great deal in common with it, can be seen on an upright stećak without arms which comes from Rogatika, and is now at the Sarajevo Museum (Figure 36). Here, the entire pillar represents the fourth level of the universe (see Map 2). It is dotted with stars and a crescent moon, and an incised path leads upwards from one of the stars to a sun-like series of three concentric circles. This abstract symbol represents the same route of ascent beyond the stars that is followed by the souls and angels in Bosch's painting. Its concentric circles lack the mathematical perspective of Bosch's layered tunnel, but they, too, are a depiction of this final path.

The Bosnian column, with its scattered symbols may not seem particularly mystical to twentieth century eyes. To the Cathars, however, it would have appeared as an otherworldly vision of the higher reaches of the universe and the path of the soul. Bosch represents the same ideas in a much more sophisticated way. He is able to portray the path to final salvation convincingly, as a shining and mystical channel approached by angels and rapt souls. But however it is depicted, this route is the last lap of the journey to our true spiritual home. It leads to the world of reality, far beyond the illusions of the material universe.

11. The Intermediary Paradise in the Sky

The need for purification

The unearthly light at the end of Bosch's tunnel, like the centre of the concentric rings on the Bosnian tombstones, is a place which is totally removed from everything to do with the physical world. The Cathar adepts might have been able to visit this realm of light briefly in their visions, but no soul which had any lingering physical ties and desires could remain in it permanently. Even the adepts, ascetic as they must have been, would not have been without some attachments to the earth, however minor. After they had died, their souls would therefore have needed at least a brief period of re-orientation and purification before they were ready to make their permanent abode in the most rarefied level of the afterworld. The ordinary Cathar believers, who were much more attached to the earth than the adepts, would have needed a longer period of readjustment before they were ready to live in the Land of Light.

The need for this intermediary period of cleansing was taken into account by the Cathars and Manicheans, and influenced their vision of the afterworld. It also plays a significant part in Bosch's paintings, as we will see soon. In the Cathar/Manichean view, this necessary purification was not achieved by punishment, as it was in the conventional Christian purgatory. Instead, it was a happy experience, which took place in a beautiful earthlike paradise, where souls could re-orient themselves gradually. This intermediary place was given various names. The Cathars and Manicheans usually called it the New Earth, but a Cathar reference to it as the Bosom of Abraham is found in an inscription on a fifteenth century Bosnian stećak from Puhovak near Zenica. The inscription, which Fine has identified as Patarene, reads:

> Here lies good Gost Mišljen to whom it was arranged by order of Abraham his great hospitality. Good lord [i.e. Mišljen], when you go before Our Lord Jesus mention us your servants. G.M. writes.[1]

The implication here is not that the Bosnian Church accepted the Old Testament prophets, as Fine suggests, but that the gost, a priest of this church, has gone to stay in the Bosom of Abraham.

The gosts were all Perfects, people who had been given the spiritual baptism before they were on their death beds, and who had followed the rules of purity during their lifetimes. Nevertheless, the reference to Abraham's Bosom on Gost Mišljen's tomb implies that he needs to go through a period of purification in the intermediary heaven, before he can move on to the Land of Light. The length of time that he will need to spend in the New Earth is not made clear. There are hints in some of the records that certain Perfects were pure enough at the time of death to ascend immediately to the highest level of the afterworld, but this was not a subject which was discussed openly.[2]

The third heaven of St Paul

As we saw in the last chapter, the Cathars visualized the heavens as a series of horizontal layers. They believed that the Bosom of Abraham, or New Earth was located in the third level. This realm was identified with the third heaven referred to by St Paul. Paul was probably talking about himself when he said:

> ... I shall go on to tell of visions and revelations granted by the Lord. I know a Christian man who fourteen years ago (whether in the body or out of it, I do not know — God knows) was caught up as far as the third heaven. And I know that this same man ... was caught up into paradise, and heard words so secret that human lips may not repeat them. (2 Cor.12:1–7)

The concept of the universe that lies behind this passage is very important if we want to understand Cathar and Manichean ideas about life after death. It was part of a cosmology that had been widespread in the Ancient World.[3] The early Christians had shared this traditional belief in a layered universe and a paradise in the third heaven. As they saw it, this paradise was a place where all (or most) souls awaited the resurrection.[4] But from about the eleventh or twelfth century, the idea of an earthly paradise in the sky disappeared from established Christianity, which came to see things in a different way. The Church now believed that all saved souls went straight to the heaven of God the Father, once they had spent the required period in purgatory. This purgatory was visualized as being somewhere on or beneath the earth, and was pictured as a kind of temporary hell. The term 'Bosom of Abraham' was not discarded, but its meaning was changed. It was now seen as a part of the heaven of God the Father, where those who were already purified would await 'a new phase of felicity.' They would experience this new phase after they had been reunited with their resurrected bodies.[5]

The Cathar New Earth was very unlike the conventional Christian Bosom of Abraham, for it had a different function, and was a totally separate area on a lower level. The Manicheans and Cathars often mentioned this terrestrial paradise in the sky. We find a reference to it in the *Secret Book*, for example.[6] But here as elsewhere, it is not described in any detail. This is probably because, as we are told in one of the Inquisition depositions, the New Earth contained a mystery which was reserved for the Perfects.[7]

Only one anonymous treatise, which was written by an Albigensian Cathar in the early thirteenth century, does anything more than refer to the New Earth by name. This work, called the *Manichean Treatise,* contains a few descriptions of the New Earth, but even these are veiled. They are given in the form of quotations from the Bible which appear traditional, but actually hold hidden meanings. We are told that the tree of life and its fruits are found in the New Earth, for example. These are allusions to Jesus as the tree of knowledge and the column of glory. The sun that does not go down (a symbol of Jesus as the spiritual sun) is also mentioned.[8] These metaphors resemble similar ones in the Coptic Manichean psalms, which describe Jesus as:

The perfect day of Light, that of the sun that does not set.
The holy bread of life that is come from the skies.
The sweet spring of water that leaps unto life.
The true vine, that of the living wine.
The joyous branch of the tree, that is laden with fruit.
The new plant of God, that of the fruits of life.[9]

The hints given in the *Manichean Treatise* begin to give us some idea of the character of the Cathar New Earth, but they need filling out. A few more indications of the Cathar ideas, which would also have been held by Bosch, can be found in an apocryphal book of the early first century AD. This work, which is called the Slavonic *Book of the Secrets of Enoch,* describes a journey to the heavens, but in a more concrete and less mystical way than the *Vision of Isaiah.* The *Enoch* was read by both heretics and conventional Christians until the seventh century, when it disappeared entirely from Western Europe. It was then forgotten in the West, and was not heard of again until 1892, when it was rediscovered in Russia. During its period of obscurity, it was known only in the Balkans, Russia, and possibly Greece. There is no doubt that the Bogomils and Patarenes of Bulgaria and Bosnia were aware of it during this time, for it had an important influence on their eleventh century *Secret Book.*[10] These Cathars did not take everything said in the *Enoch* literally, however. Instead, they interpreted the apocryphal book in a way which fitted with their dualistic view of the universe.[11] What the *Enoch* says about the third heaven is therefore a help in understanding the Cathar views, but it should be interpreted critically (see Maps 1, 2 and 3).

The writer of the *Enoch,* like the author of the Cathar *Vision of Isaiah* and the Cathars of the Middle Ages, visualized the heavens as a series of horizontal layers. Enoch visits each of the seven levels of this universe, and describes them all. He tells us that the third heaven is a beautiful garden, filled with flowering and fruiting trees. The tree of life is described as standing in the middle of the garden, with its roots reaching all the way down to the lower paradise of Eden, far below 'at the earth's end.'[12] This tree, identified with Jesus, would have been seen by the Cathars as an image of the column of glory. But in their interpretation, its base, located in the corrupt Eden on earth, would have become Satan's tree of death. As we have already seen, this

Satanic tree or column is represented frequently in the paintings of Bosch.

The garden of the third heaven is described in the *Enoch* as earthlike in appearance. It is therefore not fully separated from the material realm. But it is also beyond the earth, and consequently more spiritual. In summary, as the Slavonic *Enoch* puts it, this heaven is 'between corruptibility and incorruptibility.'[13] This description of the third heaven as a place between corruptibility and incorruptibility helps to fill out the Cathar hints, for it indicates that the New Earth is an intermediary paradise, in which souls can change their orientation from the physical to the spiritual realm. The *Vision of Isaiah* also hints at this, for Isaiah tells us that, in the third heaven, 'the glory of my spirit was undergoing a transformation.'[14]

Bosch's images of the third heaven

Although the Slavonic *Secrets of Enoch* and the anonymous *Manichean Treatise* do not give us a full picture of the Cathar vision of the New Earth, they are a great help in explaining some of Bosch's odder images of the afterworld. These images are even less conventional than the visionary tunnel of light, depicted in the *Ascent to the Empyrean* at Venice. The latter is unique and mystical, but it is not actually heretical. What is more baffling to those who see Bosch as a conventional Christian is the odd contrast between the luminous heaven at the end of the tunnel in the *Ascent to the Empyrean* and some of Bosch's other visions of the saved. These other afterworld scenes are much less mystical, and do not correspond at all well with conventional religious ideas. They show the saved souls in an earthly paradise which contains not only angels, but also small demonic monsters. These monsters symbolize sins which have no place in a traditional Christian heaven. According to medieval Church doctrines, no soul could enter the heavenly realm until all of its sins and blemishes had been expiated in purgatory. Clearly, Bosch's small demons and monsters do not correspond with this theology. They can only be accounted for if the paradise they inhabit is seen as the Cathar New Earth. This is the place where souls go before their ascent to the real heaven, and where they gradually lose their attachments to the realm of Satan.

The Paradise *panel at Venice*

One of Bosch's depictions of this transitional garden in the sky can be seen in his *Paradise* panel at Venice (Plate 68). This painting is one of the four Venetian eschatological scenes, and is paired with the *Ascent to the Empyrean* (Plate 67). It is influenced by a painting by Dieric Bouts at Lille (Plate 70).[15] Bosch's *Paradise* shows clear connections with Bouts' work, but it also contains subtle images which show that the concepts behind it are in fact very different. In the painting by Bouts, groups of souls are shown entering the Garden of Eden on earth, and ascending from there to the heaven of God the Father. This conventional medieval Eden, like the one described by Dante in his *Divine Comedy (Purgatory*, Cantos XXVIII-XXIX), is essentially empty. No one has lived there since the time of Adam and Eve. The groups of souls which enter this garden are led immediately by angels to a hill from which they can ascend upwards. For them, the Garden of Eden is nothing more than a deserted paradise which they pass through, on their way to the heaven which will be their permanent home. Birds and flowers can be seen in its idyllic landscape, and there are no small demonic monsters lurking in unexpected spots.

Bosch's green *Paradise* at Venice is very unlike that of Bouts, once one looks closely. Here, the pace is much more leisurely. The souls are obviously taking their time, and using the garden as a place in which they can think, learn and talk. One is sitting down, looking closely at a bird which represents its soul. Others, sitting or standing, engage in animated discussions with each other or with angels. Small but significant monsters are dotted about the landscape. A lion eats a deer in the upper right, for example. This vignette symbolizes the soul engulfed by matter — a subject which is no doubt an important topic in the discussions. Other monsters, symbols of sin, include a deformed bird in the lower righthand corner of the picture, and a dark, four-legged animal with a bird on its back, half way up the hill on the left. These demons are small and not very numerous, for the souls in this particular painting are sober and thoughtful, and not greatly in need of purification.

In Bouts' conventional Garden of Eden on earth, groups of souls are led by angels to the top of a hill. On their way up, they pass by a large

Gothic fountain which is decorated with angels. This is a depiction of the fountain of life, a traditional Christian symbol of redemption. Bosch's views of this fountain are made plain in the *Garden of Earthly Delights,* as we saw in Chapter 3. In his interpretation, the fountain in Eden belongs to Satan and his religion, and is the source of physical life and spiritual death. The true fountain of life is located far above it, in the terrestrial paradise of the third heaven.

The fountain in Bosch's *Paradise* is very different from Satan's fountain in Eden, for it is a source of purification and spiritual life. This same fountain is described in the Coptic Manichean Psalms as the 'place of the washing of souls' (see Chapter 10, note 3). It is associated with Jesus, who is the tree of life, the column of glory, and the dominant force in the paradise of the third heaven. When the souls have been washed in it, and have drunk its waters, they will be ready to ascend to the Land of Light, whose spiritual nature is untainted by anything to do with the earth. We see them moving upwards towards this realm in the Venice *Ascent to the Empyrean.* The fountain which is so essential to their ascent is located at the very top of a steep hill in the *Paradise* panel. A group of souls on the righthand side of Bosch's scene aspires upwards towards it. Its living waters, which will free the souls from their last attractions to the realm of matter, are a complete contrast with the waters of death in the Garden of Eden on earth.

Gibson, who sees the paintings by Bouts and Bosch as essentially the same, does not make these contrasts. Instead, he suggests that both panels depict the earthly Eden as 'a sort of intermediate stage where the saved were cleansed of the last stain of sin before being admitted into the presence of God.'[16] But the evidence for this idea is not complete. Gibson suggests that both artists took their images from certain medieval mystery plays, in which saved souls passed through the Garden of Eden on their way up to the celestial heaven of God the Father. This suggestion is interesting as far as it goes, but unfortunately Gibson does not tell us whether or not the plays made any reference to purification in Eden.[17] It is more likely that the souls in these plays were just passing through, as in Bouts' version of the scene. The traditional fountain which they pass is a symbol of redemption through the sacrifice of Christ and the Eucharist. The Roman Church would not have seen this as a place where Christian souls — already purified in purgatory — stop to remove further stains of sin.

Gibson also suggests that the anonymous mid-twelfth century *Vision of Tundale* was a second influence on the paintings by Bouts and Bosch.[18] In fact, this written account of a journey through the next world does not correspond particularly well with either of the two paintings. The author of the *Vision of Tundale* describes a paradise which contains a number of walled sections. This pleasant place can only be reached after the equivalent of purgatory (a series of hellish valleys and lakes, inhabited by sinners and devils) has been left far behind. The area on the outskirts of this paradise is called the 'field of joy.' It must be the equivalent of Eden, for it contains the fountain of life. The 'field' is apparently empty of both souls and demons, but a door opens out from it into a beautiful paradise meadow, filled with souls. Beyond this meadow, further walls lead to a series of other paradises. There is no indication that souls are purified in the Eden with its fountain, or that any of the gardens beyond it are in the sky. The author's descriptions of the gardens are probably influenced by garbled memories of the paradise of the third heaven, but many features have been changed. The 'vast tree' in one of the gardens, for example, is now called 'Holy Church,' rather than the tree of life.[19]

The third heaven after the Last Judgment

The figures in Bosch's Venice *Paradise* are different from those in any of the conventional Edens, for they are clearly purifying themselves. These particular souls are unusually sober, and must represent a group of Perfects. Most, if not all of them will be ready soon to live permanently in the Land of Light. They are less in need of purification than the majority of souls which manage to reach the New Earth. Bosch depicts these other, less advanced souls on the left wings of several of his *Last Judgment* triptychs. The hedonistic figures in these scenes behave in ways which would be most unsuitable in a traditional Christian paradise. Their actions are also out of character for Cathar adepts or Perfects.

Some of the figures in Bosch's hedonistic paradises are presumably ordinary Hearers, the people who received the spiritual baptism at their deathbeds. Others are probably the souls which are rescued at the

Figure 37. Allart du Hameel (active *c.*1500), *Last Judgment*, engraving after Bosch.

last minute by angels in Bosch's *Last Judgment*'s. These souls have been unable to leave the pleasures of the world until this very late stage. Now, however, they can manage to detach themselves from an earth which is taken over entirely by demons. The other souls, which still cannot disentangle themselves from the web of desire, must remain behind among the devils. We can see the rescue of the fortunate escapees in an engraving by Allart du Hameel after one of Bosch's *Last Judgment*'s (Figure 37). Here, a small number of the saved are rushed by angels to the top of a hill on the left side of the scene. From there, they are taken up to the New Earth in the sky, where they will learn to overcome their lingering attachments to the material world.

The souls which find refuge in Bosch's New Earth are small, naked, and similar in appearance to the little figures in the central panel of the *Garden of Earthly Delights*. Some of them are more active than others. The most lively and hedonistic ones climb the riggings of boats, swim, ride fishes, joust, and show an interest in plant shells which symbolize the body. But their paradise is different from Bosch's Eden on earth, for it contains angels as well as devils, and the waters of its fountain bring purification rather than spiritual oblivion. The souls in this garden of the third heaven are all being prepared for a future ascent to the Land of Light, but some of them are going to be ready for the transition much sooner than others.

An especially good and well preserved depiction of the intermediary paradise in the sky can be seen on the left wing of Bosch's *Last Judgment* triptych at Bruges (see Plate 31). This triptych used to be attributed to Bosch's workshop, but when the painting was cleaned in 1959, Tolnay and others who saw it became convinced that this *Last Judgment* is an original by the master himself.[20]

On the left wing of this triptych, a group of souls, escorted by angels, arrives by ship at the shores of the New Earth. In the Manichean tradition, the ship is sometimes used as a symbol of the physical body which 'carries' the soul during its earthly incarnation. Alternatively, as in Bosch's arrival scenes, it can represent the after-death vehicle of the discarnate soul.[21] In the Bruges *Last Judgment*, some of the souls move restlessly about in the boat which transports them to the New Earth. Others, whose natures are less frivolous, discuss matters seriously under the watchful eye of an angel. Those which have already made themselves at home in the landscape also behave in varied ways. Some busily climb or joust, while others are more thoughtful, and listen quietly to lectures or music played by angels. The sober ones are clearly transforming themselves, and the playful ones will presumably reach a point when they, too, become interested in the angels and their teachings.

Further signs that the paradise on the left wing of Bosch's Bruges *Last Judgment* is an intermediary place, and that there is a higher heaven located above it, can be seen if one looks closely at its fountain. This structure, which is located in the centre of the landscape, is tall, columnar, and elaborately decorated. Three souls can be seen at its base. One is sitting on the rim of the basin; another is immersed up to its head in the water, and the third stands in a doorway which leads to the interior of the fountain. The doorway is reminiscent of the openings in the fountains of Bosch's *Garden of Earthly Delights*, and its associations with the physical realm and its sins are reinforced by the sculpted demons on the level above it. Streams of water flow into the basin from the mouths of these demons, indicating that the waters at the base are not entirely pure. This corruption is not very serious, however, for the souls in the fountain do not indulge in any lewd activities.

The demons on the fountain in Bosch's Bruges *Last Judgment* show that it, like the paradise itself, is between corruptibility and incorruptibility. It presents the souls with opportunities for purification, for it is the column of glory, identified with Jesus as the tree and fountain of life. Its purity grows as it ascends, and above the demons, its corruption disappears entirely. Here, all signs of sin are absent, and an enlightened soul points upwards towards some angels in the sky. These are ascending to higher levels, and the newly purified soul seems suddenly to have realized that it can join them. Its destination, if it does so, will be the true heaven, the light at the end of the tunnel, depicted in the Venice *Ascent to the Empyrean*.

Similar ideas are expressed somewhat differently in the left wing of another of Bosch's *Last Judgment*'s. This wing has been mutilated, so that only its lower part is still extant (Figure 38). It was in the Wildenstein Gallery for several years, but has now been sold to a private collector. Like the left wing of the Bruges *Last Judgment*, this painting depicts souls undergoing a gradual transformation in the paradise of the third heaven. A decorated tent, which is a traditional medieval symbol of love and dalliance, dominates the foreground of the scene. The angel inside of it is presumably telling a soul that physical love belongs to the earth. This lesson has not yet been assimilated by the couple in the doorway of the tent, but the kneeling soul, with its head inside the cloth and its behind on the outside, is obviously wavering between the physical and the spiritual. The dark bird sitting on its bare bottom (an image that would be particularly out of place in a conventional Christian representation of paradise) makes perfect sense as a depiction of the souls' continuing fleshly temptations.

The final destination of all of the little souls in the intermediary garden was originally shown in the full panel. A reproduction of the original painting (Figure 39) reveals that its paradisical landscape was once

Figure 38. Bosch, *Terrestrial Paradise of the Third Heaven*: lower half of the left wing of a mutilated *Last Judgment* tryptich.

Figure 39. H. Met De Bles, copy of the left wing of Bosch's *Last Judgment* tryptich (Figure 38), before it was mutilated. Engraving.

212

surmounted by an enormous sun.[22] This sun is also the brilliant 'head' of Jesus, which lights the skies above the third heaven. It beckons the souls in the landscape below, and gives them an idea of the heights they will finally be able to reach, once their purification is complete and they have at last lost their longings for sensual and material pleasures.

12. The Wheel of Birth and Death

The fall back to Earth

The Cathars believed that after the Last Judgment, all movement between the world of Satan and the higher levels of the universe would be at an end. Before this time, however, the connection between earth and the heavens was always open. The link or channel, as we have seen, was the column of glory. It could be used by the soul of a Hearer who had received the spiritual baptism soon before death. Such a person could move upwards through it to the third heaven, but he or she would not necessarily remain there. Many such souls were still so attracted to the earth, despite the baptism, that they could not continue to resist its pull. These souls soon tumbled back to the physical realm. The Cathars sometimes referred to their return as the fall of a bird with a broken wing.[1]

It is not clear whether it was believed that the souls of people who had *not* received the Cathar baptism would make even this temporary ascent. Bosch's image of the falling saint or 'idol' in the Venice *St Jerome* indicates that certain of the faithful who aspired upwards would have some initial success, but that they would not be able to stay very long in the upper levels of the universe. In any case, whether or not they made a temporary foray upwards, all of the souls which were destined for reincarnation would have to spend a period of time on the earth before they could enter a new body. Their between-lives period was divided into two stages. The first of these was a restless and tormented time, when the souls were chased and attacked by devils. This unhappy phase would be followed by a second, more enjoyable period, spent in the 'place of rest' (Satan's Eden). Then, after they had finished their restorative sojourn in this Eden, the souls would be ready for reincarnation.[2]

Bosch depicts the Cathar 'place of rest' in the central panel of his

Garden of Earthly Delights, as we saw in Chapter 3. The fall back to earth, and the period of torment which precedes the spell in Eden, are also illustrated in Bosch's works. We can see depictions of them in the third and fourth panels of his *Visions of the Hereafter* at Venice.

The third panel of the Venice quartet, traditionally called *The Fall of the Damned into Hell* (Plate 72), shows the unhappy souls, which are not yet saved, tumbling back to earth after a brief period in or near the terrestrial paradise in the sky. This image appears at first to be conventionally Christian. It is influenced by a similar painting by Dieric Bouts which is also entitled *The Fall of the Damned into Hell* (Plate 71). This painting is a companion to Bouts' *Paradise* at Lille (see Plate 70), which was discussed in the last chapter.[3] Bouts' two paintings correspond with conventional religious ideas, and Bosch's panels are influenced by them. But, as always, a close look at the details reveals that Bosch's versions contain subtle changes which imply an entirely different view of the universe.

The main oddity in Bosch's *Fall* scene is easy to overlook. It is only when one begins to think about it that one starts to wonder why Bosch's figures, unlike those of Bouts, are falling through clouds. The fires of hell might produce some smoke, but they would not be responsible for filling the entire hollow interior of the earth with the thick, nebulous atmosphere of Bosch's scene. Clouds such as these have no place in depictions of souls descending into the earth's interior, and for this reason, they do not surround the figures in traditional religious paintings such as that of Bouts. Bosch's imagery is different, because it is based on a different premise. The souls which it depicts are falling to hell, but this hell is not the conventional one. Instead, it is the Cathar hell. In other words, it is the earth itself. The cloud-filled ether which surrounds it resembles the nebulous atmosphere, sometimes filled with devils, which surrounds the earth in several other paintings by Bosch. Similar clouds can be found, for example, on the reverse of the *St John on Patmos* or on the outer panels of the *Garden of Earthly Delights* (see also Map 2).

The clouds around Bosch's world are dark, and demons reach out spindly arms to catch the souls which fall through them towards the earth below. The figures are lit up in places by bursts of red and yellow flame, which shoot in and out among the murky clouds. Certain Cathar depositions before the Inquisition talk of the similar flames, called the 'fires of Satan,' which burn the soul between incarnations. The pains of these fires can only be eased by entry into a new body.[4] This is because they are likely to be mental rather than physical. They are the burnings of longings and desires for physical pleasure; the torments of disembodied souls which are not yet ready to leave the earth for good.

In Bosch's fourth Venetian panel (Plate 73), the disembodied souls have landed on the surface of a hellish earth, where the 'fires of Satan' light up a cloudy sky. This sky, with its thick clouds, is again not typical of traditional depictions of hell. Its fires are reflected in a lake in which devils are swimming, and men seem to be drowning. In the Cathar tradition, water is the element of Satan, and the chief symbol of the material world. The man who sits next to the lake, with his head in his hand, appears to be regretting his condition. Nevertheless, he is clearly under the power of the malevolent demon which holds onto his arm, and the serpent of lust which twines around his left leg. The soul to the right of him lies back in a semi-crucified position. This is a posture which Bosch uses frequently as a symbol of entrapment in the material world. It can also be found, for example, in the central panel of the *Garden of Earthly Delights*.

Bosch and the Bosnian stećci

We have already compared Bosch's mystical images of ascension through the column of glory with parallel examples on certain Cathar tombstones. But, as we have just seen, Bosch also devotes space to more pessimistic visions of the soul's continuing entrapment in the world of matter. Are any of the subjects on the Cathar tombstones similarly pessimistic? In fact, perhaps surprisingly, a considerable number of them just might be. The cosmic crosses which we looked at in previous chapters are important, but they are only one example of what can be seen on the tombstones of Bosnia and Herzegovina. There are numerous other stećci whose iconography is very different. These have intrigued scholars for many years. Some of their mysterious carvings show an influence of the designs on the ancient Roman tombstones in Bosnia, but they never copy them exactly. Instead, they alter the Roman motifs, and add some from folk traditions and various other sources. The result is a set of images which is highly unusual, and very difficult to explain.

Some authors suggest that the baffling carvings on the stećci are merely ornamental; that they are for decoration only, and have no symbolic meaning. This explanation contradicts what we know about the purpose of the decorations on Egyptian, Greek, Roman, Renaissance, Victorian and many other tombs. It is only when we do not know enough about the iconography of tombstones or burial places (as in the case, for example, of the Basque tombs in Northern Spain) that people suggest their decorations are merely aesthetic. When we learn more, we discover that the symbols do have a meaning. Even twentieth century atheists and their families attach some significance to what is written or depicted on their tombstones. Why should this not also have been true of the people who lived in fifteenth century Bosnia and Herzegovina? These people, like others of their day, were highly religious.

Other scholars (most notably Fine and Wenzel) try to explain the stećci in traditional terms. They maintain that the majority of Bosnians were either Christians of the Roman Church, Greek Orthodox Vlachs with a pagan heritage, or members of the Bosnian Church which (according to Fine) was not dualist or Cathar. In the view of these authors, the images on most of the stećci express the conventional Christian doctrines or pagan rituals of the local people.[5] But the fact remains that these symbols do not correspond well with any traditional iconography. They are as eccentric as those of Bosch. The result of trying to match them with the norm, either pagan or Christian, is a set of interpretations which never quite works.

The unconventional symbols on the stećci are puzzling, but we should not be surprised by this fact. Why should they be traditional, when most of the Bosnians did not believe in the established religions? The Bosnian Church was the state religion of the country, and the documents show without doubt that its members (also known as Patarenes) were dualists and Cathars. As we saw in Chapter 2, they were in close contact with the Cathar Patarenes of Northern Italy. The two groups visited each other and exchanged religious ideas, but unlike the Italians, the Bosnian Cathars were hardly touched by the Inquisition. Their heresy was able to expand and persist unopposed, and between the thirteenth and the late fifteenth centuries it became the chief religion of the land. Its dominance is revealed by a papal epistle of c.1319, addressed to a Bosnian ruler. The epistle was written in reaction to the reports of some Franciscan Inquisitors who had travelled in the area and reported their findings to the Pope. According to the Franciscan report, church life in Bosnia had completely disintegrated. The Roman and Greek Orthodox churches were deserted, the clergy had been completely wiped out, and no one honoured the cross of Christ.[6] The same conditions had existed in the Languedoc when Catharism was flourishing there.[7] In Bosnia, where the heresy was even more widespread, the people had turned away from the established churches because they had found a new religion which they preferred. Since this religion was Catharism, it seems reasonable to suppose that most of the Bosnian tombstones of this period were made for Cathars. And if this was the case, we would have to expect that the mysterious symbols on these stones depict Cathar ideas about the afterlife.

As we saw in earlier chapters, the anthropomorphic Cathar crosses of Bosnia can be explained as maps of the path to the higher levels of the cosmos. But what about all the other stećci, with their many puzzling images? The first western European to suggest that the odd symbols on these tombstones might express Cathar ideas was Sir Arthur Evans. He noticed them in 1875, when he was travelling by foot through Bosnia on his way to Crete.[8] Since then, his idea has been followed up by a number of other scholars, including Soloviev, Bihalji-Merin, Nelli, Roché, Kutzli, and Papasov. All of these writers have analyzed at least some of the symbols on the tombstones in Cathar terms. They have made contributions to our understanding of their iconography, especially the image of the anthropomorphic cross. But on the whole, little has been said about the pessimistic side of the Cathar afterworld. After all, memorials are always expected to predict a happy destiny for the deceased. It is therefore not surprising that, while some authors suggest that certain symbols represent sin or the evil nature of the material world, none say that they represent an unhappy future for the soul.

Papasov makes a useful contribution to this subject when she suggests that the negative images on the stećci represent the evils which the souls of the Elect have left behind.[9] But interesting as this suggestion is, it does not seem the best way of explaining the considerable number of stećci where the symbols are entirely pessimistic. In addition to this, the five stećci which we know were made for Perfects (see Chapter 10, p.183), are either undecorated or else ornamented with positive symbols only. Taking all this into account, it seems much more likely that it was the Hearers and not the Perfects whose tombstones were decorated with negative symbols. These pessimistic images would have been meant as warnings of what could happen to souls which were still weak. Bosch depicts the 'birds with a broken wing' which fall back to earth in his two panels at Venice, and it may well be that some of the Bosnian tombstones are showing the same thing. These stećci do not depict fires or an actual fall, but they are often decorated with other symbols of the soul's torments, sensual longings and cyclical returns to the earth. Many of these images are also found in the works of Bosch.

Images of the between-lives state

Some of the most striking images on the stećci are the depictions of stags or deer which are pursued by archers, dogs, and other fierce animals. Some writers, including, for example, Bihalji-Merin, interpret these as scenes of everyday life.[10] Others, such as Soloviev and Nelli, see them as symbols of the soul chased by its sins.[11] This second interpretation corresponds with the Gnostic or Cathar meaning of the symbol, but more can be said about it. In the Gnostic tradition, the hunt represents the tormented and restless period that the 'sinful' soul will experience if it does not escape the wheel of birth and death. A similar scene, in which a hunted deer struggles through the entanglements of the physical world, is depicted on the pillar in Bosch's Lisbon *St Anthony* (Figure 40, and see Chapter 6). Bosch's hunt, like those on the stećci, is an image of demons pursuing an unredeemed soul wandering from life to life.

The hunted deer on the Bosnian stećci are frequently shown together with large, fierce birds. These are not positive images. The birds represent devils, and are likely to be depictions of the personal demon which the Cathars believed was harboured in each unredeemed soul (see Chapter 5, note 19). This concept goes back to the very beginning of Catharism, and similar images can be seen in what may well be the earliest surviving funeral monument in the Cathar tradition. The

Figure 40. Bosch, stag hunt on lower band of Satan's pillar: detail, central panel of the Lisbon *St Anthony* (Plate 45).

Figure 41. Broken sarcophagus with Cathar symbols, including camel and heron attacked by birds. Little Prespa Lake, Greek Macedonia, late tenth/early eleventh century.

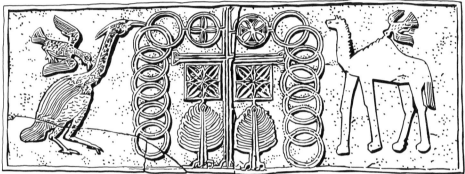

monument is a sarcophagus (Figure 41) which was found in the Church of St Achilles on an island in Little Prespa Lake, Greek Macedonia. It is generally accepted that the sarcophagus and the church both date from the late tenth/early eleventh century, soon after the Bogomil religion had originated in the area.

It is very likely that the Macedonian sarcophagus was made for a member of the newly formed Bogomil religion. The carved symbols which decorate it are in the Byzantine style, but as more than one author has said, they are unique and impossible to explain in terms of Byzantine Christianity. Instead, they correspond with the subjects and symbols of the Bogomils and Cathars. The sarcophagus (which is now broken) is decorated with a large central cross. Two evergreen trees with enormous 'stars' at the top are placed just below the arms of the cross, and seven ascending circles rise above each tree. Two large animals, a camel and a heron, stand on either side of the sacred images, looking towards them. Both of them are attacked from behind by large fierce birds. Interpreted from the Cathar point of view, the camel and the heron are symbols of the ordinary human soul. The birds which torment them are their personal demons, while the evergreen trees

Figure 42. Main face of rectangular tombstone, with deer, scenes of attack, and dancers. Brotnice, Dalmatia, fifteenth century.

Figure 43. Deer attacked by bird and dog: detail, Brotnice tombstone (see Figure 42).

Figure 44. Face (1) of tombstone from Čerin, Bosnia-Herzegovina, with stag hunt, fifteenth century.

Figure 45. Tombstone with stag hunt. Ubosko, Bosnia-Herzegovina, fifteenth century.

which they face represent their own eternal individual spirits. The two souls which stand between these positive and negative images must thus make a choice. If they opt for the spirit, they will be able to ascend through the circles of the universe by means of the cosmic cross. If not they must remain on earth, the province of Satan. It is interesting that this funeral monument, which was executed about five centuries before the stećci and the paintings of Bosch, uses such similar symbols to express the same dualistic ideas about the afterlife.

On the Bosnian stećci, souls which are still subject to the temptations of the earth are also symbolized by animals, but, as we have already seen, these tend to be deer rather than camels or herons. Their attackers are often dogs, as well as fierce birds. A particularly striking example of these images is found on a large stećak at Brotnice. On this tombstone (which will be looked at in more detail at the end of this chapter), a giant bird and a huge dog ruthlessly attack two hapless deer (Figures 42 and 43). Again, two other Bosnian stećci from Čerin and Ubosko (Figures 44 and 45) portray deer which are attacked by archers and fierce birds. The Bosnian birds often land on the backs of the deer, and, interestingly, Bosch also includes depictions of deer (souls) with dark birds (demons or demonic desires) standing on their backs in a number of his paintings. Examples are found next to the temptation of Adam and Eve in the left wing of the *Haywain*, and on top of the ruined building in the central panel of the Lisbon *St Anthony* (Figure 46). These are images which scholars who look at Bosch's works from the traditional Christian point of view have never been able to fully explain.

Other carvings on the Bosnian stećci depict small and lively figures which joust or fight. As we will see soon, these are negative symbols which also have parallels in the works of Bosch. One pair of Bosnian

Figure 46. Bosch, stag with a bird on its back: detail, central panel of the Lisbon *St Anthony* (Plate 45).

Figure 47. Tombstone from Klobuk, Bosnia-Herzegovina, with jousting figures and cosmic cross/tree of life rising from a block symbolizing the earth. Sarajevo Museum, fifteenth century.

jousters, carved on a stećak from Klobuk which is now at the museum at Sarajevo (Figure 47), confront each other at the foot of a cross. The cross, which rises out of a square base symbolic of the realm of matter, is again a depiction of the column of glory or tree of life. Like the one on the Macedonian sarcophagus, it is the channel between the physical world and the higher levels of the universe. The flowers which decorate the tops of its arms are not just pretty ornaments. They have an important meaning, for they represent the paradise of the third heaven which is located part way up the column. The jousters which pursue their sport at the foot of this cross must be at a level below this heavenly paradise. Their location at the base of the column tells us that they are in Satan's Eden, for this is the place where the anthropomorphic tree of life has its roots.

The jousting riders on the stećak at Klobuk can be compared with a pair of flying jousters in the central panel of Bosch's *Garden of Earthly Delights*. These figures, which are playing in the earthly Eden between lives, are located in the upper left of the picture (Figure 48). One is a human soul, and the other is a merman in armour. The demonic merman rides on a fantastic winged fish, brandishing a cherry on a stick. The human figure, mounted on a griffin, is armed with a leafy branch that probably symbolizes his misuse of the tree of life. A large red bird (an image of the small soul's sensuality) stands on the branch, and a froglike demon swings from the feet of the griffin. All the figures in this vignette are playful rather than serious, for Bosch never depicts scenes in which people overcome the devil through military combat. His mock fight can only be a sham, because the two figures are not really in any conflict. They are both on the same side: the side of frivolity and sensuality.

It is difficult to tell whether the conflict between the jousters on the stećak at Klobuk is frivolous or serious, but there is no sign that one of the fighters represents good and the other evil. This military scene is only one example of many on the Bosnian stećci. Not all show the joust, but there are numerous examples of male figures carrying arms such as swords, bows and arrows. Many of these warriors ride horses, but a few of them are on foot. According to Kutzli, these military figures are spiritual heroes, who triumph against evil.[12] Kutzli's interpretation is reasonable enough, but it raises certain questions. One wonders, for example, whether the Cathars, who were strong supporters

224

51. *St John the Evangelist on Patmos.*

52. (Left) Spiritual teacher and listeners: det[ail]
central panel of the *Garden of Earthly Delights*.

53. (Above) Adam and Eve with birds and g[lass]
cage: detail, central panel of the *Garden of Ear[thly]
Delights*.

54. (Opposite) *The Stone Operation.*

55. (Opposite) *St Christopher.*

56. (Left) *St James:* left outer wing of the Vienna *Last Judgment* tryptich.

57. (Right) Wayfarer figure: detail, the so-called *Prodigal Son.*

58. Wayfarer (the so-called *Prodigal Son*).

59. Wayfarer: outer wings of *The Haywain* tryptich.

60. *The Marriage at Cana.*

61. Swan, boar and bagpipe player: detail, *The Marriage at Cana*.

62. Left *Flood* panel: *Demons after the Flood.*   63. Right *Flood* panel: *Noah's Ark.*

Tondos, reverse of left *Flood* panel: (a) *Rescue of the Soul*; (b) *The Soul's Enslavement*.

65. Tondos, reverse of right *Flood* panel: (a) *Fall of the Soul*; (b) *Reunion of Soul and Spirit*.

66. (Opposite) *St Jerome:* central panel of the Venice *Hermit Saints* tryptich.

67. *Ascent to the Empyrean* (Venice *Afterworld* panels).

68. (Left) *Souls in the Terrestrial Paradise of the Th.
Heaven* (Venice *Afterworld* panels).

69. (Above) Fountain and souls: detail, left wi
of the Bruges *Last Judgment*.

70. (Left top) Dieric Bouts (c.1415-1475), *Paradise.*

71. (Left lower) Dieric Bouts, *The Fall of the Damned into Hell.*

72. (Below) *Souls falling back to Earth (Hell)* (Venice *Afterworld* panels).

73. *Disembodied souls suffering on Earth* (Venice *Afterworld* panels).

Figure 48. Bosch, souls in 'Eden' (the Cathar 'place of rest') between incarnations: detail, central panel of the *Garden of Earthly Delights* (Plate 21).

of pacifism (at least in theory) would have used armed conflict as a symbol of heroism. We cannot rule this out, but there is no denying that the concept of people using their weapons to fight evil is not consistent with the hunt scenes on the stećci. As we have seen, these show men with similar weapons chasing stags that symbolize the soul.

The placement of the armed figures is also significant. The soldiers and horsemen on the stećci often pursue their activities beneath twining vines with clover shaped leaves. These vines could be symbols of either the entanglements of life or the terrestrial paradise in the sky. Either way, the warrior figures are below them. This placement must mean that the figures have not yet managed to free themselves from the lures of the material realm. Even the man who confronts a serpent or dragon on a stećak from Konjik is placed below vines (Figure 49). This warrior is reminiscent of St George, but he is not necessarily victorious. His 'princess' has one hand inside of the dragon's mouth,

225

Figure 49. Tombstone with knight, princess and dragon. Konjik, Bosnia-Herzegovina, fifteenth century.

and the other on the horse's muzzle. She could represent the temptations of the flesh, or an attempt to resist them, and he could be nothing more than an ordinary knight, struggling against the demons of his own desires. Escape from the wheel of birth and death is difficult, and many souls fail to achieve it.

As we have seen, Bosch uses a circle of animals in the *Garden of Earthly Delights* as a symbol of the soul's continuing fleshly desires and rebirth on the earth. But the circle is only one of several related images of the wheel of birth and death. The spiral and the labyrinth are two others. These are complicated, many-layered symbols which can symbolize either reincarnation on the earth, or birth into the spirit world.[13]

Spirals which are sometimes very large and coiled are often depicted on the stećci, emerging from the shaft of the anthropomorphic cross (see Figures 34 and 50 from Jela Šuma and Radimlja). Their meaning must be related to the ancient symbolism of the spiral and labyrinth. Sometimes these spirals are hung with grapes, and Soloviev has interpreted them as the curling tendrils of Jesus the true vine.[14] This must

226

Figure 50 (left). Tombstone showing anthropomorphic cross/tree of life, with radiant 'head,' stars and vine with grapes. Radimlja, Bosnia-Herzegovina, fifteenth century.

Figure 51 (right). Tombstone with figures performing a line or circle dance below a vine. Radimlja, Bosnia-Herzegovina, fifteenth century.

be part of their symbolism, but not all of it. A few of the vine tendrils curl above the arms of the cross, but most grow out of the base, or even the ground. It is likely that the two sets of spirals or 'tendrils' are dualistic symbols, related to the two kinds of tree or vine. The higher ones are associated with Jesus and spiritual life, while the lower ones, which appear most often on the stećci, are identified with Satan and spiritual death.

The grapes that are attached to the lower tendrils can produce the wine of Satan, but they could also be depictions of the light kernels of the fallen souls. These light particles hang down from the coils which have entrapped them. In many of Bosch's works, including the *Garden of Earthly Delights,* grapes and other fruits have this same significance.

Folk dances in which the steps trace out circular, spiral or labyrinthine patterns are also common in the Balkans and many other areas of the world. Their symbolism is again related to death and rebirth, whether on earth or in the spirit world.[15] It is therefore particularly interesting that dancers who hold hands, and seem to be moving in lines or circles, are frequently represented on the stećci. It is also significant

Figure 52. Tombstone with sword dance and figure eaten by flying serpent. Kalinovic, Bosnia-Herzegovina, fifteenth century.

that these dancers are often placed below twisting vines, and never above them. An example from Radimlja (Figure 51) is typical of many. Its male and female figures perform their steps beneath a cloverleaf vine. They are joined by an animal which could be either a deer or a horse. On other stećci, the dancers are sometimes accompanied by warriors who hold swords or shields. These symbols tell us that the dancers are trapped on earth, in the wheel of birth and death.

Soloviev sees the small and lively figures with their joined hands as people performing funeral dances.[16] Bihalji-Merin believes that the dances are pagan in spirit, and express the pleasures of life.[17] Kutzli interprets them as Cathar celebrations of nature and the cosmos, which were part of the religious service.[18] Perhaps these dances *were* part of a Bosnian Cathar ritual, but if so, could it really have been a positive one? Many early peoples would have seen the concepts of earth and reincarnation symbolized by these dances as a good thing, but not the Cathars. For them, this kind of rebirth was a regrettable event which represented a victory for Satan. Their real view of these dances is made clear on a stećak from Kalinovik (Figure 52). On this stone, the line of dancers is surmounted by a flying serpent. This creature, which is symbolic of the physical world, swallows a female figure. Her fate symbolizes the plight of the dancers below her. Like the serpent's unfortunate victim, they too are entrapped by Satan and 'eaten' by the realm of matter.

228

The soul's choice

Negative images such as the ones discussed above are found on a great many stećci. Looking at them, one might think that the Bosnian Cathars expected the majority of their believers to remain entrapped in the realm of Satan. In fact, this is not necessarily the case. It is much more likely that these images, like those on the Macedonian sarcophagus (Figure 41), represent *possibilities*. Bosch often depicts souls which are trapped on the earth, but if we look at his works from the Cathar point of view, it becomes plain that he believes there is still hope for them. His main message has to do with choice. Hearers who have received the Consolamentum can ignore the earthly demons and move beyond their sphere, or they can succumb to their temptations and fall back to earth. They may be 'drunk' or 'asleep,' but as long as they are spiritually alive, they will be capable of choosing their destiny. If these souls can manage to wake up and understand their predicament, this understanding will eventually lead to freedom and ascent to the higher realms through the column of glory. The same idea of choice can be

Figure 53. Face (2) of tombstone from Čerin (Bosnia-Herzegovina), with ascending figure surrounded by doves (see Figure 44).

229

found on many of the stećci, expressed by some of the same symbols that are used by Bosch.

On certain Bosnian tombstones, the contrasting destinations of the soul are depicted by entirely separate scenes, which seem to contradict each other. A stećak from Čerin which is now at the Museum of Sarajevo is a good example of this. A deer hunt is carved on one side of this comparatively small block (Figure 44). This represents the sufferings of a soul chased over the earth by demons. The other side of the tombstone (Figure 53) shows a completely different post-mortem experience. It depicts a soul which is free of the torments of the earth, rising upwards to the higher levels of the cosmos. The soul reaches a realm which contains doves. These symbolize the spirits of the saved souls which are found in this part of the universe. Like Bosch's paintings at Venice, these two contrasting scenes appear to illustrate the baptized soul's choices in the next life. It can remain in the world of light, or it can fall back to the world of darkness.

The circle in the sky

Certain stećci, such as the one from Rogatika (Figure 36), are decorated only with positive images. These are the tomestones which are most likely to have been made for the Perfects. They illustrate the column of glory, with the light at the end of its tunnel. These tombstones represent the highest levels of the mystical channel, and do not show the entrance at its base. The latter is depicted on some of the other stećci, made for the Hearers. Here, it appears as a circular hole in the sky — a round 'doorway,' which is shown in contrast with the world, and offers a choice.

Once we think in these terms, it begins to look as though some of the suns, moons and stars above Bosch's depictions of the earth are also images of this doorway or entrance to the column of glory. Perhaps, for example, the small and distant star, unobserved by the figures in the Prado *Adoration of the Magi* (see Plate 2), is really the opening into the spiritual tunnel which can take the soul away from an evil world.

The moon above the scenes of the *Arrest of Christ* on the left outer wing of the Lisbon *St Anthony* (see Plate 43) might also be an image of the column of glory, seen from below. It is painted in the form of a ring, and floats in a break in the clouds. It could be a subtle but important clue to Bosch's interpretation of the story of the young man who slipped out of his linen cloth when Jesus was arrested, and ran away naked (Mark 14:51f). For Bosch and the Cathars, the young man could have exemplified a newly baptized soul which had managed to escape from the realm of Satan. This would correspond with what is said in the single remaining fragment of an ancient and secret version of the Gospel of Mark. Morton Smith, who discovered this fragment in 1958 in the Monastery of Mar Saba in the Judean desert, suggests that the original Secret Gospel was written between 75 and 90 AD. He believes that only a few copies ever existed, and that these were destroyed in persecutions of about 210 AD.[19]

The Secret Gospel was probably written and destroyed in Egypt, but it is still possible that the Cathars (who kept so much of the early Christian esoteric tradition alive) might have preserved a copy. As we have seen, they acquired a number of esoteric texts from the Messalians. Even if they did not have the book, the ideas within it might have been passed down to them. In any case, Bosch's scene seems to be hinting at esoteric ideas which are the same as those in the fragment of the Secret Gospel, which describes the initiation of a youth (apparently Lazarus) who was raised from the dead by Jesus. The young man then begged 'to be with him,' and:

> ... after six days Jesus told him what to do and in the
> evening the youth comes to him, wearing a linen cloth over
> [his] naked [body]. And he remained with him that night,
> for Jesus taught him the mystery of the kingdom of God.
> And thence, arising, he returned to the other side of the
> Jordan.[20]

Smith explains this story by suggesting that the well-known events of Jesus's 'agony in the garden' were 'probably pure invention.' Instead, Jesus really spent the night before he was arrested performing the youth's initiation.[21] This explanation could well have been true, but it would not have concerned Bosch. As a Cathar, Bosch would have believed that Christ's historical Passion and Crucifixion were illusory, and his real sacrifice was his descent and temporary ensnarement in matter. It would have been in keeping with Catharism for Jesus to have performed an initiation on the night of his apparent arrest, but it would have been the symbolic meaning of the story that was seen as really important.

In Bosch's version of the *Arrest of Christ*, the youth's escape contrasts with what is happening in the rest of the scene. Here, as we saw in Chapter 6, St Anthony's soul (the pilgrim) and his spirit (Jesus) are both caught and ensnared by the forces of darkness. In the middle of all this, we can see the youth's abandoned cloth (a symbol of his physical body) lying on the banks of a stream. This subtle image is a sign that he has risen and 'returned to the other side of the Jordan.' In other words, once he was spiritually awakened and taken out of his 'tomb' by Jesus, he went on to learn the mystery and was given the spiritual baptism. Having been properly prepared, he was then able to die physically and leave the earth for good. The chalice of living water at the top of the steep hill in the upper right is a symbol of his spiritual baptism (see Chapter 8). From this hill, already well above the scenes of capture and suffering, the youth's path to the higher levels of the universe leads directly towards and into the hole in the sky. He is not depicted in the scene below because he has already ascended far beyond it.

Sometimes Bosch depicts the entrance to this same tunnel as a large gap in the clouds, with an image of salvation in its centre. We can see examples of this in the *Haywain*, where Bosch depicts Jesus in the middle of the gap (see Plates 16, 17, and Chapter 5). In the left wing, Jesus holds a blue ball, an image of the New Earth. A similar vision is painted in the upper left corner of Bosch's Berlin *St John* (see Plate 51). Here, a spiritualized and diaphanous mother and baby sit on a crescent moon, in the midst of a golden circle surrounded by clouds. This scene represents the traditional woman clothed in the sun of Apocalypse 12:1, but it could also have a second Cathar meaning. Seen from this point of view, it becomes a vision of the Land of Light at the end of the column of glory. Here, far from the heaviness of earth and wearing her crown of glory, Mary is revealed in her true angelic form. The tiny baby which she holds seems to be a depiction of Jesus, but it might also be a soul which has finally reached the protection of its true home in the Land of Light.

On the Bosnian stećci, the openings or rings in the sky above the

Figure 54 (left). Tombstone showing ascending figure with raised hand. Radimlja, Bosnia-Herzegovina, fifteenth century.

Figure 55 (right). Tombstone with dancers approaching large circle. Kupres, Bosnia-Herzegovina, fifteenth century.

earth are frequently contrasted with symbols of the soul's entrapment in Satan's world. As in Bosch's paintings, they seem to be pointing out the choice which the soul will have to make after death.

Symbols which almost certainly show a Hearer's choice between the two paths are found on some of the most famous of all the stećci. These blocks, which come from the graveyard of Radimlja, depict men who are sometimes shown with their wives and children (Figure 54 is one example). These men have large hands, and they hold one or both up in the air. They seem to be rising upwards. Some are placed under twisting vines, and in every example, a circle is depicted on one side of the man's head, and a bow and arrow on the other. The bow is usually interpreted as a sign that the deceased was a soldier, but it might be a image of earthly actions and interests. If so, the two symbols would represent the two alternative possibilities. The man and his family can rise upwards through the column of glory, or they can return to life in the world of matter.

Another stećak, which comes from Kupres, depicts a line of dancers

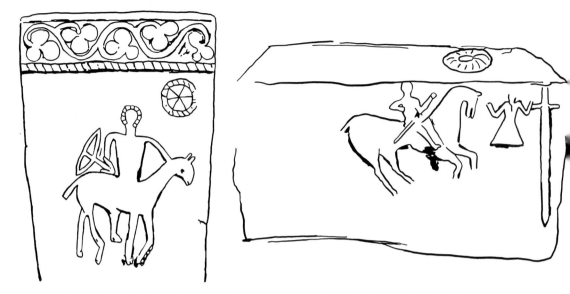

Figure 56 (left). Tombstone with horseman and circle. Stolac, Bosnia-Herzegovina, fifteenth century.

Figure 57 (right). Tombstone with horseman and circle. Nevesinje, Bosnia-Herzegovina, fifteenth century.

with an animal bringing up the rear. These figures approach a large moving circle that looks almost like a cosmic whirlwind (Figure 55). The dancers seem to have a choice between this route to the light, and the animal at the end of the line, which symbolizes the body. In this case, their leader reaches out towards the circle, and is clearly aware of it, but on many other stećci, the small souls look as though they are bound up in their earthly activities. As in the works of Bosch, they seem totally unaware of the entrance to the higher worlds which hovers above them. The horsemen on the tombstones from Stolac (Figure 56) and Nevesinje (Figure 57), are examples of this. Most likely, their horses are symbols of the physical body, to which they are still firmly attached, at least in their minds. Like the acrobats who ride the circling wheel of animals in the central panel of the *Garden of Earthly Delights*, these figures are still imprisoned on the wheel of birth and death. If they remain unaware of their plight, they will eventually move back into incarnation and life in a new body.

The tombstone at Brotnice

Nearly all of the typical Bosnian images of salvation and return to the earth can be seen on a particularly large and interesting stećak in the small settlement of Brotnice. This village is near to Dubrovnik, and the monument, which is still in the village graveyard, is the furthest south of all the stećci. It must have been made for someone whose family had the money to pay for an elaborate tombstone, and it was probably executed sometime after the 1460's, when many Bosnians had fled to the Dubrovnik area to escape the Turks.[22]

This stećak is upright, rectangular, and decorated on all sides with many motifs. A number of these show connections with the images in Bosch's paintings. The tombstone's inscription, which is located on one of the narrow faces of the block, is in Cyrillic (Figure 58). The Cyrillic alphabet was used by Patarenes and members of the Greek Orthodox Church, but not by the many Roman Christians of the Dubrovnik area. As one might expect, these Christians used Latin. The content of the inscription may seem fairly innocuous, but it contains an oddity which could be quite important. It tells us that: *The person who is writing (or carving?) this is Ratko Utješenić, grandson of A(n) Druška Ljuboe and a nephew of (Avros) tjan Luboević.*[23]

What is unusual here is the fact that this inscription gives us details about the writer of the words, rather than the person buried beneath the stone. This might hint that it was written by a Cathar priest for an ordinary Hearer, who had received the Consolamentum or Cathar spiritual baptism from the Perfect. Other inscriptions which we know were made for members of the Bosnian Church have a similar wording. As we saw earlier, Fine has identified eight of these, of which three tell us that a particular *gost* or *krstjanin* (titles of clerics in the Bosnian Church) had something to do with the placing of the stone or the writing of the inscription. The other five say that the person buried beneath the stone was himself a *gost, krstjanin* or *stroinik* (good person). On one of these (that of Gost Mišljen, referred to in Chapter 11), the person who wrote the inscription is also named, and here the wording says that it was written by a 'servant' of the gost.[24] This 'servant' must also have been a baptized priest, for the 'good people' or *krstjanin* who had a lower clerical rank than the gosts, are known to have acted as their helpers.[25]

Figure 58. Narrow face (1) of the tomb-stone at Brotnice (see Figure 42) with inscription, rider and cross.

Figure 59. Narrow face (2) of the tomb-stone at Brotnice (see Figure 42) with orant figure ascending towards the spiritual sun.

The many images on the Brotnice stećak vary between the very positive and the very negative. The contrast between them could stress the choice which the deceased will have to make after death. This corresponds with the hints given in the inscription, for it, too, suggests that the person buried beneath the stone was a Hearer. If this soul manages to resist the temptations of the world, and succeeds in remaining in the upper levels, its eventual destination will be the mystical Land of Light.

The tombstone's elaborate decorations, with their dual symbolism, are particularly interesting. Every side of the block is covered with carvings. The inscription which was discussed earlier is located on one of the two narrow faces. Above it one can see an elaborate anthropomorphic cross which symbolizes the Saviour as the column of glory.

This contrasts with the image below the inscription, which depicts a horse rider holding a hawk. This figure could be an image of the soul which is still mentally attached to its body. If (or when) it leaves the 'horse' behind, it will be ready to rise upwards through the cosmic cross.

The other narrow face of the Brotnice stećak has no lettering, but is carved with a scene that has particularly interesting parallels in the works of Bosch. Here, another horseman at the base is separated by a horizontal line from an ascending orant figure with raised arms (Figure 59). The orant position denotes prayer. It was the usual pose of saved souls in the early Christian catacombs in Rome. By the fifteenth century, Byzantine images of the Virgin Mary still held their hands upwards, but this position was no longer used by Roman or Greek Orthodox artists when they represented souls ascending to heaven. Nevertheless, figures in the orant position can still be seen in Cathar art. We find them on several fifteenth century Bosnian stećci, and an orant figure is also depicted in the lower righthand corner of Bosch's *Ascent to the Empyrean* at Venice (Figure 60).

The orant on the tombstone at Brotnice, which seems to be wearing a large hat, ascends with arms outstretched towards the highest levels

Figure 60. Bosch, orant figure: detail, the Venice *Ascent to the Empyrean* (Plate 67).

of the cosmos. Two lines, probably denoting a path, rise upwards from near the outer edges of the soul's winged hat. The path leads directly to a circle with a radiant rosette of light inside of it. This is the 'sun,' or 'head' of Jesus that can be seen at the end of the mystical tunnel. The style of this relief is cruder and less sophisticated than that of Bosch, but, once we look beyond the differences in style, we can see that the comparatively primitive and naive-looking carvings on the tombstone contain a message which is much the same as the one in Bosch's *Ascent to the Empyrean* at Venice. Both scenes depict the soul's final return to the spiritual Land of Light. This land is its true home; the realm which it left behind and forgot during the many years of its entrapment in the world of Satan.

The carvings on the wider faces of the tombstone (Figure 42, for example) are a complete contrast. Both of them are covered with depictions of hunted deer, large fierce birds, and dancers with linked hands. These images, which were discussed earlier in this chapter, represent the experiences of souls which have not yet escaped from the grip of Satan; souls which are still attracted to the material world, and are consequently destined for rebirth in another body.

These opposing images of salvation and entrapment could be depictions of a future choice, or (less likely) an escape which has already been accomplished. Either way, they express the dualism of the Cathar/Manichean tradition. This dualism is also found in the paintings of Bosch, which constantly remind the viewer of the two worlds, and the two possible destinies of the soul.

13. Bosch's Spiritual Legacy

The Cathar story of the soul's fall, capture, earthly experiences, and ultimate choice between a final ascent to the Land of Light or a terrible end in the physical universe, can all be seen in the works of Bosch. Many ordinary Cathars must have believed that these events were real. And yet, looking at Bosch's works, one feels more and more that what he is actually depicting is a world of dreams. He has often been called a surrealist because of this. His fantastic monsters, fountains, buildings, plants, and so on, all seem to be images that are found in our subconscious minds. Some come from the lower depths explored by modern psychologists, and others from the spiritual levels experienced by mystics of all periods. The human figures in this mental world tend to be weightless — more like the light and active people in our dreams than the slower, heavier figures in our everyday lives.

Bosch's art is dreamlike, but, on the other hand, his images and symbols can be understood as expressions of actual events. Perhaps this apparent conflict actually reflects the thinking of the Cathar adepts. It is possible that Bosch is expressing the idea, frequently put forward by mystics, that the physical world is essentially unreal. The creation of the world, and our fall into it, have often been described by seers as a dream and an illusion. The Gnostic, Manichean and Cathar tradition itself often compares the unenlightened state with drunkenness or sleep. This does not make these illusions any the less strongly felt by us, however. They are 'real' in that sense, but when we return to our true spiritual home, they will all be seen as the dreams they really were. In Bosch's universe, even the terrestrial paradise of the third heaven is still illusory, for it is an earthlike transition point. Only the World of Light towards which the souls move in the Venice *Ascent to the Empyrean* is genuine.

Bosch's thinking up to this point is in the tradition of the great mystics. But what about his seemingly heartless condemnation of so many erring souls to the fires which will follow the Last Judgment? As we have seen, Bosch believed that the souls of ordinary folk (those who were not the very rich, the very powerful, or intolerant promoters of Church doctrines) were fallen angels, whose souls contained a spark of light. Although these people were 'asleep,' their sparks were still spiritually alive. With the help of the Perfects and the Cathar spiritual baptism, they would be able to wake up and escape from the world of matter. Most of them were too weak to manage this on their own, however, and it is this weakness that lies at the root of Bosch's pessimism. By the end of Bosch's lifetime, Catharism had been all but extinguished by the Church in Western Europe. Where it did still exist, as in Northern Italy, its doctrines must already have begun to alter radically. The sixteenth century records of Scandella's neo-Cathar ideas provide a good example of changing Cathar beliefs. In the Byzantine world, Catharism had already been swamped by the Muslims in Macedonia and Bulgaria, and the same process had now begun in Bosnia. Bosch would have believed that if Catharism was destroyed, the hope for most (even if not all) souls would go with it. And yet, despite all this, Bosch was not entirely pessimistic. When he shows the tragic end of the souls which miss their chance to be 'awakened' he is issuing a warning. This implies that he thinks there is still hope for the people he warns.

Most of Bosch's pictures were sold to conventional believers, but there may have been some which were intended for the secret Cathars of his day. We do not know how many of the latter still existed in Western Europe during the fifteenth and sixteenth centuries. There were probably very few, but as the stories of Hans Thon and Domenico Scandella (the two sixteenth century heretics whose unorthodox Cathar views did come to light) show, there must have been more than we are aware of. We should not assume that where there are no records of Cathars, no Cathars existed. The authorities' total ignorance of Thon's religion and anyone who practised it shows that centuries of persecution had taught at least some of the heretics how to survive undetected.

Because the presence of Catharism was not suspected in Brabant any more than it was in Thuringia, the conditions in Bosch's home-town would have been favourable for heretics who wanted to keep a low profile. With luck and prudence, a small group of Cathars could have lived undiscovered in 's-Hertogenbosch for years or even centuries.

Assuming that this is just what did happen, it is fortunate (for us as well as for the Cathars) that Bosch appeared among them when he did. With what must have seemed an exceptionally ingenious mind, as well as an unparalleled skill in portraying both light and darkness, he had just the right abilities to become the undetected spokesman for his underground dualist heresy.

Bosch's background was Netherlandish and his style grew out of the Late Gothic tradition of the north. But Bosch was not just an old-fashioned artist in a small backwater, as some writers have suggested. Though his trip to Venice in c.1500 did not make him into a High Renaissance painter, there is no doubt that it had a formative influence on his art. As we have seen, some of his images and certain details of his style reveal that he had contacts with Leonardo and Giorgione. His meetings with the Venetian group of Cathar adepts must also have affected him, adding to his mysticism and deepening his ideas. The dating of his paintings is difficult and controversial but although he was already at least forty years old in 1500, it is possible that all of his developed works (that is, all the ones which have been discussed in this book except for the Philadelphia *Adoration of the Magi*) were executed during or after his stay in northern Italy. There is much that we do not know about Bosch's visit, but it does seem to have been a major milestone in his life and work. It was during this trip that he perfected his ideas, images and techniques. And once he had done this, he was able to produce an illustrated record which would preserve all the main tenets of Mitigated Catharism before it vanished completely.

Bosch's coded records have lasted over the centuries, just as the artist and his circle must have hoped they would. Together they form a set of pictures which is unique in the history of western painting. The symbols and layers of meaning in these works are continually fascinating, and the pictures themselves are brilliantly painted and full of strange and frequently beautiful images. Through a combination of intelligence, mysticism and broadness of vision, they depict the Cathar universe with all its heights and depths. The spirituality of Bosch, as well as his dualism and his Cathar message, are visible in every painting he produced.

Appendix

Some thoughts on the Cathar spiritual baptism

As we saw in the text, the Cathars believed that the soul's final spiritual transformation could be accomplished by a single ceremony: the spiritual baptism. In their view, this baptism by fire and the Holy Spirit would purify any soul which received it, reunite it with its spirit, and end its bondage to the material world. Supposedly, the baptism involved the passing on of the Holy Spirit from person to person through the laying on of hands. Ordinary Cathars (the Hearers) were not baptized until they were on their deathbeds, and could no longer live a physically-orientated life. The Perfects, or priests, who were thought to be more pure to start with, were baptized earlier. But even they were normally given this initiation only in middle age, after they had had their children and lost most of the passions of youth. Whatever their natures, it was hoped that this ceremony would help everyone who had it to escape forever from the desires which drew them back into the cycle of rebirth on earth.

But what exactly *was* this all-important Cathar initiation? The Cathars claimed that it was the same baptism by fire and the Holy Spirit that Jesus had at the Jordan, and the Apostles had at Pentecost. But what do these words *really* mean? Most likely, they cover an ancient esoteric secret which was known to the Ancient Egyptians and the genuine alchemists, and is still known and practised in India. Some of the hidden facts about it are revealed by Elizabeth Haich in her books *Initiation,* and *Sexual Energy and Yoga.* They are also hinted at in some of the books on alchemy — Jacques Sadoul's *Alchemists and Gold,* for example. It would appear, from all this, that the Cathars' spiritual initiation was another version of what the Hindus call the rising of the kundalini. According to Elizabeth Haich, this is experienced as a burning, white-hot sensation in the spinal cord and chakras. What is happening at this time is a complete transformation of the sexual energies, and it profoundly alters the person who undergoes it. Among other things, the energy change that it brings results in a full unity of the personality with the higher, spiritual self. It also brings a new orientation towards the spiritual world, and away from the physical one.

After this baptism of fire, the candidate's personal and sexual life will come to an end. He or she will separate mentally (and probably also physically) from family and home, and will live an ascetic, God-oriented life, devoted to helping people in need. All of this sounds very much like the descriptions of the Cathar spiritual baptism, and the life that the Perfects led afterwards. The Manichaeans had a similar priesthood made up of people who were called the Elect, and these, too, must have been initiated. There are indications in the Manichaean *Kephalaia*, and the Coptic Manichaean psalms (both found in the Egyptian Fayum) that their initiation also involved the laying on of hands, as well as experiences of fiery, burning energies. (For more on this, see Chapter 8.)

The rising of the kundalini is a major transformation, however, and one which should not be taken lightly. The person who *genuinely* experiences it runs great risks, for those who slip back into a material and sensual way of living afterwards will fall lower than they had been before. This 'baptism by fire' should only be given to people who are entirely ready for it, and there are very, very few people who qualify. It is certainly unlikely — even impossible — that all the Cathars who received it had reached this stage. The Perfects underwent a long period of preparation beforehand, and this must have helped, but it did not do enough for all of them. The records tell us that some of them had love affairs, or broke the rules in other ways after their baptisms. These fallen Perfects were initiated a second time if necessary, and continued with their lives. They do not seem to have suffered any serious personal consequences as a result of their actions. This indicates that, although their baptisms may have brought them nearer to genuine transformation, they had not yet achieved it.

We might wonder at this stage whether the Cathar baptism by fire and the Holy Spirit ever did cause a genuine transformation of energy. Perhaps it was always an imitation of the real thing. There is certainly no doubt that the Cathars themselves took it seriously, and believed that it was real. What seems most likely (though of course we can't know for certain) is that the spiritual baptism was not the same for everyone. Instead, it had different effects on different people. Its most important feature, as said above, was the touching of the candidate by someone who had already been baptized. This, as Haich says, can be enough to bring on the transformation in someone who is truly ready for it. Some of the Cathars could therefore have been genuinely changed by the baptism, while the others who received it only imagined that it had affected them. In many cases, their belief in it would have been enough to change their lifestyles completely, and no one would have known that the baptism had not been entirely effective.

Notes

Introduction

1. Baldass 1960, p.89.
2. Walker 1983, p.12.
3. Grant 1961, p.17.
4. Widengren 1946, pp.65 and 66, taken from Witzel, *Tammuz-Liturgien*, pp.345:39ff, and p.396:11–14.
5. Widengren 1946, p.67, taken from Witzel, *Tammuz-Liturgien*, p.92: 10–13.
6. Widengren 1946, p.66, taken from Witzel, *Tammuz-Liturgien*, p.168: Rev.9.
7. Widengren 1946, p.100f, taken from Witzel, *Tammuz-Liturgien*, p.96: Rev.III 17 and p.446:11.
8. Widengren 1946, p.10f.
9. Obolensky 1948, p.31f and 44f.
10. Angelov 1987, p.14f.
11. Widengren 1965, p.44.
12. Loos 1974 is particularly good on Bosnia. See especially his Chapter XIX.
13. Anselm, Canon of Liège, *Gesta episcoporum Leodiensium* 1043–1048, reproduced in Wakefield and Evans 1969, p.90.
14. Widengren 1965, p.123; and Pederson 1988.
15. B. Gui, *The Conduct of the Inquisition of Heretical Depravity 1323–24*, Chapter I, reproduced in Wakefield and Evans 1969, p.379.
16. See Widengren 1965, pp.36 and 74; and Lieu 1988.
17. *New Catholic Encyclopaedia* 1967, Vol.IX, p.155.
18. Wakefield and Evans 1969, p.464.
19. Jackson 1930, p.195.
20. Jackson 1930, p.197.
21. See for example Duvernoy 1976, p.96, including n.27; Loos 1974, p.278; Obolensky 1948, p.137f; and Oldenbourg 1961 (1), p.38.
22. See Augustine, *De Haeresibus*, reproduced in Müller 1956, p.97, for the Manicheans, and Wakefield and Evans 1969, p.464 or Bozoky 1980, p.83 for the Cathars.
23. See Fine 1975, p.376f. and Stoyanov 1994, p.209.
24. These ideas are summarized in Mâle 1958, p.23ff, and elaborated on in later chapters. The are also discussed in Huizinga 1987, p.206f.
25. Nicholls 1980, p.28.
26. Nicholls 1980, p.29.
27. See for example Huizinga 1987, p.120.
28. Brand Philip 1980, p.193.
29. See F. de Guevara, *Comentarios de la Pintura (1560–63)*, in Snyder 1973, pp.28–33.

Chapter 1

1. Slatkes 1975, p.345.
2. Marijnissen 1987, p.11.
3. Baldass l960, p.83.
4. Baldass 1960, p.85.
5. Panofsky 1964, p.357.
6. See Clasen 1963.

7. See Snyder 1973, pp.28–43; or Marijnissen 1987, p.23f, for the early sources. See also Gombrich 1967, pp.403ff for a discussion of the way that sixteenth century viewers reacted to Bosch's triptych, the *Garden of Earthly Delights*.
8. Parker 1978, pp.56f and 162.
9. Brand Philip 1953, p.285.
10. Fray José de Sigüenza, *Tercera parte de la Historia de la Orden de S. Gerónimo*, Madrid 1605, translated and reproduced in Tolnay 1966, p.402, and Snyder 1973, pp.34–41. The reminiscenes of Francisco de Melo are discussed in Heidenreich 1970, pp.191–95.
11. Baldass 1960, p.234.
12. Gibson 1973 (1), p.112.
13. See Tolnay 1966, p.296, Brand Philip 1953, p.280, and Ewing 1978, pp.122–27.
14. Brand Philip 1953, p.268.
15. *Psalm Book* (Allberry 1938), pp. 62:7–8 and 152:33.
16. Moneta of Cremona, *Summa against the Cathars c.*1241, Book II, quoted in Wakefield and Evans 1969, p.319f.
17. See Singleton 1980, p.9f, for commentary on the *Inferno*, Canto I.30.
18. Brand Philip 1953, p.276.
19. For more on the headgear of this eccentric figure, see the discussion of Bosch's Venice *St Jerome* in Chapter 10.
20. Brand Philip 1953, p.274.
21. Brand Philip 1953, pp.268ff.
22. Gombrich 1969, pp.80ff.
23. Gui, *Conduct*, IV, in Wakefield and Evans 1969, pp.426f and 433.
24. Lea 1888 Vol.II, p.355.
25. Duvernoy 1976, p.227 and Loos 1974, p.266.
26. Obolensky 1948, p.216f and Ivanov 1976, p.105.
27. See Gui, *Conduct*, IV, in Wakefield and Evans 1969, pp.427 and 433.
28. *Psalm Book* (Allberry 1938), p.60: 26f and p.61:25f; Loos 1974, pp.265, 278 and 354; Widengren 1946, p.55; and Ladurie 1980, p.315.

Chapter 2

1. These are the known beliefs of the Brethren of the Free Spirit (see Lea 1888 Vol.II, pp.320ff and 355ff; Clasen 1963 and *Hastings Encyclopaedia* II, 1909, p.842f).
2. The records of these persecutions are discussed in Lea 1888 Vol.I, pp.110ff and II, 115ff; Runciman 1946, p.121f, and Wakefield and Evans 1969, pp.126ff, 243f, and 265ff.
3. The heretics persecuted by Conrad of Marburg were of several varieties. In Lea's interpretation, none of them were Cathars (1888 Vol.II, p.334), but according to Wakefield and Evans, a German chronicle written at Trier in 1231 reveals that some heretics in this city were Cathars. These were the ones described as performing a second baptism (the Cathar spiritual baptism), and rejecting the Eucharist (1969, pp.265 and 268). This chronicle also tells us that some of the Trier heretics performed devil worship. According to Loos, this accusation was probably a fantastic invention in which Cathar dualism was turned upsidedown (1974, p.196).

4. The Cathars' many attempts to flee the Inquisition are covered most thoroughly in Lea 1888 Vols.I and II.
5. Lea 1888 Vol.II, pp.240ff.
6. See Loos 1974, p.287f. These records are also discussed in Lea 1888 Vol.II, p.255f.
7. These letters are discussed in Loos 1974, Chapter XIX.
8. See Loos 1974, pp.321 and 328, n.134. The map drawn by S. Ćirković, and referred to by Loos is reproduced here as Map 4. This map is based on Turkish documents and other data from Bosnia and Dubrovnik. It shows the locations of the Patarenes in Bosnia, during the Middle Ages and under the Turks.
9. Loos 1974, p.320.
10. Nicholas Davidson (Dept of History, University of Leicester) 1993, unpublished material for a forthcoming book. See also Lea 1888 Vol.II, pp.249ff and McNeill 1974, p.174.
11. Ginzburg 1992, p.19. For the judges' references to Scandella's 'Manicheism' see Ginzburg 1992, p.92 and del Col 1990, LIV.
12. Ginzburg 1992, p.107f. For the records of the Venetian *Vision of Isaiah*, see Ivanov 1976, pp.135, 152, 157; and Turdeanu, 1950, p.214f. The earliest reference to this heretical work that has come down to us is in Sixtus Senensis, *Bibliotheca sancta* I, II, Paris 1610, p.62, col.2. The name of the Venetian publisher is not mentioned in this record.
13. Clasen 1963, p.406f. The rejection of New Testament doctrines such as the Virgin Birth, is mentioned as point number nine in a list of 'Manichean' errors of 1461. This was prepared by Franciscans in Bosnia for Cardinal John of Torquemada in Rome. It referred specifically to the beliefs of the Bosnian heretics. (See Fine 1975, p.355; Duvernoy 1976, p.353; and Loos 1974, p.319f.) Its information does not seem to have reached the clerics of Northern Europe, who were no longer interested in Catharism. The Bogomil and Cathar views on the Trinity varied, as Loos has said (1974, p.86), and Thon's beliefs on this subject would be in keeping with many of them.
14. For a good description of the Cathar priests and priestesses see Oldenbourg 1961 (1), pp.62ff. The Cathars of the Languedoc are also brought to life in her two historical novels, 1961 (2) and 1963.
15. Clasen 1963, p.392.
16. These records are listed and discussed in Mosmans 1947, pp.7 and 72.
17. Lea 1888 Vol.I, p.113.
18. Guido Jansen, personal communication, April 1989. See also Filedt Kok 1972–73.
19. Marijnissen 1987, p.11.
20. Slatkes 1975, pp.337ff and 344.
21. Slatkes 1975, p.343f.
22. Slatkes 1975, pp.340ff.
23. Wind 1969, pp.4ff. For the *Three Magi*, see for example Settis 1990, especially pp.20ff.
24. See for example Tolnay 1966, pp.397f and 407f, for more on Bosch's patrons. See Gombrich 1967 for Beatis.
25. Guido Jansen, personal communication, April 1989.

26. *Psalm Book* (Allberry 1938), p.52:23.
27. Guiraud 1935, p.71f; Runciman 1947, p.76; and Bozóky 1980, p.69.
28. See Steinberg 1984, especially pp.61–72, for the ideas about Jesus' circumcision.
29. See Tolnay 1966, especially p.341f, for the interpretation of the Philadelphia *Adoration*.
30. For the Cathars' views of Jesus and Mary, see Guiraud 1935, p.70f; Runciman 1947, p.81; and Bozóky 1980, p.69. Scandella's views on the Virgin are discussed in Ginzburg 1992, pp.34f and 102.
31. See Tolnay 1966, p.341; and Cooper 1982, p.164, for the images of the swan and the lily.
32. See Bax 1979, p.295, for the pigeons, and pp.120 and 295 for the swan.
33. Bax 1979, p.195.
34. Guiraud 1935, pp.75ff. For more on Cathar ideas about Jehovah's religions, see Chapter 6 below.
35. Tolnay 1966, p.340, and Marijnissen 1987, p.12.
36. Tolnay 1966, p.340.
37. See Oldenbourg 1961 (1), pp.62–70 and 1961 (2).

Chapter 3

1. Ivanov 1976, p.159.
2. See Lieu 1985, p.7 and Baedecker's *Egypt*, p.186f for Medinet Medi; and *Psalm Book* (Allberry 1938), p.xix-xx, for the history of the Coptic Manichean psalms.
3. See Runciman 1947, pp.23f, 86 and 90f.
4. For the owl as Satan, see Cooper 1982, p.124. For the owl's identification with the Jews see Brand

Philip 1953, p.275; Beagle 1982, p.43; and Janson 1952, p.178.
5. Images of the owl as a cruel, gluttonous and evil creature which attacks other birds in darkness are found in the *Dialogus Creaturarum*, a text published in Gouda in 1490. This text and the symbols of cock and fox are discussed by J. Rosenberg in his article of 1961, reprinted in Snyder 1973, pp.118ff.
6. See Bozóky 1980, pp.45–49 and 55f for the Cathar creation, as described in the *Secret Book*.
7. For Satan and the fall of the angels, see Bozóky 1980, pp.49ff. The Cathar belief that two sorts of soul had followed Satan down to earth can be found in the Inquisition records (see Duvernoy. 61f, and Anselm of Alessandria, *Notebook*,(4) *c*.1266, trans. in Wakefield and Evans, p.364).
8. For the soul as a small bird, see Janson 1952, p.178.
9. Bozóky 1980, p.59.
10. Bozóky 1980, p.59.
11. Brand Philip 1980, p.66.
12. *Psalm Book* (Allberry 1938), pp.162:12, 210:18f, and 218:25f. The Manichean image of souls as valuable jewels, which the forces of darkness want to steal, is also discussed in Klimkeit 1982, p.14. For the Cathar images, see note 23 of this chapter.
13. Fraenger 1952, p.62f. For Fraenger, however, the owl is a not a negative image, but a symbol of esoteric wisdom (1952, p.66f).
14. Dixon 1981, p.20.
15. These Cathar ideas about baptism by water are found in many of

the Inquisition records. See for example Duvernoy 1976, p.144f; and Guiraud 1935, p.64f. For the Cathar attitudes towards John the Baptist, see Chapter 6 below.

16. Van Oudheusden and van Mackelenbergh 1985, p.29.

17. Bozóky 1980, p.61.

18. See Duvernoy 1976, pp.94ff; Guiraud 1935, p.59f; and Ladurie 1980, p.352, for Cathar ideas of metempsychosis. For the differing views of the Absolute and Mitigated Cathars, see Bozóky 1980, Gloss no.5, p.91 and the interpretation of it on p.176.

19. The Cathar/Manichean belief that ordinary souls (the good fallen angels) can be damned is discussed in the Introduction, including notes 22 and 23. See also Chapter 4, note 3.

20. See Gloss 6 in the Vienna copy of the *Secret Book* (Bozóky 1980, p.91).

21. Ladurie 1980, pp.349 and 349n.

22. See Jonas 1963, p.126n. for a summary of this allegory.

23. These ideas can be found in Bozóky 1980, p.65 and 138; Duvernoy 1976, p.114f; Moneta, *Summa Against the Cathars*, c.1241, I, in Wakefield and Evans 1969, p.313, and Söderberg 1949, pp.154ff.

24. *Psalm Book* (Allberry 1938), p.143:25f.

25. Widengren 1965, p.104f.

26. See Loos 1974, p.259, and Gui *Conduct*, I, in Wakefield and Evans 1969, pp.379 and 382.

27. *Psalm Book* (Allberry 1938), p.220:4–6.

28. Gibson 1973 (1), p.86.

29. Jackson, 1925, p.265.

30. Brand Philip 1956, p.5.

Chapter 4

1. Bozóky 1980, p.83 (see Introduction here for more on this).

2. See for example Duvernoy 1976, p.93.

3. Cathar ideas about the punishment of sinners can be found in Bozóky 1980, p.83; Duvernoy 1976, p.101f; and in Sacchoni, *The Summa of Brother Rainerius of the Order of Preachers on the Cathars and the Poor of Lyons* 1250, (2), in Wakefield and Evans 1969, p.330. Manichean ideas are found in Augustine *De Haer.*, Müller 1956, p.97, and in Jackson 1930, pp.185ff.

Chapter 5

1. For the Manichean views on the soul and the spirit, see for example Jackson 1932, p.12f; and Jonas 1963, p.125. The Cathar ideas on the difference between the soul and the spirit can be found in Duvernoy 1976, p.67f.

2. For more on the subject of the spirit and the soul, see · *New Catholic Encyclopaedia* 1967, Vol.IV, p.238 and Vol.X, p.769. See also *Encyclopedia of Religion* 1987, Vol.13, pp.455ff, and *Encyclopaedia Judaica* 1971, Vol.6, p.880f.

3. Lieu (1985, p.51) and Doresse (1986, p.95) both see connections between the Manichean religion and the *Hymn of the Pearl*. Layton suggests that the *Acts of Thomas*, which were probably written in Edessa in *c.*200 AD, influenced Mani. He is not certain, however, whether the *Hymn of the Pearl* was an original part of this body of

works, or added later (Layton 1987, p.361 and 367ff). For a particularly perceptive translation and interpretationation of the *Hymn of the Pearl,* see Jonas 1963, pp.112ff.

4. Söderberg 1949, p.189.

5. The relevant quotation from the *Liber Supra Stella* is discussed in Söderberg 1949, pp.216ff.

6. Theodore bar Khoni, *Liber Scholiorum,* quoted in Jackson 1932, pp.249ff.

7. See the *'Manichaean Treatise'* VI, Wakefield and Evans 1969, p.500, or Chapter 10 here for the Cathar images of Jesus and the tree of life. The Coptic Manichean Psalms, which associate Jesus and the tree of life are found in *Psalm Book* (Allberry 1938), pp.112:21–22 and 116:7. Finally, Widengren also discusses the identification of Jesus with the tree of life in Manicheism and esoteric Christianity. See Widengren 1946, pp.124–30.

8. Gloss no.6 in the Vienna copy identifies the plant the fruits grow on as a forbidden vine (Bozóky, 1980, p.91). The same vine of seduction is referred to in the Early Christian *Apocalypse of Baruch,* which is known to have influenced the Cathar *Secret Book* (see Ivanov 1976, p.184 and 191).

9. Lieu 1985, p.19f, based on Augustine, *Haer.,* XLVI (115–17).

10. *Psalm Book* (Allberry 1938), p.144:19.

11. *Psalm Book* (Allberry 1938), see for example pp.70:30 and 159:31.

12. Doresse 1986, p.216.

13. See Klimkeit 1982, p.31f.

14. This very helpful information, which is relevant to the iconography of Bosch, was kindly provided by Dr Lore Sander, Museum für Indische Kunst, Berlin, personal communication, October 1991.

15. Doresse 1986, p.216f.

16. Fraenger 1952, p.54.

17. See Dixon 1981, p.16 for the alchemical explanation. Calas comments on the fact that Christ's face is 'disturbingly unattractive, distorted, even,' when seen in the original. She also remarks on the lack of nimbus in this particular depiction (1980, p.13).

18. See Bozóky 1980, p.53 for Satan's face, p.61 for the seduction of Eve, and p.91 for gloss no.7.

19. For the Bogomils, see Zigabenus quoted in Obolensky 1948, p.213. For Scandella, see Ginzburg 1992, pp.5, 72 and 88ff; and also del Col 1990, LVII.

20. Duvernoy 1976, p.82.

21. Layton 1987, p.15 and 30.

22. Gibson 1973 (1), p.35 and 1973 (2), pp.220ff.

23. C. Justi, *The Works of Hieronymus Bosch in Spain,* 1899, reprinted in Snyder 1973, p.50.

24. Gibson 1973 (2), p.208.

25. Marijnissen 1987, p.329.

26. See Sigüenza 1605, in Tolnay 1966, p.403.

27. For more on Van Eyck's mirror, see Panofsky 1964, pp.174 and 203.

28. Stein Schneider 1984 (1), pp.14ff.

29. See Duvernoy 1976, p.148 and 148n for the desc or discus; and Wakefield and Evans 1969, pp.474 and 492 for the relevant parts of the Rituals.

30. Wakefield and Evans 1969, p.475 and 490.

31. For more on this tapestry, see Kurz 1967.
32. Ivanov 1976, pp.84f and 255f.
33. *Psalm Book* (Allberry 1938), p.219:4–10, 24–26.
34. The important Manichean image of Christ's death and crucifixion on every tree (i.e. in the physical world) is discussed, for example, in Pederson 1988, pp.174ff; Jonas 1963, p.228f; Klimkeit 1982, p.11; and Asmussen 1975, p.47. There are no extant records of a similar Cathar belief, but the idea may be hinted at in the reference to the Crucifixion in the Cathar *Secret Book*. See Bozóky 1980, p.69.
35. *Psalm Book* (Allberry 1938), p.214:1–20.
36. Tolnay 1966, p.307.
37. For further details, see Tolnay 1966, p.375.
38. For more on the attitudes of the Cathars towards secular authorities, see Guiraud 1935, pp.59 and 77; Oldenbourg 1961 (1), p.38; and Obolensky 1948, p.137f.
39. Foster and Tudor-Craig 1986, p.65f.
40. Foster and Tudor-Craig 1986, p.62f, and Tudor-Craig, *The Secret Life of Paintings*, BBC 2, 1987.

Chapter 6

1. Obolensky 1948, pp.131 and 214; and Runciman 1946, p.77.
2. Loos 1974, p.294 and N. Davidson, unpublished material 1993.
3. Cooper 1982, p.160.
4. Guiraud 1935, p.61.
5. Duvernoy 1976, p.191f and Gui 1323–24, quoted in Wakefield and Evans 1969, p.382f.

6. Bozóky 1980, p.69 and Guiraud 1935, p.61f.
7. A description of the soul with a 'deer's form surrounding her,' wandering in the labyrinth of ills on earth, is given in a Naassene (early Gnostic) psalm (Mead 1964 Vol.I, p.191).
8. The image of the living Jesus or twin is discussed in Layton 1987, p.359, and found in the *Book of Thomas* 138:7–19 (Layton 1987, p.403); and the *Gospel according to Thomas*, (1) 32;10 (Layton 1987, p.380).
9. Bax 1979, p.197.
10. Beagle 1982, p.114.
11. See for example *Psalm Book* (Allberry 1938), pp.87:17, 152:12, and 193:26.
12. Bozóky 1980, p.71. See also Duvernoy 1976, p.87 and Loos 1974, p.140.
13. See for example Guiraud 1935, pp.64f; and Obolensky 1948, pp. 129f, 213 and 228.

Chapter 7

1. See for example Duvernoy 1976, p.88.
2. This idea about the spiritual baptism is stated in the Provençal Ritual (Wakefield and Evans 1969, p.489). For more on the tradition of the spiritual baptism, see also Loos 1974, p.117f; Söderberg 1949, pp.224f and 227; and here Chapter 8.
3. Wakefield and Evans 1969, p.467.
4. Scott 1980, pp.114 and 193ff, including caption of Figure 130.
5. Oldenbourg 1961 (1), p.47.
6. Stein Schneider, Autumn 1984 (1), pp.11ff.

7. Bax 1979, p.182.
8. *Hastings Encyclopaedia*, Vol.II, 1909, p.399.
9. Bax lists the eight occasions on which this headgear is worn (1979, p.181).
10. Gibson 1973 (1), p.40.
11. *Hastings Encyclopaedia*, Vol II, 1909, p.400.
12. Gibson 1973 (1), p.101
13. Jonas 1963, p.55f.
14. Jonas 1963, p.113. Jonas goes into more detail about the Gnostic concept of the stranger on pages 49–51.
15. Bax 1979, p.302. See also Brand Philip 1958, p.70.
16. Jonas 1963, p.83.
17. See for example Jonas 1963, p.115.
18. Wertheim Aymès 1975, p.39, and Stein Schneider 1984 (2), p.59f. See also Cooper 1982, pp.156, 170.

Chapter 8

1. See Duvernoy 1976, p.97f and Gui, *Conduct*, I, in Wakefield and Evans 1969, p.380.
2. *Psalm Book* (Allberry 1938), p.81:13 and p.154:7.
3. Doresse 1986, p.95, and Widengren 1946, p.110.
4. *Hastings Encyclopedia*, Vol.V, 1912, p.571.
5. For some analyses of the two groups and some alternative interpretations of the scene, see Tolnay 1966, pp.70 and 339ff; Bax 1979, pp.287ff and 389; and Gibson 1973 (1), pp.28ff.
6. See for example Bozóky 1980, p.87.
7. Jackson 1930, p.179.
8. The images of cold water and fiery wine are both found in *Psalm*

Book (Allberry 1938), p.184:10, 12–13. The interpretation of the cold water image has to be somewhat conjectural, as much of this particular psalm is missing. Nevertheless, physical water was the element most identified by the Cathars with Satan and the material world (see Obolensky 1948, p.213 and Ivanov 1976, p.269).
9. For Nazarius, see Anselm of Alexandria, *Notebook* (3), in Wakefield and Evans 1969, p.363.
10. Details of the *Missal of Duke Hrvoj of Split* at Istanbul can be found in Soloviev's article of 1948, pp.490 and 529. Duke Hrvoj, a heretical Bosnian nobleman, is discussed in Fine 1975, pp.222ff; and Soloviev 1948, p.529f.
11. Gibson 1973 (1), p.98.
12. Origo 1959, p.288n.
13. Bax 1979, p.290.
14. *Psalm Book* (Allberry 1938), p.56:15–30.

Chapter 9

1. Latin Ritual of the Consolamentum, in Wakefield and Evans 1969, p.478f.
2. Wittrock 1979, p.58f.
3. Moneta, *Summa*, in Wakefield and Evans 1969, p.319f.
4. See Widengren 1946, Chapter IV.
5. Balai, translated in Widengren 1946, p.62f.
6. Widengren 1946, pp.68ff.
7. Widengren 1946, p.79.
8. For this Apocryphal book, see Ivanov 1976, especially p.204f.
9. *Psalm Book* (Allberry 1938), p.152: 15–23. For the symbolic connection of body and house see also Jonas 1963, p.56.

10. Duvernoy 1976, p.99 and 102.
11. See for example Duvernoy 1976, p.99.
12. Jonas 1963, pp.122ff and Obolensky 1948, p.215.

Chapter 10

1. *Psalm Book* (Allberry 1938), p.59:17.
2. *Psalm Book* (Allberry 1938), p.178:25f.
3. *Psalm Book* (Allberry 1938), p.139:19–24.
4. See Roché 1947, p.122f, and Stoyanov 1994, pp.193 and 194f, for more on Cathar refugees from the Languedoc and other parts of Western Europe.
5. The development of the tombstones of Bosnia is discussed by Wenzel in her article of 1962. In her view, only a very small minority were made for Cathars.
6. Fine 1975, pp.260ff. (For more on this, see Chapter 11 here.)
7. See Papasov 1983, p.154 for the statistics of the stećci, and pp. 156ff for the question of Hearers and Perfects.
8. See Nelli 1966, p.117.
9. Guiraud 1935, pp.284ff.
10. See Nelli 1966 (especially p.16f); and Soloviev 1949 (especially p.57) and 1954 (especially p.103).
11. Langdon 1964, 150.
12. Le Coq 1923, 26.
13. For the locations of these stele see 'Signalisations de Sépultures et Steles Discoidales, Ve-XIXe Siècles,' *Actes des Journées de Carcassonne* 4–5–6 septembre 1987, Carcassonne 1990; and J.M. Miro i Rosinach, *Esteles Funeraries Discoidals de la Segarra*, Barcelona

1986. For more on Celtic crosses, see J. Streit, *Sun and Cross*, Edinburgh 1993.
14. Guiraud 1935, 293.
15. Bayley 1988, p.261 and Goblet d'Alviella 1894, p.179f.
16. The inscription, which is in Cyrillic (an alphabet used only by the Greek Orthodox Church and the members of the Bosnian/Patarene Church) reads 'this is the cross of Cvietko Dragišić] he died in (to the?) great suffering these....' This English translation is based on the German one by C. Truhelka, in 'Altbosnische Inschriften,' *Wissenschaftliche Mittheilungen aus Bosnien und der Herzegovina* V, 1897, p.293.
17. See *The Vision of Isaiah* in Wakefield and Evans 1969, pp.449ff.
18. For the two sets of heavenly bodies, in the Inquisition records, see Bonacursus, *A Description of the Catharist Heresy* 1176–90 (Wakefield and Evans 1969, p.173), and Moneta, *Summa, c.*1241 (Wakefield and Evans 1969, pp.308f and 318). For the discord, see *The Vision of Isaiah* in Wakefield and Evans 1969, p.450.
19. The tunnel of light in Bosch's Venice *Ascent* also reminds Tolnay of the Manichean column of praise (another name for it), but he does not conclude from this that Bosch was a Manichean or Cathar (Tolnay 1966, 354).
20. Duvernoy 1976, p.98f; and Loos 1974, p.91.

Chapter 11

1. Fine 1975, p.262.
2. For hints in the Bogomil records, see for example, Loos 1974, p.91. For a Cathar example from the Languedoc, see Guiraud 1935, p.83.
3. For more on the origins and development of the concept of a layered universe and a terrestrial paradise in the sky (as distinguished from the paradise of Eden on earth) see Vuippens 1925. For the subject as it appears in the Inquisition records, see Duvernoy 1976, pp.100f and 375; and Söderberg 1949, p.258.
4. Vuippens 1925, pp.25ff.
5. Boase 1966, p.235.
6. Bozóky 1980, p.49.
7. Duvernoy 1976, p.100.
8. *Manichean Treatise* of c.1218–22, Part VI, reproduced in Wakefield and Evans 1969, p.500.
9. *Psalm Book* (Allberry 1938), p.193: 19–24.
10. For more on the Slavonic *Enoch* including its connections with the Cathars, see Charles and Morfill 1896, Ivanov 1976, pp.161ff; Duvernoy 1976, p.363; and Crane and Guthrie 1974, Part Two, pp.81ff.
11. Ivanov 1976 gives a particularly good analysis of the Cathar ways of interpreting the Slavonic *Enoch*. See especially pp.180ff.
12. Crane and Guthrie 1974, Part Two, p.83.
13. Crane and Guthrie 1974, Part Two, p.83f. The Eden which is located on the earth is also described in the Slavonic *Enoch* as being 'between corruptibility and incorruptibility.' This part of the description does not correspond with Cathar ideas. The Cathars interpreted the *Enoch* in their own way, as Ivanov points out. As they saw it, Eden on earth had been created and planted by Satan as a trap for souls, and was entirely corrupt. But the *Enoch*'s description of the higher paradise of the third heaven as an intermediate area dominated by Jesus was fully in keeping with their cosmology.
14. *The Vision of Isaiah*, Chapter II, in Wakefield and Evans 1969, p.451.
15. Chatelet discusses Bouts' panel in his article of 1965, and shows that it (along with a hell scene which will be discussed in Chapter 12) was executed in 1468 (1965, p.17). He suggests that these two paintings by Bouts influenced Bosch's eschatological panels at Venice (1965, pp.27ff).
16. Gibson 1973 (1), p.63.
17. Gibson 1973 (1), p.64.
18. Gibson 1973 (1), p.64.
19. For a translation of the *Vision of Tundale*, see Patch 1980, p.112f.
20. Cinotti 1969, p.109.
21. We find these various ship images in the Manichean psalms – see *Psalm Book* (Allberry 1938), pp.139:30, 147:34–37, 217:24–30, and 218:1–5.
22. Bosch's mutilated Wildenstein panel was copied by H. Met de Bles. The copy, which showed the entire triptych, was once in the Maeterlinck Collection in Ghent. It is now lost, but reproduction of its two wings can be seen in Tolnay 1966, p.440.

Chapter 12

1. A beautiful reconstruction of the Cathar vision of souls falling back to earth like wounded birds is given by Oldenbourg in her excellent and well researched historical novel – 1961 (2), p.202. For a similar concept in Manicheism see Jackson 1932, pp.179 and 191.

2. These Cathar ideas are found in the Inquisition records (see Ladurie 1980, p.345ff, for the tormented phase, and p.349 and 349n for Satan's Eden). For related concepts in Manicheism see for example Jackson 1930, p.180.

3. See also Chapter 11, note 15.

4. Duvernoy 1976, p.94 and 373.

5. The pagan interpretations are found mainly in the writings of Wenzel (see Bibliography).

6. Loos 1974, p.294.

7. Oldenbourg 1961 (1), p.55.

8. See Sir Arthur Evans, *Through Bosnia and Herzegovina on Foot During the Insurrection, 1875*, London 1876. According to J. de Asboth, *An Official Tour Through Bosnia and Herzegovina*, London 1890 (p.104), the association between the stećci and the Bogomils had been a popular tradition in Bosnia even before the arrival of Evans.

9. Papasov 1983, p.156f.

10. Bihalji-Merin and Benac 1962, viii.

11. Soloviev 1957, p.163, and Nelli 1966, p.123.

12. Kutzli 1977, pp.182ff and 192ff.

13. See Purce 1974, pp.28ff, and Cooper 1987, pp.92ff and 156f.

14. Soloviev 1954, p.106.

15. See Wosien 1974, p.15f.

16. Soloviev 1957, p.163.

17. Bihalji-Merin and Benac 1962, viii.

18. Kutzli 1977, p.219.

19. Smith 1974, p.142f.

20. Smith 1974, p.16f.

21. Smith 1974, p.80f.

22. Carter 1972, p.189.

23. English translation by Dr Puvačić of the London University School of Slavonic Studies, from S. Beslagic, 'Stećci u Brotnjicama,' *Anali Historijskog Instituta u Dubrovniku*, Dubrovnik 1962, p.81.

24. See Fine 1975, p.262.

25. See Papasov 1983, p.157; and Fine 1975, p.262.

Bibliography

Allberry, C.R.C.(ed.), *A Manichaean Psalm-Book,* Part II, Stuttgart 1938.

Angelov, D., *The Bogomil Movement,* Sofia 1987.

Asmussen, J.P., *Manichaean Literature,* Persian Heritage Series No.22, Delmar, New York 1975.

Baldass, L. von, *Hieronymus Bosch,* London 1960.

Bax, D., *Hieronymus Bosch: His Picture-Writing Deciphered,* Rotterdam 1979.

Bayley, H., *The Lost Language of Symbolism,* New Jersey 1988.

Beagle, P.S., *The Garden of Earthly Delights,* London 1982.

Bihalji-Merin, O. and Benac, A., *The Bogomils,* London 1962.

Boase, T.S.R., 'King Death. Mortality, Judgement and Remembrance,' in Evans, J., *The Flowering of the Middle Ages,* New York, Toronto, London & Sydney 1966, pp.203–244.

Boczkowska A., and A. Wiercinski, 'Hieronymus Bosch's Self-Portraits,' *Ars Auro Prior,* Warsaw 1981, pp 193–99.

Bozóky, E. (ed.), *Le Livre Secret des Cathares, Interrogatio Iohannis, Apocryphe d'origine bogomile,* Paris 1980.

Brand Philip, see Philip, L. Brand.

Brenon, A., *Le Vrai Visage du Catharisme,* Portet-sur Garonne 1991.

Calas, E., 'The Ethiopians in Bosch's Garden,' *Coloquio artes* XLVI, 1980, pp.12ff.

Carter, F.W., *Dubrovnik (Ragusa): a Classic City-State,* London & New York 1972.

Charles, R.H. and Morfill, W.R. (eds.), *The Book of the Secrets of Enoch,* Oxford 1896.

Chatelet, A., 'Sur un Jugement Dernier de Dieric Bouts,' *Nederlands Kunsthistorisch Jaarboek* XVI, 1965, pp.17–41.

Cinotti. M., *The Complete Paintings of Bosch,* London 1969.

Clasen, C.-P., 'Medieval Heresies in the Reformation,' *Church History,* XXXII, 1963, pp.392–414.

Col, A. del, *I Processi dell'Inquisizione (1583–99),* Padova 1990.

Combe, J., *Jheronimus Bosch,* London 1946.

Cooper, J.C., *An Illustrated Encyclopaedia of Traditional Symbols,* London 1982.

Crane, F. and Guthrie, W.N. (eds.), *The Lost Books of the Bible and the Forgotten Books of Eden,* New York & Scarborough Ontario 1974.

Cuttler, C.D., 'Witchcraft in a Work by Bosch,' *The Art Quarterly,* XX, 1957, pp.129–40.

Dixon, L.S., *Alchemical Imagery in Bosch's Garden of Delights,* Ann Arbor Michigan 1981.

Doresse, J., *The Secret Books of the Egyptian Gnostics,* Rochester Vermont 1986.

Duvernoy, J., *La Religion des Cathares: Le Catharisme,* Toulouse 1976.

Encyclopaedia Judaica, Vol.VI, Jerusalem 1971.

Encyclopedia of Religion (ed. Eliade, M.), Vol.13, New York & London 1987.

Ewing, D.C., *The Paintings and Drawings of Jan de Beer,* Ph.D. Dissertation, Michigan 1978.

Filedt Kok, J.P., 'Underdrawing and drawing in the work of Hieronymus Bosch: a provisional survey in connection with the paintings by him in Rotterdam,' *Simiolus* VI, 1972–73, 3–4, pp.133–62.

Fine, J.V.A. Jr., *The Bosnian Church: A New Interpretation*, New York & London 1975.

Foster, R. and Tudor-Craig, P., *The Secret Life of Paintings*, Suffolk 1986.

Fraenger, W., *The Millennium of Hieronymus Bosch: Outlines of a New Interpretation*, London 1952.

Fredericq, P., *Corpus Documentorum Inquisitionis Haereticae Pravitatis Neerlandicae*, II, Gent & 's Gravenhage 1896.

Gibson, W., *Hieronymus Bosch*, London 1973 (1).

—, 'Hieronymus Bosch and the Mirror of Man. The Authorship and Iconography of the Tabletop of the Seven Deadly Sins,' *Oud Holland* 87, 1973 (2), pp.205–26.

Ginzburg, C., *The Cheese and the Worms, the cosmos of a sixteenth century miller*, USA & UK, 1982 and 1992.

Goblet d'Alviella, *The Migration of Symbols*, London 1984.

Gombrich, E.H., 'The Earliest Description of Bosch's Garden of Delights,' *The Journal of the Warburg and Courtauld Institutes*, XXX, 1967, pp.403–6.

—, 'The Evidence of Images,' in C. Singleton, *Theory and Practice*, Baltimore 1969, pp.35–104.

Grant, R.M., *Gnosticism: An Anthology. A Sourcebook of Heretical Writings from the Early Christian Period*, London 1961.

Guevara, F. de, *Comentarios de la Pintura (1560–63)*, in Snyder 1973, pp.28–33.

Guiraud, J., *Histoire de l'Inquisition au moyen age*, I, Paris 1935.

Haich, E., *Sexual Energy and Yoga*, London 1972.

—, *Initiation*, London 1979.

Hamburger, J., 'Bosch's "Conjuror": An attack on magic and sacramental heresy,' *Simiolus* XIV, 1984, I, pp.5–24.

Hastings Encyclopaedia of Religion and Ethics, Vols.II and V, Edinburgh & New York 1909 and 1912.

Heidenreich, H., 'Hieronymus Bosch in Some Literary Contexts,' *The Journal of the Warburg and Courtauld Institutes*, XXXIII, 1970, pp.171–99.

Huizinga, J., *The Waning of the Middle Ages*, London 1987.

Ivanov, J. (ed.), *Livres et Légendes Bogomiles (Aux Sources du Catharisme)*, Paris 1976.

Jackson, A.V.W., 'The Doctrine of Metempsychosis in Manichaeism,' *Journal of the American Oriental Society* , XCV, 1925, pp.246–68.

—, 'A Sketch of the Manichaean Doctrine Concerning the Future Life,' *Journal of the American Oriental Society*, L, 1930, pp.177–98.

—, *Researches in Manichaeism, with Special Reference to the Turfan Fragments*, New York 1932.

Janson, H.W., *Apes and Ape Lore in the Middle Ages and the Renaissance*, London 1952.

Jonas, H, *The Gnostic Religion. The message of the alien God and the beginnings of Christianity*, Boston 1963.

Justi, C. *The works of Hieronymus Bosch in Spain*, (1899) in Snyder 1973, pp.45–56.

Klimkeit, H.-J., *Manichaean Art and Calligraphy, Iconography of Religions XX*, E.J. Brill, Leiden 1982.

Kurz, O., 'Four Tapestries after Hieronymus Bosch,' *Journal of the Warburg and Courtauld Institutes*, XXX, 1967, pp.150–63.

Kutzli, R., *Die Bogumilen. Geschichte – Kunst – Kultur*, Stuttgart 1977.

Ladurie, E. Le Roy, *Montaillou, Cathars and Catholics in a French Village, 1294–1324*, Harmondsworth, Middlesex 1980.

Langdon, S.H., *Semitic Mythology, The Mythology of All Races*, ed. J.A. MacCulloch, Vol.V, 1964.

Layton, B. (ed.), *The Gnostic Scriptures*, London 1987.

Lea, H.C., *A history of the Inquisition in the Middle Ages*, Vols I & II, London 1888.

Le Coq, A. von, *Die Buddhistische Spätantike in Mittelasien — Band II: Die Manichäischen Miniaturen*, Berlin 1923.

Lieu, S.N.C., *Manichaeism in the Later Roman Empire and Medieval China, a Historical Survey*, Manchester 1985.

—, 'Fact and Fiction in the *Acta Archelai*,' in *Lund Studies in African and Asian Religions*, Vol.I, Manichaean Studies, Proceedings of the First International Conference on Manichaeism, ed. P.Bryder, Lund University, Sweden 1988, pp.69–88.

Loos, M., *Dualist Heresy of the Middle Ages*, Prague 1974.

Mâle, E., *The Gothic Image. Religious Art in France of the Thirteenth Century*, New York, Evanston, & London 1958.

Marijnissen R. H. and Ruyffelaere, P., *Hieronymus Bosch, the Complete Works*, Antwerp 1987.

Martin, J., *Venice's Hidden Enemies; Italian Heretics in a Renaissance City*, Berkeley, Los Angeles, & London 1993.

McNeill, W.H., *Venice the Hinge of Europe 1081–1797*, Chicago & London 1974.

Meade, G.R.S., *Thrice-Greatest Hermes*, Vol.I, London 1964.

Mosmans, J., *Jeronimus Anthonis-zoon van Aken alias Hieronymus Bosch. Zijn leven en zijn werk*, 's-Hertogenbosch 1947.

Müller, L.G., *The* De Haeresibus *of St Augustine*, Catholic University of America, XC, 1956.

Nelli, R., *Le Musée du Catharisme*, Toulouse 1966.

New Catholic Encyclopaedia, New York *et al* 1967, Vols.IV, IX and X.

Nicholls, D., 'The Devil in Renaissance France,' *History Today*, November 1980.

Obolensky, D., *The Bogomils, a Study in Balkan Neo-Manichaeism*, Cambridge 1948

Oldenbourg, Z., *Massacre at Montségur. A History of the Albigensian Crusade*, London 1961 (1).

—, *Destiny of Fire*, London 1961 (2).

—, *Cities of the Flesh, or the Story of Roger de Montbrun*, London 1963.

Origo, I.,*The Merchant of Prato, Francesco di Marco Datini*, London 1959.

Oudheusden, J. van and Mackelenbergh, E. van, *St. Jan, the Cathedral of 's-Hertogenbosch*, Zwolle 1985.

Panofsky, E., *Early Netherlandish Painting, its Origins and Character*, Vols. I & II, Cambridge, Mass. 1964.

Papasov, K., *Christen oder Ketzer — die Bogomilen*, Stuttgart 1983.

Parker, G., *Philip II*, Boston & Toronto 1978.

Patch, H.R., *The Other World According to Descriptions in Medieval Literature*, New York 1980.

Pederson, N..A., 'Early Manichaean Christology, primarily in Western Sources,' in *Lund Studies in African and Asian Religions*, Vol.I, Manichaean Studies, Proceedings of the First International Conference on Manichaeism, ed. P. Bryder, Lund University, Sweden 1988, pp.157–190.

Philip, L. Brand, *The Ghent Altarpiece and the Art of Jan van Eyck*, Princeton 1980.

—, *Hieronymus Bosch*, New York 1956.

—, '*The Peddler* by Hieronymus Bosch, a Study in Detection,' *Nederlands Kunsthistorisch Jaarboek*, IX, 1958, pp.1–81.

—, 'The Prado *Epiphany* by Jerome Bosch,' *The Art Bulletin*, XXXV, 1953, pp.267–293.

Purce, J., *The Mystic Spiral, Journey of the Soul*, London 1974.

Reutersward, P., *Hieronymus Bosch*, Uppsala 1970.

Roché, D., *Le Catharisme*, Toulouse 1947.

Rosenberg, J., 'On the Meaning of a Bosch Drawing,' in Snyder 1973, pp.118–25.

Runciman, S., *The Medieval Manichee, a Study of the Christian Dualist Heresy*, Cambridge 1946.

Sadoul, J., *Alchemists and Gold*, London 1972.

Scott, M., *Late Gothic Europe, 1400–1500. The History of Dress Series*, London and New Jersey 1980.

Settis, S., *Giorgione's* Tempest: *Interpreting the Hidden Subject*, Cambridge & Oxford 1990.

Singleton, C.S., Translation and Commentary on Dante's *Divine Comedy*, Vol.I, *Inferno* & Vol.II, *Purgatorio*, Bollingen Series LXXX, Princeton 1980 & 1982.

Slatkes, L.J., 'Hieronymus Bosch and Italy,' *The Art Bulletin*, LVII, 1975, pp.335–45.

Smith, M., *The Secret Gospel: the discovery and interpretation of the* 'Secret Gospel according to Mark,' New York & London 1974.

Snyder, J.(ed.), *Bosch in Perspective*, Englewood Cliffs, New Jersey 1973.

Söderberg, H., *La Religion des Cathares, Etude sur le Gnosticisme de la Basse Antiquité et du Moyen Age*, Uppsala 1949.

Soloviev, A.V., 'Les Bogomiles veneraient-ils la Croix?' *Bulletin de l'Académie royale de Belgique*, classe des lettres, XXXV, 1949, pp.47–62.

—, 'La doctrine de l'église de Bosnie,' *Bulletin de l'Académie royale de Langues et de Littérature Française*, classe des lettres, 5th Series, XXXIV, 1948, pp.481–534.

—, 'Le Symbolisme des monuments funéraires bogomiles,' *Cahiers d'Etudes Cathares*, 1st Series, XVIII, 1954, pp.92–114.

—, 'Le Symbolisme des monuments funéraires bogomiles et cathares,' *Actes du Xème Congrès d'Etudes Byzantines*, 1957, pp.162–65.

Steinberg, L., *The Sexuality of Christ in Renaissance Art and in Modern Oblivion*, London 1984.

Stein-Schneider, H., 'Le Consolamentum cathare, peint par Hiéronymus Bosch' (1), and 'Hiéronymus Bosch et la Réincarnation' in 'Platon, les Cathares et la

Réincarnation dans l'art de la Renaissance italienne et des Flandres' (2), both in *Cahiers d'Etudes Cathares*, 2nd Series, No.103 (Autumn 1984), pp.3–19, 55–62.

Stoyanov, Y. *The Hidden Tradition in Europe: The Secret History of Medieval Christian Heresy*, London 1994.

Tolnay, C. de, *Hieronymus Bosch*, London 1966.

Tudor-Craig, P. *see* Foster, R.

Turdeanu, E., 'Apocryphes bogomiles et apocryphes pseudo-bogomiles,' *Revue de l'histoire des religions*, II, CXXXVIII, 1950, pp.22–52 & 176–218.

Vuippens, P.I. de, *Le Paradis terrestre au troisième ciel*, Paris & Friebourg 1925.

Wakefield, W.L., and Evans, A.P. (eds.), *Heresies of the High Middle Ages*, New York & London 1969.

Walker, B., *Gnosticism. Its History and Influence*, Wellingborough, Northamptonshire 1983.

Welburn, A., *The Beginnings of Christianity. Essene mystery, Gnostic revelation and the Christian vision*, Edinburgh 1991.

Wenzel, M., 'Bosnian and Herzegovinian tombstones — who made them and why,' *Südostforschungen*, XXI, 1962, pp.102–143.

Wenzel, M., *Ukrasni motivi na stećcima — Ornamental Motifs on Tombstones from Medieval Bosnia and Surrounding Regions*, Sarajevo 1965.

Wertheim Aymès, C.A., *The Pictorial Language of Hieronymus Bosch, represented in a study of two pictures:* The Prodigal Son *and* The Temptation of St Anthony, *with comments on themes in other works.* Horsham, Sussex 1975.

Widengren, G., *Mani and Manichaeism*, London 1965.

Widengren, G., *Mesopotamian Elements in Manichaeism (King and Saviour II)*, Uppsala & Leipzig 1946.

Wind, E., *Giorgione's* Tempestà, *with Comments on Giorgione's Poetic Allegories*, Oxford 1969.

Wittrock, I., 'Die sogenannte Sintflutflügel des Hieronymus Bosch. Ein Versuch zur Interpretation der drei ersten Medaillons der Aussenflügel,' *Oud-Holland* XCIII, 1979, pp.52–60.

Wosien, M.-G., *Sacred Dance, Encounter with the Gods*, New York 1986.

Photographic acknowledgments

Artothek, Peissenberg, *Plates 29, 39.*

Bartram, Adina *Diagrams 1, 2, 3.*

Bilderarchiv Preußischer Kulturbestiz, Berlin, *Plates 33, 51.*

Bridgeman Art Library, London, *Plates 12, 45, 46, 47, 54, 56, 70, 71, Figures 10, 33, 40, 46.*

British Library, *Plate 34.*

British Museum, *Figures 5, 6, 9.*

Fundación Lázaro Galdiano, *Plate 50.*

Harris, Lynda, *Plate 35, Figures 1, 2, 4, 13, 14, 18, 19, 22, 24, 26, 27, 28, 29, 30, 31, 34, 36, 42, 43, 44, 45, 47, 50, 51, 53, 54, 58, 59.*

Instituto Português de Museus, *Plates 43, 44.*

Kupferstichkabinett, Staatliche Museen zu Berlin, Preußischer Kulturbesitz, *Figure 15.*

Museo Nacional del Prado, Madrid, *Plate 1.*

Museum Boymans-van Beuningen, Rotterdam, *Plates 55, 58, 60, 62, 63, 64, 65.*

Museum für Indische Kunst, Staatliche Museen zu Berlin, Preußischer Kulturbesitz, *Plate 27.*

National Gallery, London, *Plates 10, 41.*

National Galleries of Scotland, *Figure 16.*

Österreichische Nationalbibliothek, *Figure 12.*

Philadelphia Museum of Art: The John G Johnson Collection, *Figure 11.*

Photographie Giraudon, *Plate 14.*

Réunion des musées nationaux, *Plate 15, Figure 32.*

Rijksmuseum-Stichting, Amsterdam, *Figure 37.*

Royal Collection Enterprises, *Figure 7.*

Scala Istituto Fotografico Editoriale, Florence, *Plates 2, 3, 4, 11, 16, 17, 18, 20, 21, 22, 23, 36, 37, 38, 40, 42, 49, 59, 66, 67, 68, 72, 73, Figures. 8, 17, 20, 35, 48, 60.*

Smith, Tim, *Maps 4, 5, Figures, 41, 56, 57.*

Stedelijke Musea, Stad Brugge, *Plates 30, 31, 32.*

Verlag Urachhaus, *Figures 49, 52, 55.*

Main index

Figures in italics refer to page with illustration. **Pl. is Plate No.**

Aachen (town of) and Bosch's family 71

Abraham, Bosom of 221ff *(see also* paradise of the third heaven)

Adam and/or Eve

—, 'awakening' of Adam by Saviour 27, 121ff, 125,

—, entrapment of 108–14, 159

— as fallen angels/collective human souls 27, 104, 110, 121, 177f

—, 'marriage'/seduction/temptation of 121, 125f, 223

—, physical bodies, creation of 104

Adamites (Brethren of the Free Spirit) 59f

afterworld *see* Land of Light; paradise; hell

alchemy 61, 125, 159, 243

Alexander VI, Pope 41, 152

Anabaptism 66, 67

angels

—, 'evil' fallen, *see* demons

—, 'good' fallen, *see* soul, human

—, heavenly 53, 66, 117, 128f, 156, 179, 191, 196, 198ff, 205ff, 209ff

— in traditional Christian paintings 53, 128f, 206

—, Jesus, Mary and John the Evangelist as 70, 84ff, 88, 127f, 141, 157

anger, sin of 134

Anthony, St 146, 147, 150ff, 232

Antichrist 55f, 152

Apostles

— at Last Judgment 156

—, Pentecost and spiritual baptism of 158, 163, 243

astrology 61

Armanno, Pongilupo (Cathar) 63

Arnold of Brescia 120

Augustine, St 35f, 39f, 122, 247, 252

Averroes of Cordoba 120

Balai (fourth century hymn writer) 177

Baldass, L. 23, 48, 52

baptism

— fire *see* spiritual baptism

— water *see* Church, Roman

Baroni, Pelegrino 'Pighino' (Cathar) 67f

Bax, D. 89, 90, 150, 152, 160, 164, 172

Bäzäklik (Turfan Oasis) 123

Beagle, P. 110, 152, 159

Beatis, A. de 82

Beauvais, Vincent of 42

Beer, Jan de (Birmingham *Nativity*) 53

'Beguins' 55, 56

Bernard Gui (and other Inquisitors) *see* INDEX OF SOURCES, ANTI-CATHAR

Bethesda, Pool of (John 5) 107f

Bihalji-Merin, O. 219, 220, 228

birds *see* cock; dove; heron; magpie; owl; pelican; pigeons (in loft); swan; tit; vulture; *see also* CONCORDANCE OF SYMBOLS

— on back 206, 211, 223

—, caged 150, 159, 165f

—, large, dark, menacing 138f, 165, 206, 211, 220–24

—, small and quick-flying 102, 109f, 112, 159, 165f, 206

— with broken wing 215, 220, 257

black figures in *Garden of Earthly Delights* 111

boat *see* ship

Bogomils 30, 31, 36, 96, 126, 204, 221 *(see also* Cathars)

Index of Sources

Cathar texts (including Bogomil and Bosnian)

Cathar depositions before the Inquisition

Anti-Cathar polemics (including Inquisition Records)

Esoteric Christian

Index of Bosch's Works

Concordance of Bosch's Symbols

* entry in Main Index